THE WORSHIP OF THE GOLDEN CALF

THE WORSHIP OF THE GOLDEN CALF
AN OIL-EXPORTER'S INDUSTRIAL STRATEGY, TECHNOLOGY POLICY AND PROJECT PLANNING DURING THE BOOM YEARS

Trevor M. A. Farrell

© 2022 The Estate of Trevor M.A. Farrell
All Rights Reserved

ISBN: 9798847421089

Dedicated to:

Maya

and

Kion

Table of Contents

LIST OF TABLES	VIII
PREFACE AND ACKNOWLEDGMENTS	X
PROJECTS, TECHNOLOGY POLICY AND TRANSFORMATION	1
PROJECT ANALYSIS AND THE PROJECT CYCLE: AN OVERVIEW	9
THE INDUSTRIAL PROJECTS IN THE OIL-BOOM YEARS: AN OVERVIEW	39
ISCOTT: THE VENTURE INTO STEELMAKING 1975-1977	57
ISCOTT: FROM PLANNING TO CONSTRUCTION	80
CONSTRUCTION, COMMISSIONING AND POST START-UP CRISIS	102
THE FERTILIZER STORY: PART 1	129
THE FERTILIZER STORY: PART 2	147
THE METHANOL EXPERIENCE	161
TECHNOLOGY POLICY IN THE ENERGY PROJECTS: AN ASSESSMENT	173

INDUSTRIALISATION STRATEGY, PROJECT ANALYSIS AND THE
MNC: FURTHER LESSONS OF EXPERIENCE 195

POSTSCRIPT: DEVELOPMENTS IN IRON AND STEEL, AMMONIA, UREA AND METHANOL AFTER 1985 211

REFERENCES 217

INDEX 223

LIST OF TABLES

Table		Page
3.1	Oil Revenues 1970-1983	41
3.2	Public Sector Industrial and Infrastructural Projects Proposed and Undertaken Post-1973	46-50
3.3	Membership of the Coordinating Task Force 1975-1979 and Composition	51
3.4	Major industrial Projects Actually Implemented in Trinidad and Tobago, 1974-1984	55
4.1	Time Overruns on the ISCOTT Project	59
4.2	Production Levels at ISCOTT 1981-1984	60
4.3	ISCOTT: Profit/Loss 1980-1985	61
4.4	Options for the Iron/ Steel Plant	73
4.5	Summary of Offers/Positions Taken by Potential Joint-Venture Partners in ISCOTT, 1974	74
5.1	Procurement of Major Items of Equipment	94
6.1	Analysis of Expatriate Staff Turnover at ISCOTT, 1980-1983	106
6.2	Technology Policy Issues and Possible Planning Objectives in the Case of Trinidad and Tobago's ISCOTT	120
6.3	Outline of the Complex of Activities Involved in the Project Cycle, the Areas of Possible Fit with Technology Policy Objectives and ISCOTT's Planning Response	121
7.1	Fertilizer Production in Trinidad and Tobago 1975-1984	134
8.1	Actual vs projected profit and Loss for Fertrin and Tringen Plants 1979-1983	146
8.2	Ammonia Prices (US Gulf Coast) 1981-1983	147
8.3	The Financing of Tringen	150
8.4	Comparison of the effects of the Mode of Financing Tringen Using Part Loan (TT$99.8 million) as Compared to Equivalent Equity Injection	151
8.5	The Financing of Fertrin	154

PREFACE AND ACKNOWLEDGMENTS

Trevor M.A. Farrell lectured in the Economics Department at UWI St. Augustine from 1974 to 2007. He taught International Economics initially and then taught Oil and Energy Economics, Industrial Economics, Technology Policy and Political Economy of Planning. While he conducted research and wrote many pieces over the years, some of his more important work which inspired post-graduate research, remained unpublished. Much of his early work addressed the problems of unemployment and development strategy. He also was interested in economic and social planning and developed his AFROSIBER nine-point planning methodology published in *Social and Economic Studies*. However, in considering a suitable memorial of his more influential work, I thought there would be little point in republishing already published pieces, some of which could be found in *Social and Economic Studies*, *OPEC Review,* and in various book chapters. Other work, such as his lectures compiled by the OWTU as *The Economics of Discontent*, were dated and would have little meaning for the reader today.

From 1980 to 1982, he was Senior Research Fellow at ISER and Regional Coordinator of the Caribbean Technology Policy Studies II (CTPS II) programme, which brought together economists, engineers, and management specialists to study technology policy in the Caribbean context. From August-September 1982, he visited steel mills and automobile factories in Japan to see how electronics and robotics were being used. While in Japan, he studied firsthand the Japanese system of organisation for formulating and implementing industrial policy and technology policy. He also visited South Korea and Hong Kong. His work on the CTPS II programme produced several articles and two monographs. The first monograph (1985) was a study of the Vehicle Assembly industry (with A. Mel Gajraj). The second, this work, *The Worship of the Golden Calf,* was completed in 1987. However, like many of the CTPS II studies, although it was the intention to do so, it was never published. I was alerted to its existence and its relevance to contemporary policy by one of his former students. While Trevor did some work and publications in the early 2000s on Caribbean economic integration, this study is probably the last major piece of academic writing he did.

Trevor was not a theoretical economist, nor did he seek to employ econometric methods which were becoming popular in the 1970s and 1980s. He averred that those tools were in his 'bottom drawer', but somehow, he never seemed to need to reach that drawer, probably because the problems in which he was interested were not conducive to those tools. He was an empirical economist who preferred to use interviews and survey methods to understand the problem he was addressing. He believed that problems could be solved by rational thinking applied systematically and rigorously. He immersed himself in detail and then sought to draw conclusions which he usually expressed with the utmost confidence and certainty. He would make lists of factors which affected a problem and analyze each thoroughly. This approach is very evident in this study. He conducted numerous interviews with key players, accessed critical project documents, including contracts and feasibility studies, and read widely and deeply on every topic. His background in Science at secondary school level also helped his analysis. The result is a detailed exposition, particularly of the iron and steel project, which is both revealing and insightful. Methodologically, he uses the lenses of both project planning and technology policy to make his assessments of the success or failure of the Point Lisas projects.

He enjoyed working and interacting with professionals outside of his discipline, particularly scientists, engineers and medical doctors, attracted perhaps by their rigour and attention to detail. Many of the examples he adduced were drawn from those fields.

After the National Alliance for Reconstruction (NAR) came to power following the general election in December 1986, he was deputy chairman of the National Economic Advisory Council. He was also a director of the National Energy Corporation (1987-1988) and chairman of TRINTOPEC (1987-1989). For much of his career he was also what is today described as a 'public intellectual'. He was an excellent public speaker and lectured widely in the region to university and business organisations, and also wrote several opinion pieces for *Caribbean Contact* as well as local and regional newspapers.

Between 1991 and his retirement in 2007, he devoted most of his time and energies 'downtown' as deputy chairman of Scotiabank Trinidad and Tobago and chairman of Bourse Securities, and consulted overseas with the World Bank, the Commonwealth Secretariat and CARICOM. He also lectured and consulted in management, specifically in the area of strategy with many public and private sector organizations in the region. He had hoped to get back to some of his earlier work with the intention of publishing these, but was afflicted with an eye disorder which severely impaired his reading and writing.

This publication is first and foremost a memorial to an academic economist who made a significant impact on economic research at UWI St Augustine between 1980 and 1987. He energized the Masters programme in Economics and supervised the dissertations of many students such as Elizabeth Parsan, Auliana Poon, Gregory McGuire, Dennis Phillip, Ronald Ramlogan, Gillian Marcelle, Lou Ann Barclay, and several others who have gone on to distinguish themselves academically and otherwise.

Secondly, while the book details the experience of the ISCOTT project and also the early years of the ammonia and methanol projects, and arguably can now stand on its own as a work of economic history, its lessons continue to resonate down to today. The lessons which he drew from the ISCOTT experience in particular, were not learned and practiced and hence project failures are to be expected. He noted in this book:

We can see ...the consequence of the often-blind faith in, and reliance on, metropolitan analyses and projections which blinker planners and policy makers in the ex-colonial countries of the Third World. The counterpart of this faith is of course a rejection of locally-produced analyses and warnings, and a failure to think things through for oneself.

Trevor would not have been surprised at the outcomes of Petrotrin's Trintomar and Gas to Liquids projects, the demise of Petrotrin itself, or NGC's Train 1 misadventure.

I have appended a short factual postscript which updates the developments in respect of the iron and steel project and the ammonia and methanol projects. I am aware that Carlos Hee Houng and his collaborators are proposing to publish a major review of the Point Lisas projects which will likely complement this work, in part because it details the growth and development of the early generation of local engineers and managers within the successful operations at Fertrin and the methanol and urea companies.

Trevor died on November 14, 2013. On behalf of Trevor's family, I would like to thank the UWI St Augustine Library for facilitating access to the study which was housed in its West Indian collection. I have made minor editorial corrections recognizing that the manuscript was written 25 years ago, but I have otherwise made no changes. Our brother, Carlyle, Professor at Ryerson Business School in Toronto, Canada, reviewed the manuscript and corrected numerous errors which had escaped me. I would also like to thank Gabby Woodham who designed the cover in keeping with the theme.

Terrence W. Farrell
September, 2022

When the people saw that Moses was a long time before coming down the mountain, they gathered around Aaron and said to him, 'Come, make us a God to go at the head of us; this Moses, the man who brought us up from Egypt, we do not know what has become of him. Aaron answered them, "Take the gold rings out of the ears of your wives and your sons and daughters, and bring them to me. So they all took the gold rings from their ears and brought them to Aaron. He took them from their hands and, in a mould, melted the metal down and cast an effigy of a calf. 'Here is your God, Israel, they cried, who brought you out of the land of Egypt! Observing this, Aaron built an altar before the effigy. Tomorrow, he said, will be a feast in honour of Yahweh. And so, early the next days they offered holocausts and brought communion sacrifices; then all the people sat down to eat and drink, and afterwards got up to amuse themselves.

EXODUS 5:32

1
PROJECTS, TECHNOLOGY POLICY AND TRANSFORMATION

Introduction

One of the fascinating phenomena of recent years has been the remarkably similar experiences of a variety of oil-exporting underdeveloped countries around the world as they responded to sudden and unexpected wealth. The weakening of oil prices beginning in late 1981, and the actual fall in nominal prices which was formalized in 1983, signaled that the heady years of the 1970s were finally coming to a close. For some countries, such as Mexico, Venezuela and Nigeria, the end of the boom, precipitated serious economic and social crisis, with the usual political fallout as a result. For many of these countries, the end of the boom came as swiftly and as unexpectedly as the start.

Around the world, rather like the morning-after the night before, sober appraisal has now begun of the course and consequences of the oil boom years for the oil-exporters. It is already apparent that in at least some the question can seriously be posed: whether particular countries have really ended up any better off than they were in 1973 despite all the windfall oil wealth they have enjoyed.

In so many of them the litany of problems is the same — horrendous inflation ignited during the boom years (especially in real estate); destruction of domestic agriculture and of traditional export activities, as countries overpriced themselves out of international markets; wages and salaries driven way out of line; the deterioration of the work ethic and the destruction of traditional values, endemic corruption, prestige projects gone sour, bloated bureaucracies, large sums wasted on armaments, overloaded infrastructure and congested cities.

Much of this is now quite familiar and can be easily compared with past booms in history. One area however, is of very great importance for analysis and has so far not received as much attention as it deserves. This is the 'instant industrialization' that most of the oil exporters attempted, once the capital became available.

In country after country, governments saw the petrodollar windfall as the opportunity to transform their underdeveloped, backward nations into modern, industrial societies and to do so within a few short years. Despite the massive expenditures over the last decade, it is increasingly clear that this objective is not so easily achieved. In several cases, it turns out that the shiny new industrial plants are likely to be economic failures producing the commodities of yesteryear, in competition with other new suppliers impelled by the same vision, all aiming at markets which are either highly protected or have lost their growth dynamic or both.

Whether the new industries set up are economically successful or not, it has also turned out to be the case that the technological capacities that these countries hoped to acquire through operating these new facilities, somehow turns out to be somewhat more elusive than expected.

It turns out once again that transformation is not quite so simple. In the case of Iran, the experiment of instant industrialization coupled with major social and cultural changes in a traditional society, led to an explosion and to an Islamic Revolution which affirmed traditional values that were directly opposed to the 'modern' ones touted under the Shah.

The formulae for successful industrialization, technological development and social reorganisation are clearly still not perfectly understood. Some countries seem to suddenly get it all together, and are able to do what is necessary. Japan after 1868, and South Korea in the 1970s are apparent examples. Other countries seem to bring together all of the ingredients the experts suggest are necessary – capital, access to technology, certain industrial and intellectual activities, determined leadership, and so on – and either fail or go nowhere.

In our search for answers to the riddles of successful industrialization, technological development and economic transformation, the experience of the world's oil exporters over the last decade is extremely important. Studied assiduously, it will certainly yield valuable clues and important lessons for the future.

This study chooses as its focus one slice of the instant industrialization experience of the 1970s, project planning and management, and locates it spatially in one of the world's oldest but smallest oil producers, Trinidad and Tobago, a Caribbean country and non-OPEC member Both the choice of focus and of country require some explanation.

Why Project Planning and Project Management?

Project planning and project management are critical in the industrialization and the transformation process for least four reasons. First, projects are the concrete expression of development plans and dreams. Whether we are talking about addressing 'basic needs' or about riding the product cycle, it means, if we are serious, that at some point these notions have to materialize in the 'bricks and mortar' of an irrigation project, a new hospital or polyclinic, the construction of a machine-tools facility or a petrochemical complex. Whether and how projects are planned and managed has an enormous bearing on the practical attainment of development goals.

Poor project conception leads to partial or complete failure to achieve stated developmental goals whether these are the provision of adequate water or electricity supplies to some target population, or the easing of costly transportation snarls, or boosting exports and foreign exchange earnings. Bad project planning and management can lead to the same results even if the basic project conception was sound.

Experience makes it quite clear that the success or failure of many activities can be directly traced to the original conception of the activity, how it was planned, organised and put into effect. Genesis, gestation and parturition can stamp an activity for life. In the areas of development and industrialization, this basic truth holds. Project planning, project management and project implementation are often key determinants of the success or failure of industrial ventures. Once a badly planned and implemented industrial venture comes on stream, subsequent remedial efforts are often costly or ineffectual or both.

A second reason for focusing on project planning and management lies in the growing significance of technology and technology policy issues for economic transformation in today's world. It turns out that all of the technology policy issues with which current analysis is concerned, are often most vividly exemplified, and can be studied most closely and concretely, in projects especially large-scale industrial projects. Similarly, the technology policies of countries, whether implicit or explicit, often find their concrete expression in actual projects and their planning and management.

Issues such as building a country's technological capability, the acquisition of foreign technology, the cost and terms of such acquisitions, the impact of technologies used on the environment, the economy, culture, etc., are all often expressed, and can be concretely observed, in projects, and decisions about which projects will go forward, and how and where they will proceed.

It therefore pays the student of technology policy issues to study what happens in the planning and management of projects. Important lessons are often to be learnt here. In fact, it is in many cases more rewarding to pursue this line of approach than to study the written technology policies of governments, the speeches on the subject by ministers, and the functioning of state or parastatal organizations supposedly concerned with formulating and implementing technology policy. It is after all commonplace to observe that people can say anything. It is often more important to watch what they do, rather than what they say, or what they say they are doing.

An important corollary of this argument is that for technology policy recommendations to do the most good, they often have to be taken down to the level of project planning and management. They cannot be left, as they so often are, at the level of pious recommendations on the procedures to be followed by state research institutions and line ministries, or recommendations on macro-policies to be pursued by Central Banks and other organs of the central government.

These latter are very often important in their own right, but as we shall see in this study, they very often suffer from the fact that they can be totally undercut by, or proceed in abstraction from implicit technology policy decisions which are subsumed in decisions on project planning and project management These latter technology policy decisions are often characterized by (1) their implicitness, (2) the fact that they are subsumed and effectively hidden, (3) their frequent contradiction of explicit, official technology policies, and (4) their concreteness, in the sense that they are the policy decisions which are real and manifest, as opposed -to the rhetoric of official speeches, and the abstractions White Papers, the mission-statements of official institutions, and even enacted legislation.

There is a third reason for the significance of project planning and project management decisions. In a study of what goes on here, we can often see capsuled or embodied many of the critical international issues of the cut-throat modern world in which we live. For example, we see underdeveloped, culturally backward countries with unsophisticated bureaucracies, either being persuaded by metropolitan experts, or themselves picking the wrong industries to go into industries or activities that have lost their growth dynamic, and are in the mature or declining phases of their product cycle. In some cases, these countries have rushed (or been pushed) into activities which are about to experience dramatic technological change, leaving the host countries with shiny new plants which are technologically obsolete at the ribbon-cutting ceremony or soon thereafter. All of this is often traceable to project conception and project planning.

Studying project planning and management in the 'new states' we can see up close as well, the abrupt collision between archaic, somnolescent, colonial bureaucracies and modernity It is especially marked in the suddenly affluent oil exporters in the post-1973 world. Officials in a bureaucracy that had been originally designed to do little more than collect taxes, issue stamps and maintain the 'Queen's order', suddenly found themselves having to deal with international banking consortia, make decisions on technological choice, choose among the competing tenders of international construction companies, respond to problems involving licensing agreements, shipping conferences, the validity of feasibility studies done by prestige names Like Arthur D. Little, and evaluate alternative financial proposals involving different debt-equity ratios and something mysterious called 'leverage'.

It is in the arena of large-scale industrial projects in these countries, their planning and management, that we get perhaps one of the best cockpit views of the results of colonialism, neo-colonialism and backwardness. Here, like perhaps nowhere else, we can also see learning taking place and trace the impact of increasing sophistication in some Third World countries as they engage in negotiation and bargaining with large U.S. transnationals and phalanxes of international bankers. Suddenly, these countries have to learn to sue or defend suits in international courts. Suddenly too, they are plunged into the icy-cold waters of protectionism, as the doors to metropolitan markets abruptly slam shut against the products of their new multi-million dollar plants. Several of these countries today find themselves stranded on the rocks of their illusions about 'free trade', 'market opportunities' and 'being part of the free world'.

Fourthly, the resources that can be committed to a large industrial project can be nothing short of immense, especially for an underdeveloped country. Steel plants, LNG trains, petrochemical complexes, etc. are all frightfully expensive. These projects can represent a major share of the investment capital a country is ploughing into the future. Further, the economic significance of such projects may be even greater than implied by their share of a country's gross or net capital formation.

For example, wastage of resources here can have really very serious economic and social implications. Badly conceived or badly planned projects which fail (e.g. an LNG facility in a world with an embarrassing gas surplus) can be devastating for an economy, especially that of a small, Third World country. While not on the same scale perhaps, cost and time overruns can imply significant resource costs, especially of precious foreign exchange.

Project planning and project management are crucial to what happens in a country with respect to these issues. In fact, it is quite surprising that economists have not focused much more heavily on these areas of study. Enormous attention has been given to refining rarefied measures of social costs and social benefits in project analysis. Relatively little has been paid in the mainstream economics literature to the broader set of issues involved in project planning and management.

Trinidad and Tobago as a Case Study

On one level, it might seem that there would be relatively little likelihood that students of transformation and technology policy problems, would find any useful lessons of general applicability emerging from a study of Trinidad and Tobago's experience. Trinidad and Tobago does not have the physical size or the population size that partly underlies the significance of a Nigeria, an Indonesia or a Mexico. Neither does it have the natural resource abundance or the geo-political importance of a Saudi Arabia.

As countries go, Trinidad and Tobago is tiny, with a population of just over one million (1,079,000 in 1980) and a land area of under 2,000 square miles. Its proven oil reserves (600-700 million barrels) are miniscule when viewed in world scale, and its oil production at its all-time 1978 peak was no more than some 234,000 barrels per day. By 1984, this had declined to just under 170,000 b/day. What little significance it had in the oil world during the 1960s and 1970s, derived more from its role as part of the complex of offshore refineries set up in the Caribbean by the oil companies to produce residual fuel oil for the US East Coast, than from its contribution to world oil output.

Trinidad and Tobago is interesting however, for at least two reasons. One is that it is in the 'classic' small, underdeveloped, resource-based, ex-colonial mould. In many ways it is a pure case. It proves to be a fertile testing-ground for several of the hypotheses and assertions of both recent and current development theory, including theory about technology policy in developing countries. The life of the analyst is not clouded and complicated by extraneous factors and special difficulties. There is little of the complicating factor of international politics as in an Iran or a Saudi Arabia.

The population is small and almost wholly literate, and despite its plural nature, does not come close to matching up with the problems of a huge, very heterogeneous and tradition-bound population as in the Nigerian case for example.

Trinidad and Tobago is one of the world's oldest oil exporters. It has been in the business of exporting petroleum and petroleum products since the early years of the 20th century (1909-1910), long before many of the current giants of the oil world (Kuwait, Nigeria, Saudi Arabia, Britain, etc.) Unlike most of its English-speaking Caribbean neighbours, Trinidad and Tobago has had the advantage of a lucrative natural resource over a long period. The particular resource, oil, is characterized not only by lucrativeness (especially post-1973), but also by the potential it offers for linkages and for spin-off industries. Properly used, the industry can provide a fruitful base for genuine industrialization and transformation. In the 1970s, this general potential was suddenly allied to the available capital needed to realize it. There was, in addition, a propitious international climate, as the metropolitan world reeled before an apparent energy shortage. Trinidad and Tobago is also an important laboratory for studying the impact of foreign capital and the multinational corporation on the transformation of the less-developed countries. On a per capita basis, it has been one of the 'major hosts for foreign capital among developing countries. Its hosting of foreign capital goes back a long time as well.

It has played host to the transnational oil corporations for more than seventy years. (Shell Oil entered Trinidad in 1913). One finds exhibited in the Trinidad and Tobago case, pretty much the full range of relationships between foreign capital (private and institutional) and host governments in underdeveloped countries. Relationships which range from wholly-owned subsidiaries through joint ventures, to a variety of contractor and consultant arrangements, management agreements, technical assistance and licensing agreements, and so on. All of this has taken place within a context of consistent docility on the part of the government where foreign capital is concerned. For those who aver that foreign capital and the TNC do, or can, play a catalytic role in economic transformation, it is necessary to come to grips with the Trinidad and Tobago experience.

Second, Trinidad and Tobago is a fascinating study because it is small. One of the consistently most intriguing issues in development theory is the implication of small size for transformation strategy. Do small countries suffer special disadvantages because of their size? Does the absence of a large, domestic market demand particular economic strategies, and rule out others? Are economies of scale really important? Does small size necessarily imply inability to reap economies of scale? Can the application of modern technology (micro-electronics, biotechnology) effectively vitiate the problem of scale? Is it not true that small countries are bound to be exporters and cope with the rigours of the international marketplace? If so, how should they organize to do this effectively, and what kind of strategies make the most sense for them?[1]

All these issues arise to haunt both the analyst and policy maker when the problem of choosing among alternative project ideas arises. So do several others. If small size is a disadvantage, then how do we explain the fact that some (or even, many) of the most successful countries on the

---

[1] See Demas (1965), Best (1966), Thomas (1974) and Farrell (1982).

international scene are small? What is the secret of their success? What strategies do they employ that can be used by other small countries?

This concern about the supposed advantages and disadvantages of size bedevils not just development economics. Similar debates can be found among agronomists and agricultural economists with respect to whether small farms are inherently more efficient than large. It also arises in the organization and management literature with respect to firm size and business success and among students of technology policy with respect to firm size and innovation.[2]

The industrialization strategy of a small oil exporter offers the opportunity of illuminating some of these issues through a study of the actual industrial ventures entered, the fate of these ventures and the reasons why. In the case of Trinidad and Tobago, we see a country which has had the experience of seeing virtually none of the large, expensive industrial projects it started in the boom years (steel, fertiliser, methanol) fulfil the expectations held for them.

Was this simply a case of bad planning, or of being outfoxed by the transnational companies with which it dealt, and the metropolitan world behind them? Or, seeing that many similar projects in the metropolitan countries also failed, is it an example of the problem of being small?[3] Was it that the industrial strategy pursued was completely wrong?

The significance of small size also arises in a very special way in the Trinidad and Tobago case from the point of view of technology policy. Some of the now popular suggestions as to the desirable technology policy strategies for underdeveloped countries are seriously called into question from a study of the Trinidad and Tobago experience (e.g., strategies of learning by doing over several projects as a way of building technological capability. Let us now turn to an examination of precisely what is involved in industrial project planning and management before addressing the Trinidad and Tobago experience in greater detail.

---

[2] See Peters and Waterman (1982), Ch 11-12, Freeman (1974, Ch 6), Koch (1980, Ch 9),
[3] See for example, Peters and Waterman (1982, p. 141). If large country A attempts 20 projects and 5 fail, the system as a whole may do very well and easily write off the failures. If small country B attempts 6 projects and 5 fail, (the same 5 as in country A), disaster may ensue.

2

PROJECT ANALYSIS AND THE PROJECT CYCLE: AN OVERVIEW

Introduction

The process by which a large project such as a steel mill, a medical complex, a new airport or a petrochemical plant, finally materializes into finished, operational form is generally long, always complex, and often very expensive. The ordinary industrial plant may easily take three to five years just to construct. In the case of nuclear power plants, this can easily stretch to a dozen or more years. This is just construction. If one takes into account the length of time a project may have been on the drawing boards, before construction, the gestation period for many projects is staggering. To give just one example: Trinidad and Tobago's new methanol plant which came onstream in 1984 took some three years to construct. However, the initial pre-feasibility study was undertaken in 1978, some three years earlier than construction start-up, and serious official interest in a methanol project was stimulated in 1974, four years before that. Thus, from conception to commissioning, a decade had elapsed. This is not unusual.

The planning, management and execution of a large project is also extremely complex. It involves the initiation and coordination of what is often hundreds of different activities, drawing upon a variety of different disciplines and areas of expertise. Several branches of engineering are generally involved, as are marketing, finance and accounting, industrial relations, the management of complex organisations and systems, economics, ecological sciences, physical planning and, not infrequently, a liberal dash of politics. The management challenge often covers thousands of workers and dozens of different organizations.

In today's world, a large industrial project is often enormously expensive as well. A price tag running into hundreds of millions, or even billions of dollars is not uncommon. Two or three large projects can easily swallow up most or all of the investment budget of a small or medium-sized country for several years. In addition, cost and time overruns can make the original price tag, however high, look modest by comparison with the final cost. Expenditure overruns and or mistaken project decisions, both of which may lead to failure and large financial losses can easily drive a major corporation to the wall or plunge a small country into effective bankruptcy.

In order to make sense of any of the complex of issues that find expression in the execution of a large project, whether these are issues of technology policy, better planning techniques, finance, or broad development problems, it is necessary to disaggregate a project into its constituent stages and aspects. Let us attempt this exercise now, keeping in mind as we do, two important points. First, while the setting out of the various stages of a project from planning through management to execution and start-up may seem mechanistically clear-cut, in practice this is not the case. Activities overlap or are repeated several times in various stages. Stages do not necessarily follow each other in linear sequence as we shall set them out here. They may be undertaken with a greater or lesser degree of simultaneity, depending upon the circumstances. Some may even be undertaken 'out of turn' at times. In addition, stages and activities often shade into each other. Second, the delineation and ordering of stages or activities we shall present below is just one, hopefully useful approach to disaggregation. Other schema are possible, though most seem to vary in the degree of disaggregation undertaken, rather than in the activities identified.

We can break down the process of planning and executing a project into the following broad stages:

Stage	Activities	Key Actors Involved
Project Conception	Gestation of project idea Approval of Concept	Client's In-house staff/ Consultants/ 'Serendipity'
Project Planning	Preliminary Analysis Feasibility Analysis Approvals Organisation Set up Financial Arrangements Formal Project Development & Project Planning Engineering Design	Client/ Consulting Engineers Specialist Consultants (Finance Feasibility Studies, etc.) Financial Organisations Project Manager Design Engineers
Purchasing/ Procurement	Preparation of books of tender Evaluation of bids Negotiation and contractual arrangements Choice of suppliers, contractors, sub-contractors Detailed Engineering	Client Consulting Engineers Project Managers Contractors, Sub-Contractors Suppliers Consultants
Construction	Delivery, Inspection, installation of plant and equipment Site Preparation Plant and building erection Infrastructure and ancillaries; Manpower planning, recruitment, training	Project Managers Contractors, Sub-Contractors Specialist Consultants (e.g. manpower training) Consulting Engineers
Commissioning and Running-in	Plant start-up and handover Troubleshooting	Project Managers Specialist Consultants/ Consulting Engineers/ Client

Before beginning a discussion of what is involved in each stage of the project planning and execution cycle, it would perhaps be useful to provide an overview of the key actors and their roles, since many non-engineers may be unfamiliar with the relevant details.

Project Planning and Management: The Key Actors

It is useful to identify certain key actors or organisations that are generally involved in the planning, design, and execution of projects, and to briefly describe their roles.

(i) Client: The client is the owner/ initiator of the project being planned or constructed.

(ii) Consulting Engineer: Since the client (perhaps a state enterprise or government ministry) may have little technical expertise in either plant construction or the specific project area, a firm of consulting engineers may be hired:

(a) To advise the client on technical matters;
(b) To represent the client's interest in negotiations with contractors, suppliers, etc.;
(c) To maintain oversight of the project during construction and commissioning in order to ensure the client's interests are being properly looked after;
(d) To assist in the evaluation of bids and in the preparation of books of tender, as well as the choice of contractors, suppliers, etc.;
(e) To perform specialist services such as finding executive talent for the new facility, organizing manpower training, assisting with feasibility studies and so on.

In some cases, consulting engineers may be hired, not because an organization does not have the technical expertise in-house, but because its own staff are busy with regular duties, and it is deemed wiser to have the relevant functions undertaken by someone who can accept full responsibility for their successful execution.

(iii) Project Manager: The project manager is essentially concerned with the coordination and control of the complex of activities that are involved in the construction and commissioning of a project such as a new plant. These activities may number in the thousands. It is the responsibility of the project manager to coordinate and control the various activities, and to liaise with and supervise the work of various sub-contractors concerned with matters such as instrumentation, piping, foundation and civil works, electrical installation, plant erection, and so on.

The project manager also necessarily plays an important role in the procurement process. Equipment and materials ordered from outside suppliers have to be decided upon, physically ordered, transportation and payment arranged, inspection conducted (on-site and/or at source), storage organized, and general control over use exercised. Much of this either falls within the project manager's direct jurisdiction or impacts sufficiently on it that he necessarily has an important voice in decision-making on these matters.

Because of the project manager's function in control, coordination, and supervision, it is clear that especially on large, complex projects, the project management staff must possess a great deal of technical expertise and experience. It is also clear that good or bad project management can save or cost a client a great deal of money. The efficiency of the project manager, his budgeting, costing and planning, and his ability to operate to budget is of very great significance to the success of the project

Project management may be entrusted to the same firm that functions as the consulting engineers. (This in effect means that there is no specialist consulting engineer). It may also be carried out as an in-house function, either using an ad hoc group created from within the client's own organisation and entrusted with the responsibility, or there may be a particular permanent unit within the organizational structure charged with the project management function. In developing countries of the Caribbean type, large projects seem to almost always involve the hiring of an outside firm to act as a specialist project manager.

The project manager is also in some cases the same firm that does design engineering work for the plant or facility being built. This situation may be preferred especially when dealing with sophisticated or complex technology. Here the designers of the facility may need to be kept in close contact with the process of its construction so that bugs may be ironed out and specialist knowledge applied which the initiators of the technology may best possess. Having the same firm that manages the project do the design may also improve efficiency, in some cases. Separation of the design function from project management can sometimes lead to responsibility falling between stools. Where the functions are integrated, one organization has the clear responsibility to see that the design works as it is supposed to.

On the other hand, for a developing country the integration of the two functions may lose the chance to develop and deepen its technological capability by carrying out the project management function itself. In simple projects, involving standard processes, equipment, etc. there is probably little to be gained by contracting out both these functions to the same, foreign firm, and perhaps a fair amount to lose.

(iv) Design Engineers: The design engineers are the professionals who undertake such functions as :

(a) Area layout for the plant;

(b) Determining the process flows through the plant
(c) Determining the sizing of vessels, the specifications of equipment and machinery required, the interconnections necessary, designing, piping, instrumentation, electrical installations, etc
(d) The foundations required and other civil engineering specifications, e.g., drainage, sewerage, etc.
(e) Working out the bill of materials for the project.

The design engineers produce the set of drawings which enable a host of other people to do their work. Equipment suppliers can fabricate the necessary vessels, pipelines, instruments, etc. exactly as required when the specifications have been determined and given to them. Standard equipment such as pumps, compressors electric motors, etc. which can come in various sizes, with different performance characteristics and capabilities, can be bought once the design engineers have indicated what would be needed to perform a particular function. The same thing applies to the purchase of materials such as catalysts and other raw materials and intermediate goods.

The design engineers would specify such things as the amount of water the new plant would need, and the type of water, whether steam would be needed and where in the process, what type of alloys should be used in the manufacture of pipes or vessels depending on the pressures to which they would be subjected, the corrosive materials to which they would be exposed and so on.

The design engineers play a key role in the business of technology and its concrete application in a facility. In some cases, they have either developed processes or equipment in-house. They may also have knowledge of, and experience with, alternative technological options for carrying out a particular function. They may therefore play an important role in not just designing a plant, but in pushing certain technological choices. It is here that the knowledge and experience of the project managers and particularly the consulting engineers may be needed as an effective counterweight.

Similarly, the materials specified by the design engineers, the equipment and machinery required may either preclude or open up opportunities for local suppliers. It is often the case that if the motivation exists, a plant can be constructed with what is effectively, a mix of technologies. Not only can equipment and machinery be sourced from a wide variety of countries and suppliers, depending upon which is best and which is cheapest, but different functions of the plant can be carried out at different levels of technological sophistication. This, of course, has implications for the development of local supply capabilities. Similarly, the fact that there are in many cases, alternative choices with respect to materials used, again has implications for the development of local (or regional) capabilities.

To perceive and identify these possibilities implies the need to penetrate right down into the details of the work of the design engineers and the further need to be able to intervene at that level. The discussion of 'unpackaging or 'unbundling' in the literature on technology policy is of great relevance here.[1] The motivation and orientation of the design engineers is clearly important to the final outcome, not just economically in terms of project cost and subsequent operating costs and operating efficiency, but also in terms of broader issues of technological development. By necessary corollary, so too is the role of the client's in-house technical staff, their orientation and motivation, and that of the consulting engineers and project managers, since all these people, assuming that they are all separate entities, participate in the decisions on design.

(v) Contractors and Suppliers: Sub-contractors are hired to carry out particular specialist functions, such as civil works, land clearing and site preparation, electricals, piping, building construction, installation of vessels, machinery and equipment, furnishing of offices, etc. There may be dozens of sub-contractors hired to work on a project at various times during its construction and commissioning. The availability of such specialists, their skill, expertise and reliability, is an issue not just for completion of a project within time and cost budgets, but also in terms of the technological development of a country. One frequently encountered problem in Caribbean underdeveloped countries is the relative lack of such specialists, (outside of relatively straightforward areas such as civil engineering), who are at least good enough to be given an opportunity to develop, even if they cannot yet compete on an even footing with foreign rivals. Part of the problem here is small size and its implication for what I have elsewhere called the 'Blackman Effect'.[2] This relates essentially to the lack of sufficient opportunities for the practice of specialized skills in a small country.

There are also numerous suppliers who are drawn upon in the process of constructing a large project for everything from nails and staples, to giant compressors and specially constructed plant. These suppliers may be required to do the detailed engineering necessary for actually carrying out a function specified by the design engineers, or producing specialized pieces of equipment. Once again, the availability of the relevant skills locally or regionally is one of the critical issues for technology policy. For example, without an indigenous capital-goods industry, there may be

---

[1] See Junta del Acuerdo de Cartagena (1976) and Sercovitch (1980).
[2] See Farrell (1982).

no chance of local producers playing a role in the supply of equipment, machinery and certain other inputs required in plant construction.

(vi) Other Specialists: There are a variety of other specialist organizations whose skills may be drawn upon over the course of a project's gestation into an operating facility. These range from consultants who specialize in doing feasibility studies, to financial specialists who help to plan and arrange financing, law firms who may be called in to assist with contracts and firms that specialize in manpower planning and providing training. These people may help in finding and training the eventual work force for the plant. There may also be a need for industrial relations consultants, information specialists, and so on. Let us turn now to the detailed examination of the various stages and activities involved in the concrete realization of project.

From Project Planning to Plant Start-Up

Essentially, we can distinguish five broad stages in the progress of a project from initial gestation to an operational facility. These are:

1) Project Conception

2) Project Development, formal approvals and project planning

(3) Purchasing and Procurement including negotiations and contracts

(4) Construction

(5) Commissioning

Project Conception

This activity involves the birth of the idea that will later take the form of a specific project. This may be an idea for a new product at the level of the firm. It may be a political response to the pressure of some group of citizens for relief of their water woes, or for electricity to reach their community. This pressure may be translated into an order from a political figure to a government bureaucracy or a state enterprise to do something to address the problem. The idea may be the intellectual offspring of technocrats charged with responsibility for planning or industrial development, or whatever.

Experience shows that original project ideas can spring from the most unlikely sources. The process is often far from rational. This is not to say that such projects are never successful. Far from it. Two examples, both drawn from the Caribbean, illustrate the point. It was reported to the author that the idea for a project to make a new product (yogurt) came from the wife of the chairman of a holding company which owned a large food and agro-processing subsidiary. The chairman's wife had reportedly tasted the product on a European holiday, liked it, and asked the chairman 'Why don't you make yogurt?' They did and the new product reportedly enjoyed considerable success initially when it was launched.

The second example relates to a new maternity hospital set up in Trinidad and Tobago. A group of the author's students sent out to study the planning that went into that project and brought back the startling news, which they insisted was correct, that the genesis for that project lay in a 1968 Conference on the need for Family Planning. Nobody could explain to them the process by which the presumed concern of that meeting had been translated into the need for a new maternity hospital.

A project idea can then be born in any of several different ways: by an enterprise's response to perceptions of threat or opportunity, by a process of rational deduction, starting deduction, starting from an identification of some social need, by serendipity, by the desire to take advantage of some new technology that has been developed, by formal brainstorming sessions in a corporate or governmental office, etc.

Any of several things can happen to an idea after conception. Much depends upon who was the initiator, and in what circumstances the idea was born. In some cases, ideas languish for years in desk drawers or in consultants' reports, before something happens that leads to their abrupt resurrection. For example, the idea of a steel industry or some component of it floated around in one agency of the Trinidad and Tobago government (the Industrial Development Corporation) for two decades, beginning in the mid-1950s. The development of direct reduction technology led to more serious consideration of the idea around 1971, when large reserves of natural gas materialized. However, it was only when the OPEC oil price hike of 1973-74 abruptly conferred windfall oil wealth on the country, that this idea took concrete form as a project.

In other cases, the time span from original idea to a functioning project can be quite short. Often, when the chairman of the Board proposes, nobody dares oppose, and everyone scurries to dispose. Where the idea eventually proves to have been hare-brained, much regret is subsequently expressed, and murmurs are often heard about the wisdom of formalizing the process of generating and vetting new project ideas. When the idea proves a brilliant success (as did Sony's Walkman, a product apparently of its Chairman Akio Morita's ad hoc inspiration), tributes are paid to the progenitor's vision and acuity. Talk about formal method evaporates.

For our purposes here, three aspects of the business of conception stand out. First, it is often at this stage that success or failure is really determined. As we shall see, the formal processes of feasibility analysis that are supposed to separate the rice from the husks, are riddled with methodological flaws. Therefore, especially when one factors in the role of politics and power in organizations, and their implications for how decisions are in fact made (whatever the numbers say) the quality of the original conception is in many cases, key.

Second, there can be little presumption that formalized methods for generating project ideas carry guarantees of eventual success or are necessarily better than non-formal methods in the sense of having a superior track record of coming up with winners. There is no substitute for the acute perception of the creative mind that something will work. It matters little whether this perception is mediated by formal processes (e.g., roundtable brainstorming) or not.

Third, one of the most sobering problems in project work is the often long time between original conception and activity start-up. In a situation where conception, analysis and decision can take say 3 to 5 years (not unusual), construction another 3 to 5 years, and then commissioning, shaking out the bugs, and running production levels up to design capacity another 2-3 years, one can find then that anywhere from 7-12 years can elapse between conception and a plant in full flight. One's guess that something will work or be profitable, in many cases, has to be related to what will be happening perhaps a decade or more into the future.

Project Development and Project Planning

There are perhaps six key activities or issues that fall under this rubric:

(2a) Preliminary Analysis

At some stage, an idea begins to be taken seriously in an organization. At this stage, the crucial activity of preliminary analysis begins. This involves: -

(i) Data-gathering: Collecting information about the particular industry, commodity, activity that is being considered, what is happening in domestic and/or international markets, etc.

(ii) Preliminary Engineering Analysis: Here consideration is given to what will be involved in setting up a particular plant. Issues such as alternative output levels, type of products possible, possible suppliers and contractors, various technological options, alternative approaches to handling the project are subjected to some analysis.

(iii) Preliminary Cost Estimates: Rough, rule of thumb estimates of costs are generated. In some cases, these are ballpark figures quoted by suppliers or potential contractors, based on experience with roughly similar sized projects elsewhere. These figures are of course usually quite far from the estimates produced at later stages of the project and from the eventual final figure. In any event, these are the figures that the basis of the initial, economic feasibility studies.

(iv) Field Visits: Trips may be made to functioning factories or ongoing projects in the same or other countries, in order to get a feel of what is likely to be involved, and get some feedback from the experience of others

(v) Options for Financing: Preliminary analysis undertaken of the options for financing the potential project. Preliminary or exploratory discussions with financial institutions may be held both to get an idea of the cost of financing and the level of interest the project would generate in the financial markets.

(vi) Initial Decision: At the end of this exercise, a decision may be taken to either drop the project or to pursue it further, perhaps with major or minor alterations to the original conception. This stage is an extremely critical one in the life of any project. Decisions made here often largely determine the approach to the project and what happens after According to one author, "During this phase, which will cost only a small fraction of the overall project, decisions are made which determine 90 per cent or more of the cost of the project and largely determine its operating profitability; the wrong process chosen, whether to go ahead or not, the wrong size of plant, the wrong type Of equipment whether to contract the work out or not, the timing, the speed of the work etc. Wrong decisions on these could lock the company into unprofitable investment for many years".[3]

At this stage, basic decisions are made that are an expression of implicit or explicit technology policy. Certain technologies may be ruled out of consideration either for philosophical reasons or as a derivative of the choice of product and/or choice of plant. Decisions as to how the project should be pursued, for example, whether on a turnkey basis or with local project management and an eclectic approach to putting together activities, technologies and suppliers, have tremendous portent for the organization or country's development of its technological capability. Even decisions as to whether to proceed with the project or not can be of great, though at the time unrealized, significance.

---

[3] Harrison (1981), pp 52 -53

Part of the problem often encountered here is that these initial, critical, decisions are in many cases being made based on information that is rather sketchy very far from being comprehensive, and with figures of a rather rough sort. Another problem is that the planners may have very little or no experience with the particular technologies, industry or markets that the project involves. For example, a small developing country with no prior experience in metals production, would naturally find itself few or no people experienced enough in metallurgy, steel production, the nature and record of firms in the industry, etc. to reliably make the kind of sound investment decisions on a new steel mill that Nippon Kokan of Japan would make. Experience shows that while high IQs and intellectual brilliance may be assets of some value, there is nothing like thorough knowledge of an area and in-depth familiarity with all the actors associated with it as a basis for wise decision-making.

In short, operational experience can confer significant advantages However, it would not do to overstress this. Sometimes, too much familiarity leads to blinkered vision. This is the problem of the experienced expert who believes that because something has been done the same way for the last thirty years, that is the only way to do it, or that because something happened in certain circumstances in 1950, apparently similar circumstances necessarily mean the same denouement in 1990.

Also, history does record several instances of companies or countries making successful entrances into business of which they previously knew nothing. Transformation in fact demands precisely that. New activities, new industries, new methods of doing things. The real point is that there is a learning curve, and that inexperience often means ignorance which can be costly, if not fatal.

The essential lesson of experience is that considerable time, care and effort need to go into this stage of project planning. Careful, detailed, painstaking and thorough information gathering and analysis will pay rich dividends. This may sound so obvious as to be trite and even platitudinous. In fact, in an operational situation this stricture is not at all obvious. There are several reasons why it is so often ignored.

For example, very thorough and detailed study at this stage may cost what, at the time, seems like large sums of money to say nothing of time. It often involves large expenditure on travel and data collection. Considerable time and effort may have to be diverted to collecting information about minutiae. Now psychologically, many managers are instinctively reluctant to fork out sums which may run into hundreds of thousands of dollars, for the pursuit of investigations which may at times appear to be meandering rather aimlessly, and which may not result in anything concrete and profitable. A simple example is staff requests to investigate comprehensively all the technological options for a particular process, or all the options for a piece of equipment, when "everybody knows" that so-and-so is used by 90% of the people in the industry".

(2b) Organisation

At some point in time, either before the preliminary analysis is undertaken, or after it, a decision usually has to be made about organisational arrangements for pursuit of the project. In some organisations, a special, ad hoc group may be created to take charge of the project planning exercise. In others it may be simply given to an existing staff in an organisation as part of their routine responsibility. Once again, a great deal depends upon the decisions taken in this regard. The quality of leadership of a project group, its vision, dynamism and values play a very great role in the quality of work it does, and the management decisions its analyses precipitate. A project entrusted to the dead hand of a tired, archaic bureaucracy in the line ministry of a government may be doomed from the start.

(2c) Formal Project Development and Project Planning

At some stage after the preliminary analysis undertaken, the results of this analysis and recommendations as to the development or cessation of the proposed project, have to be decided upon by top management, whether at board level in a corporation, or at ministerial or even Cabinet level in a government. The quality of the analysis submitted, and the competence of the decision-making body to decide, are two crucial, interrelated issues.

If a board of directors, or a ministerial policy committee, or a Cabinet is comprised of knowledgeable, experienced people, they will tend to know what information to look for in a staff report, how to evaluate it, what weight to give to the figures proffered, and what questions to ask. Often in underdeveloped countries, the decision-making body does not have the necessary competence. Its members not only may have little personal expertise in the area of the proposed project but may not have expertise on any related areas that could be brought to bear.

For example, it is clearly of little use to put forward a refinery or petrochemical project to a Cabinet for decision, if the Ministers of Health, Education, Works, Finance and External Affairs are ignorant not only of the petroleum and chemicals industries and what is happening to them, but also have no experience with what happens in large industrial projects or what is involved in running a business. They will either be prisoners of the numbers and analyses put before them, or they will make the decision on irrelevant or spurious grounds. Human beings, it might be noted, en passant, often seem not to be bothered by, or even aware of, their own ignorance, and frequently do not allow it to disqualify them from having an opinion or making a decision. All that happens is that a decision on a particular project will turn on such considerations as who is putting it up, whether they are liked or disliked, respected or disrespected, whether all the bureaucratic formalities in putting a proposal forward have been followed to the letter, 'gut feelings', suspicions as to the ambitions or political machinations of particular individuals or organisations and so on.

Whether competently or incompetently made, once a decision to proceed has been arrived at, we now enter a stage of formal project planning and project development. This involves: -

(a) Giving formal consideration to how the project will be organized, what procedures will be followed, etc. Sometimes this is handed down as an order accompanying the decision to proceed.

(b) If this has not been done before, consulting engineers may be hired to give advice on how the project should be approached, to assist in the planning of the technical details and the actual choices that would have to be made, and later on to represent the client's interest and act on his behalf

(c) Firmer decisions are now made on exactly what is wanted, details of the products to be manufactured are hammered out, as are production volumes, target markets, estimates of time to completion and start up, etc. Plans are drawn up for how the project would proceed, who would be involved, and so on.

(d) Approaches are made to design engineers (if this is being contracted out) project managers are interviewed and perhaps chosen (again, if this is being contracted out), other more detailed discussions may begin with banks or other possible sources of finance. Until some work has been done with respect to the design of the new facility, it is usually not possible to begin to generate any detailed figures about likely costs, nor can firm quotations be obtained from equipment and other suppliers since these generally have to have some idea of the engineering specifications to which they would have to produce.

This is yet another crucial stage in the life of the project, and it is one that often overlaps with, and shades insensibly into the two preceding it, or the ones following it. The original conception begins to take on a little firmer shape. However, there are characteristically many alterations and modifications to the original idea, discussions proceed with potential suppliers, more information is gathered, initial grandiose conceptions are found to be impractical, and reports of superior new processes or equipment performance, turn out on more detailed analysis to have been exaggerated.

(2d) Engineering Design

Often in a small developing country, a large industrial project involves hiring foreign firms to do the engineering design work. Sometimes the same firm may also be hired as project manager. Sometimes the two activities are contracted out to two different firms. In a large corporation some of the basic design decisions may have been taken at the preliminary analysis stage and only the detailed work is left to be done. In a developing country such as Jamaica or Trinidad and Tobago, it is often the case that most of the engineering design work only now gets into full swing.

The client, the consulting engineers and the design engineers/project managers, begin to work very closely together at this stage. This is one of the most important processes for technology policy decisions. It is here that, many of the hard decisions are in fact made. The design engineers, who are often foreign, and may be large, international engineering firm with proven experience and expertise, may have their own ideas as to what will work and what will not. They would have knowledge of the alternative chemical processes for manufacturing methanol for example and have views as to which is preferable. The decision would carry with it a long train of consequences for equipment supplies, possible local involvement, costs, and so on.

Arrayed against this is the local client, say a government ministry or state corporation, whose personnel may not have sufficiently broad international experience with the industry in question, and the client's consulting engineers. Often in the Caribbean region, the local engineering consulting firms are rather weak, lacking both in the breadth and depth of their expertise. As Cyril Solomon's analysis of the region's capabilities in this area attests, local firms are not as strong as necessary in such areas as mechanical, electrical, chemical, and mining engineering.[4]

Frequently, therefore, the consulting engineers are also foreign firms who may or may not have a local firm as a tag-along to help secure the contract. In some cases, the use of foreign engineering consulting firms is lubricated, if not mandated, by the conditions of donor agencies in cases involving financial aid.

The significance of this is that neither the design engineers nor the engineering consulting firm may be highly motivated to use the project as an instrument for developing local technological capabilities At the same time, the local client, private firm or state enterprise, may lack the

---

[4] See Solomon (1983, pp 109-115) for a summary of his conclusions of the region's capabilities in the area of consulting engineering firms.

knowledge and experience themselves to insist on choices that would have a positive repercussion on the development of local capabilities.

Not infrequently as well, the local client may not be conscious of this as a desirable goal. To compound matters, the logic of the situation may in fact militate against this. A corporation, whether state owned or privately owned, is generally concerned, and should be, with the 'bottom-line'. It is therefore interested in executing its projects with maximum efficiency, at minimum cost, in the shortest time, and with the best operational results possible. Strategies that may develop local capabilities in the long run, can easily conflict with this desirable (shorter run) objective. Local suppliers for example have to travel up the learning curve. This means concretely that they will make mistakes initially, produce work that is inferior and/or costlier than that available from more experienced, foreign suppliers.

It may be desirable for the society as a society to pay the costs of learning, but no individual manager wants to be the actual paymaster through having his new factory subjected to frequent breakdowns as a result of poor-quality equipment. Neither is he willing to be forced to bear higher costs than necessary through inferior technology, or bad plant lay-out. It must be recognised therefore that often it is not just the foreign design engineers/project managers, and the foreign consulting engineers who, faced with the choice of cheaper, more efficient, more reliable but foreign technological choices, or more expensive, less reliable local choices, opt for the former.

To these strong, valid arguments from the foreign organisations involved in these projects, there must be added, for analytical purposes, a recognition of other, less noble motives also at play. Foreign engineering firms may opt for particular solutions in part because these have been tried and tested by them over time. They are comfortable with them, know them, and therefore do not want to change. In addition, they may have an implicit, or explicit bias, not just to familiar equipment and processes, but to those of their own home country. They may genuinely believe these to be the superior technical solutions, or they may be interested in boosting their country's exports of its capital goods and technical services, or they may have direct or indirect interests (financial) in the supply of equipment and processes. They may therefore be looking forward to not just the profits from the project, but to a much longer-term flow of profits from royalties, spare-parts sales, etc., or they may just prefer to deal with certain, familiar supplier firms in whom they have confidence.

The actual design work involves such things as deciding on and specifying via drawings the vessels, equipment, pipelines, etc. that the new plant requires, designing the layout of the facilities, the process flows, specifying the foundations required, the materials to be used in construction, the ancillaries required (emergency equipment, stand-by generators, etc.) the location of the buildings, and so on.

On the basis of this work, a bill of materials can be drawn up, detailed specifications for the manufacture of equipment (pumps, generators, compressors, pressure vessels, piping, etc.) can be outlined, and tenders for supply invited. Firmer and more detailed plans for the scheduling of work on the project can be prepared, and various sub-contractors for specialist jobs can be hired.

(2e) Feasibility Studies and 'Go' Decisions on Projects

The question may have already arisen in the mind of the reader of exactly what role feasibility studies (the economic and financial analysis of projects) plays in the project planning phase, and at what stage it arises. The first point one should note here is that in most large projects economic/financial analyses are performed not just once but repeated at several different times. In addition, several alternative variants of the project are typically analyzed, especially nowadays with the widespread availability of computerized spread-sheet analysis. These permit a project to be considered from any of different angles, varying product mixes, financing options, output levels, expected product prices, etc. These computerized techniques have really permitted sensitivity analysis to be taken to a very high level.

In most commercial projects, the emphasis is on financial analysis i.e., on Discounted Cash Flow analysis to calculate present values and estimate Internal Rates of Return. Despite the frowns of the theoretical purists, considerable emphasis also tends to be placed on computations of the payback period. Where projects are being financed in whole or in part by international donor agencies, there is usually a greater chance that economic analysis of a project will also be undertaken in an attempt to assess the social benefits and costs of the investment.

It is a rewarding exercise to review the feasibility studies conducted for several projects in the past and compare the projections with the eventual out-turn. The results raise very serious questions about the usefulness of current methodologies. In this study we shall see this concretely with respect to the large industrial projects undertaken in Trinidad and Tobago in the 1970s.

Part of the problem lies in the timing of the feasibility studies in relation to decisions about the viability of the project. Usually, a basic 'Go/No Go' decision is taken at some stage after the results of the preliminary analysis are delivered. In theory, this decision can be subsequently rescinded if fresh, or further information seems to warrant it. However, when the initial 'Go/ No Go' decision is made, this can lead, if positive, to considerable expenditure for design work plus negotiations and the entering into contractual agreements with several parties -- design engineers, project managers, suppliers, and so on. Psychologically at least, the project begins to acquire momentum which can prove difficult to stop.

It is generally at some point in the formal design stage that really 'firm' information as to costs begins to become available. Previous estimates tend to be ballpark or rule-of-thumb data. It is when equipment suppliers, civil engineering contractors, and other professionals are given precise specifications of what would be required of them, that they can give 'precise' estimates of the costs involved. Observation suggests that these new estimates are almost always rather more than first thought at the rule-of-thumb or 'ballpark' stage.

The first problem that arises then, is that the initial feasibility studies on which the formal decisions are made are often based on inferior numbers. Conceptually, the use of sensitivity analysis should help. In practice since the decision has to be made on the basis of some 'most likely' or 'best guess' figures, the availability of sensitivity analysis does not obviate the need for some judgement as to the expected eventual cost of the project. This is made on the basis of what is known at the time. Sensitivity analysis might help to set up boundaries, for example, as long as actual costs do not rise by 2% or more above estimated costs, the project should be profitable.

However, when once a decision is taken on this basis (a particular best guess estimate), the problem of psychological momentum can arise. If subsequently at the design stage it is found that in fact cost estimates are likely to be 20% or 25% above the expectations arrived at in the preliminary analysis, the response in many cases seems to be to find some way to juggle the project parameters -- reduce the size of the plant, alter the output mix, cut back on systems or sophisticated equipment. Often, the people charged with developing the project have developed a psychological bond with it and do not want to see it die. They believe in it, or their jobs, promotions, and prestige come to be bound up with its continuation and success.

If the top management to whom reports are made is not sophisticated and experienced, a project like this, one where the prognosis indicated by the numbers from firm estimates is much worse, can slip through.

The essence of the problem here then, is that a reasonably detailed set feasibility studies with reasonably good numbers can often only be done after a certain point in the design and project development stage has been reached. However, at this point, the fundamental decision to proceed has already been taken. While conceptually, it can be reversed, there are often strong psychological and organisational pressures that militate against this. The key to dealing with this situation seems to lie in the thoroughness and the quality of the work done in the preliminary analysis stage, before the basic 'Go/No Go' decision is taken.

Here the quality and experience of the consulting engineers and/or the quality of the client's own in-house engineering and technical staff can turn out to be critical. The reason is that the greater the quantum of the basic design decisions made at the preliminary analysis stage, the easier it is to obtain firm or firmer quotations from potential suppliers of materials and services. Similarly, the more exhaustive the analysis of the options, the more detailed the data that can be incorporated into the initial economic and financial analysis.

There should be no illusion however, that even the data arrived at the design stage will generally prove to be the final figures. One of the most worrying problems for any project manager is the threat of horrendous cost overruns, far beyond any contingency allowance. In a recent analysis of the problems of cost estimating in process plants, one author identifies five different types of cost estimates (differing according to the stage of the project at which they are prepared) and offers estimates for the degree of error associated with each. According to Desai, the error, plus or minus, associated with each stage, is in general, as follows:[5]

Type of Estimate	Error +/- (% difference between estimated and actual final cost)
Order of Magnitude	40-50
Study	25-40
Preliminary	15-25
Project Control	10-15
Detailed	5-10

It is readily apparent that with a project costed at, say $1 billion, an error of 5-10% in the detailed estimate can involve a sum of $50 million to $100 million. A decision on a project costed out at such a sum in the preliminary estimate, can involve an error of $150 million to $250 million.

---

[5] See Desai (1981)

That errors in cost estimates can in fact be extremely large is amply confirmed by experience. Harrison, for example, gives figures for reported cost escalation on different types of projects: 50% on petrochemical projects, 140% in North Sea Oil projects, 210% on nuclear power stations, and 545% on Concorde.[6] Such enormous variations in cost, if they are in an upward direction, can clearly destroy the economic viability of a project.

Bad as this is, there is yet another very serious problem that arises with project analysis. Every price in project analysis exercise is, by definition, a future price. Prices quoted for construction costs, or plant and equipment may be prices relating to deliveries of goods or services a few months away, or perhaps a year or two away. Changes here, for example due to inflation, are as we have seen, problematic enough. What is even more problematic are expected prices for the final product to be manufactured in the new facility.

When the relevant analysis is being done, the prices it is assumed the output will fetch may be prices starting up 3, 4, 5, even 10 years into the future, and stretching out 10 or more years beyond that, depending upon the time horizon over which the project is being evaluated price forecasts are often based on historical prices, with some escalation factor applied. So it may be assumed that if prices for the product in question have grown on average by 2% over the last decade, they can be projected to grow at this percentage over the next ten or fifteen years A range may be used in practice, around some most likely figure.

However, this approach often proves with hindsight to have been quite unsatisfactory as a method of proceeding. Structural changes taking place in the industry in question, or in a related industry may radically alter the future trajectory of prices. Technological change taking place in distant areas, geographically and sectorally, may be on the verge of throwing up substitutes which would dramatically throttle the market prospects for the products of the new plant now in gestation. The usual methodology for arriving at expected product prices, based on assumed, often arbitrary, escalation factors, generally fails comprehensively to take account of this. Recent experience with projects in the oil and energy field provide vivid examples of this. While economists in metropolitan countries have spent large amounts of time trying to refine social discount rates, shadow exchange rates, and methods of measuring the immeasurable, these major methodological flaws at the very heart of project analysis techniques go

---

[6] See Harrison (1981) p. 147

unremedied and often unremarked.[7]

Errors in estimates of future prices for a project's output can again lead to dramatic failures. This is of course a commonplace, and it happens with projects everywhere, as do cost overruns and the problems they generate. What is significant for our purposes here is the implication of these mistakes in major projects in small, developing countries. The losses experienced by large firms or by developed countries because of bad decisions on projects, and/or errors in estimates, can be, and often are, shrugged off. With both large firms, and large developed countries, one or two or even several failures which are written off are more than compensated for by the successes.

For a small firm, or a small country and especially a small, poor country, virtually everything, including the proverbial kitchen sink, may be gambled on just one or two large industrial projects. Failure here may mean the demise of the small firm taking the gamble, or the virtual bankruptcy of a small, developing country. A couple of large projects may represent, as indicated earlier, almost all of a small country's investment budget for several years. Not only can it not afford to lose the capital involved, but the haemorrhage of funds and of foreign exchange to subsidize uneconomic public- sector projects can help plunge the government's budget and the country's balance of payments into deficit, and eventually drive the country into the trauma of an IMF embrace.

Small countries (and small firms) are much more vulnerable than their large counterparts, especially, these are not just large, but rich and diversified. The body-blows the latter can absorb, the former cannot. Therefore, the weaknesses of current project analysis methodologies is of especial significance for small firms and small countries. Such entities, have to make sure that they do their homework better, and that their guesses are consistently more correct. They can less afford to be wrong.

The organisation which is doing the feasibility study can be very important. The issue is not just the competence, knowledge and experience of the analysts involved, but their awareness of the cost of mistakes, and the cost of failures. The practice in small, developing countries of the Caribbean type of hiring foreign consultants to conduct their feasibility studies, runs into precisely this problem. These organisations may employ their customary methodologies, without either an awareness of the implications of the forecasting problems mentioned above, or a grasp of the real significance of error for such countries. In

---

[7] Experience with most of the widely used reference books on project analysis methods provides striking confirmation of this. See for example, Little and Mirrlees (1974) or Squire and Van der Tak (1975)

any event, they have little incentive to do better than they do. This applies, as we shall see later, to even the most prestigious names in the field, firms whose fundamental competence is widely conceded.

(2f) Financing

Arranging financing for large projects is a complex, technical and often delicate matter. The financial arrangements can hamstring the way in which the project proceeds and how the finished plant operates. Such factors as the tying of financing to particular countries as suppliers, or to particular equipment or technology or product line (for example, when aid agencies are involved) can frustrate the objectives of a developing country's planners. In addition, the debt burden the facility carries can, if not intelligently arranged, prove to be an incubus on the back of the new plant.

Where large projects are involved, financing is very often arranged nowadays through a consortium of banks. The consortium is put together by one lead bank and the members of the consortium may put up varying proportions of the total financing the project requires. In many cases, the consortium is international, in the sense that the banks or other credit agencies involved are drawn from several different countries. This is sometimes a deliberate strategy on the part of the lead bank, in order to increase the security of the loan. The theory here is that default is less likely when the debtor, in calculating the risks and costs of default, has to confront the possibility of angry reactions, and perhaps trade boycotts, by several different countries, not just one. It is expected of course that a bank's home government and sister institutions, to say nothing of its home country's legal institutions would all line up behind it a confrontation with a defaulter.

It is also often the case that international development agencies such as the World Bank may play crucial roles in either financing a project or arranging finance. Similarly, export credit institutions in plant and equipment supplying countries often play an important role in providing finance. (e.g., the US Ex-Im Bank or Japanese Ex-Im Bank).

Commercial bank financing has tended to have fewer strings attached than either aid agency financing or Ex-Im bank-type financing. In many cases however, commercial banks, finding it difficult to assess both political and commercial risks in developing countries, rely on signals of creditworthiness from international institutions such as the World Bank or IMF in making decisions on loans. The banks may also establish credit limits for individual countries or regions in an effort to diversify their portfolios and reduce their overall risk exposure.

Typically, lending institutions will want to screen a project closely where large sums of money are involved. However, given the weaknesses of project analysis techniques with respect to reliable forecasting of future prices and other imponderables, the scrutiny of the commercial banks, especially in boom times is hardly fail-safe. The quality of the names associated with the project not infrequently has considerable influence on financing decisions.

From the point of view of the borrower, there are certain critical factors that have to be given consideration in arranging financing. These include such basics as the interest rate quoted, whether it is fixed or variable, if variable, the basis of variation, the term of the loan, the fees being charged by the financiers, the guarantees required, how highly leveraged is the project (the debt-equity ratio), and the consequent implications for project cash flows, whether the financing is tied or not, and the provisions written into the loan agreement relating to such matters as the circumstances under which the loans can be called.

Purchasing and Procurement

As a result of the work done in the project planning and development stage, two major sets of functions can now be undertaken. First, if this has not already been taken care of, project managers can be selected, and contractors and sub-contractors can be hired. Secondly, arrangements can be made for the supplies of equipment, machinery, materials, and so on.

As intimated earlier, it is sometimes the case in large industrial projects in developing countries such as those in the Caribbean, that the same firm may be hired to do both design and project management or to do both design and the consulting engineer's function. Sometimes in larger, more sophisticated countries, large firms may do their own project management, or specialist institutes can sometimes be found doing this in some more advanced developing countries. Whatever the actual situation, it often seems to be the case that one way or another, by the time this stage is reached, the issue of the project's management has already been decided.

One important issue that arises with respect to both the main contractor/project manager and to other sub-contractors is the type of contract entered into. First, there is the question of how cost is dealt with. There are two basic types of contract(a) Fixed price, and (b) Cost-plus. There are several variations, permutations and mixtures of these two types in practice. A fixed price contract as the term implies, involves a specified price agreed on beforehand for the completion of a job. A cost-plus contract involves the addition of an agreed-on percentage mark-up, or other addition, to final costs as defined and agreed by some formula.

Each type of contract has advantages and disadvantages especially in its 'pure' form. A cost-plus contract gives the contractor no incentive to control costs and imposes no penalty for failing to do so. A fixed-price contract may avoid this type of problem, but gives the contractor every incentive to cut corners and compromise on quality and standards. While in principle any escalation of costs beyond what was anticipated, or any underestimate of price by the contractor, is not the client's concern with a fixed-price contract, cost escalations which threatens the contractor with a serious loss or even bankruptcy can create problems for the client. He may be left with an incomplete job despite the availability of litigation as a remedy.

Several recent contracts examined by the author contained elements of both fixed-price and owner-account costs. Also, there are in some cases incentives built in in the form of either explicit bonuses, or bonuses from the sharing of savings, for a contractor completing a job within time and cost budgets.

Apart from the question of price, contracts may differ in terms of what responsibility is given to the contractor, especially the main contractor, or project manager. At one extreme is the turnkey contract, in which the main contractor/project manager has responsibility for virtually every aspect of the project. This includes design; detailed engineering; procurement decisions; responsibility for actual procurement; hiring of construction and other contractors and sub-contractors; training and even recruitment of staff for the new facility.

As the term implies, with a turnkey contract, the client essentially walks into a completed facility at the end of the project and makes little or no intervention into the details of its design and construction after the initial planning phase. At the other extreme is in-house project management in which control over and coordination of all aspects of the project are handled by the client's staff. In between these two types, considerable variation is possible.

In both the acquisition of contractual services, and the provision of various supplies (materials equipment, etc.) tendering is frequently used as a basis for selection. There are various types of tendering processes possible. Tenders may be invited from specific organizations; they can be arranged in stages so that there is an initial open competition, a short-listing, and then a final selection. Firms may be required to 'pre-qualify' before being allowed to enter a bid. Various constraints may be placed on who can qualify. The evaluation of bids and the decision on awards may also be carried out in any of several ways. These may be designed to boost or to block the chances of certain organisations being successful. Similarly, there can be considerable variation in the degree of detail required in tenders, and in the extent of the investigation mounted into firms entering bids.

In some cases, the financiers of the project may impose constraints on the tendering and selection process. This is frequently the case where funding coming from international aid agencies. Political pressure from other countries is also often encountered in practice. These pressures are often designed to boost the position of metropolitan firms, though the arguments are generally couched in terms of the efficient execution of the project (which is however a real and important issue).

The choice of process technology often sets up boundaries as well in terms of the selection process where suppliers of services and physical inputs are concerned. In some cases, once the process is specified, the business about suppliers is, ipso facto, settled.

This stage of procurement and purchasing is clearly one of the most critical with respect to technology policy issues. There is often the dilemma of choosing between cheaper costs, better quality and the promise of greater operating efficiency on the one hand, and higher short-run or medium-run costs, lower quality and some operational inefficiency but the start of the development of local technological capabilities, on the other. While it often does not take much thinking to recognize that the latter choice is often in principle the wiser, the real problem that arises is how much should be sacrificed now to achieve the long-run gains from learning? What mechanisms must be set up in order to ensure that learning and the development of domestic technological capabilities in fact takes place from giving opportunities to local suppliers? How does a small country with no existing nucleus of a capability get off the ground? How does a small country with perhaps just one or two domestic firms in an area, avoid both the evils and inefficiencies of monopoly and the problems of the 'Blackman' effect.[8]

In some cases, the problems are at an even more basic level. Policymakers and planners may not understand at all the significance of the decisions made about projects and the details of projects for the development of local technological capabilities, or for the acquisition of needed foreign technologies. The project may be viewed purely in terms of its hoped-for boost to foreign exchange earnings, or its alleviation of some domestic need. In such cases any contribution of the project to the country's technological advancement may be little more than fortuitous.

---

[8] Farrell (1982, p.9)

It is important to emphasize clearly the significance of the first two stages of the project cycle for the technological advancement of backward countries. First, experience demonstrates clearly that in many modern plants, the critical technology involved in them is the technology built into them. The skills involved in running many of today's highly automated, sophisticated plants are often not that great.[9] The real skills are involved in their design, construction, and sometimes repair. Second, precisely for this reason, the important point of intervention in terms of developing technological capability is in these areas. Third, the scores, and even hundreds, of activities and technologies that are brought together, directly and indirectly, in the planning and construction of a large project provides unmatched opportunity for technological development and industrial advance. It is in the first two stages of the project cycle that the critical decisions bearing on these possibilities are made.

Three specific issues that loom large in the second stage need to be also illuminated rather more fully here First, much of the business of procurement involves, directly or indirectly, the acquisition of foreign technology. Often, the processes that the new facility will use are patented. The catalysts required may be proprietary and their exact composition a secret. Alternative technological processes may exist. Different suppliers may be willing to offer greater or less access to their technologies, their plants and facilities abroad, or local participation in special design and development work that have to be done for the new facility.

The issues of cost of technology therefore arises frequently here. Licences may have to be acquired. Their cost and the technology available through them need to be addressed. Other issues of commercialization arise, for example, what are the channels, open and hidden, through which the project manager/ consulting engineer, the various contractors, consultants and suppliers, are seeking to receive payment for their technology? Are the prices quoted 'fair' or 'exorbitant'? Can better deals be had? What mechanisms must be negotiated into the various agreements, and what systems must be set up domestically in order to ensure that the technologies sought are in fact acquired? Has there been proper identification of what technologies are required, what can be acquired, from whom, on what terms?

Whether these questions were posed at all at the project planning and development stage, and how, if at all they were answered, now finds concrete expression at this phase of procurement, purchasing, negotiation and bargaining.

---

[9] See for example Braverman (1974) for an early, insightful articulation of this point.

The second specific issue that arises here is the criticality of knowledge and experience. Ignorance and inexperience at this stage manifest themselves as a costly disadvantage. The value of experience arises in several different dimensions responding to arguments offered by the design engineers as to why something cannot be done or is best done in one particular way; knowing what technological options exist, what supply possibilities exist; knowing what is currently a 'fair' price for a particular service; familiarity with the track record of various suppliers offering their services. Here the weakness of a country's public service, state enterprises, and engineering consulting firms is concretely seen as a serious disadvantage.

If one is inexperienced, perhaps little can be done about this except to acquire the experience. But it is certainly true that method, organisation, and the sophistication of one's general understanding of the dimensions and dynamics of the game can provide some compensation. This raises the third specific issue that arises at this stage This is the importance of method of proceeding and the importance of information.

Painstaking, thorough investigation and information gathering can do a lot to palliate the disadvantages of inexperience and lack of knowledge. A country with no previous experience of steel production or methanol production, that decides to go into these industries is well advised to pay careful attention and devote considerable resources to information gathering and to search.

Search may involve detailed and careful investigation of large numbers of potential suppliers (in the aggregate), located in many different countries. It may mean considerable travel, studying and evaluating the experience of others. It will mean a great deal of information about technologies, operating experience of various plants, searches of patent records, study contractual agreements signed by others and especially by metropolitan organizations faced with similar decisions.

The detailed information and analysis conducted is one of the important bases for the determination of one's specific objectives. This is in turn the basis of one's strategy in the procurement and contracting stage of the project cycle and in the approach to negotiations with contractors, sub-contractors and suppliers. Needless to say, this kind of exhaustive preparation can be both time-consuming and expensive. Little wonder that officials in many an underdeveloped state think it a mark of wisdom to eschew it. Little wonder then that their countries, if not they themselves, ultimately pay enormous costs through errors committed with respect to this business of procedure.

Construction, Commissioning and Plant Start-Up

The construction phase of the project involves a series activities such as:

- Earth moving and site preparation
- Foundation work (piling, excavating, etc)
- Civil engineering work - drainage, sewerage, road building, etc
- Testing and installation of machinery and equipment
- Laying down of pipelines, cables, etc
- Erection of buildings
- Setting up of ancillary systems for such things as steam generation, water purification or cooling, stand-by electricity generation, etc.
- Linking various systems together, instrumentation work, etc

The work in this phase of the project cycle may overlap with that of the previous phase i.e., procurement. In fact, it may even begin before all of the design work has been completed. Also, other activities such as recruitment and training may start up during the construction phase.

The role of the project manager is really critical at this stage. A host of details have to be covered and coordinated. Small slippages, little inefficiencies often seem to cumulate into major problems. Crisis management is very much involved as well, whether this relates to sudden flare-ups of industrial relations disputes, or to the discovery of design errors which would be costly to correct, or to unexpected problems with suppliers.

Planning of activities, time-phased and costed, is an important aspect of the project manager's job during the construction phase. On large projects, such techniques as PERT/CPM (Critical Path Method) are sometimes used for monitoring and control. On small ones and even some large ones as well, the older techniques of Gantt or bar-charts are used. More and more, computerized methods of planning, budgeting, monitoring and control are finding application.

Things never go according to plan. During the construction phase, it is generally necessary to constantly revise and juggle plans and projections. It is also important that good mechanisms for financial monitoring and control be developed and installed. Several kinds of problems arise which generate cost and time-overruns. Often time overruns end up being cost overruns.

Suppliers may miss delivery dates. This may or may not be their fault. It could be operating inefficiencies in a supplier's plant, a dock strike in the supplier's country or any of several other causes. Over the life of a project, costs may go up because of macro-economic related inflationary factors. Higher wages may be squeezed out of contractors as a result of union or other industrial action. Sub-contractors may not work out and have to be replaced with attendant cost escalation.

In some cases, what seem to be cost and time overruns are in fact the result of faulty estimates at the start. The project manager has to undertake the job of staying on top of all these issues and attempting to control the project so that it is completed to specification and as much within time and budget as possible.

Also important during construction is the phasing, supervising, and coordination of the work of the many different specialist sub-contractors that are brought in to perform various tasks. Over the life of a large industrial project, thousands of people and hundreds of different organisations may be involved at one time or another. Their work has to be planned, costed, integrated with that of others, checked and paid for.

Quality control is one of the critical functions during the construction phase. It arises with the work of the various contractors and sub-contractors It also arises with respect to the equipment procured, and the procedures for installation and testing.

Finally, there are minor and ancillary matters that crop up. Such issues as security, adequate storage, public relations, managing relations between the various organisations that interface on and off the project site, including the client, all have to be attended to.

Finally, at the end of the construction phase, when the new plant is mechanically complete, the business of commissioning and start-up has to be dealt with. In a sense, this is the moment of truth. It is also often a very important and highly technical stage in the project cycle. Commissioning activities can require several weeks to be successfully completed. In some cases, specially trained personnel may be involved. At the end of it all, a new plant is operationally ready, output begins, and now the real moment of truth arrives. Will the new plant work as intended? Will its product sell? Was it a good project to have gone into'? What benefits will it really provide to its owners?

3
THE INDUSTRIAL PROJECTS IN THE OIL-BOOM YEARS: AN OVERVIEW

Armed now with the conceptual apparatus of the project cycle and its components let us now begin our evaluation of Trinidad and Tobago s experience with its large industrial projects in the oil boom years.

When oil prices abruptly quadrupled in the 1973-74 period, Trinidad and Tobago had been an independent country for just over a decade and had had full internal self-government (1956) for some seventeen years. Though Trinidad was an oil producer and exporter, and consequently had always been somewhat better off than its Caribbean neighbours, the years since independence had not been very good. In fact, by 1973, the country was plainly in the throes of economic crisis.

Unemployment which had been 6.4% in 1956 had risen steadily over the years to nearly 17% in 1973.[1] The government's fiscal deficit between 1965 and 1975 had expanded at an annual rate of 21.4%. The current account of the balance of payments was likewise in a condition of chronic deficit. By the end of 1973, the country's foreign exchange reserves stood at some TT$67.3 million, equivalent to just six weeks' worth of imports.

Not surprisingly, the economic crisis had produced serious social discontent and a political crisis. In 1970, the country's capital city, Port of Spain, had exploded in anger and frustration in the Black Power riots which featured unemployed youths as the rebellion's shock troops. An army mutiny sparked off by the disturbances, plus the riots themselves, shook the government to its very foundations.

---

[1] See Farrell (1978, Table 2)

It was crystal clear that the development strategies the government had pursued had not worked. Two such strategies may be identified. The first, associated with the name of Arthur Lewis, was predicated on the attraction of foreign capital which would function as the engine of development. The second, borrowed from Latin America, and grafted on to the first, emphasised import substitution as a way of dealing with the balance of payments crisis which had materialised within a few years of formal independence. The failure of the government's economic strategies meant that by the early 1970's, there were massive unfulfilled social and economic needs -- jobs, education, infrastructure, and material welfare.

By late 1973, the combination of economic and social crisis had led the then Prime Minister Eric Williams to announce his imminent retirement from public life. Within a few short weeks of this however, the first oil price shock sparked off what was to be a dramatic reversal in Trinidad and Tobago's fortunes.

The seeds of such a reversal had already been planted. Beginning in the late 1960's, there were major new discoveries of oil and gas offshore Trinidad's east coast by Amoco Oil Company. In 1972, the first fruits of these discoveries had begun to be realized in the form of significantly increased oil production. In fact, from the nadir of 1971, oil production grew by 8% in 1972, 18% in 1973 and 12% in 1974, and from there continued to grow steadily until it peaked in 1978. The increases in production coincided neatly with the dramatic surge in oil prices after 1973 to produce an abrupt windfall for Trinidad and Tobago.

A few simple statistics tell the story. In the eight years before 1974 (1966-1973) government revenues totalled just TT$2 billion dollars. In the eight years after 1974, i.e., roughly to the end of the boom which we can date as 1981, government revenues amounted to TT$29 billion dollars. Expenditure soared concomitantly, from less than TT$600 million in 1973 to over TT$7 billion in 1981.

The government's wage bill rose more than six-fold in the eight years from 1973 to 1981. Foreign exchange reserves moved from TT$67 million in 1973 to over TT$7 billion in 1981 equivalent to 21 months' worth of imports. Revenues from oil soared from TT$80 million in 1972 to TT$898 million in 1974 and TT$4,253 million in 1981 at the crest of the boom (Table 3.1).

Table 3.1

Oil Revenues, 1970 -1983

Year	Central Government Recurrent Revenues	Oil Revenues	Oil Revenues/ Recurrent Revenues (%)
1970	313.2	72.3	23.1
1971	341.9	69.7	20.4
1972	398.2	80.3	20.2
1973	476	107.2	22.5
1974	1297.9	898.1	69.2
1975	1788.4	1257.2	70.3
1976	2219.2	1446	65.2
1977	2971.2	1770.5	59.6
1978	2928.1	1733.5	59.2
1979	3852	2371.1	61.6
1980	6202.4	4136.5	66.7
1981	6818.6	4253	62.4
1982	6824.7	3274.2	48.0
1983	6438.8	2461.4	38.2
1984	6526.1	2696.5	41.3

Source: Central Bank of Trinidad and Tobago, Annual Reports

Opportunity and Response

Prior to 1973 in the desperate years of the early 1970s, the government had been busily seeking out new ideas for breaking out of the economic crisis in which it was mired. A great deal of intellectual attention came to be focussed on the possibilities of utilizing the large reserves of natural gas, which Amoco's exploration had thrown up as a by-product of the search for oil. The dramatic rise in oil prices and the windfall oil revenues it produced, now opened the way for certain ideas that had been marinating for several years to find concrete expression. The Prime Minister, Dr. Eric Williams, reversed his earlier decision to leave political life and his government threw itself into the task of using the new-found financial opportunities to deal with the country's needs and transform the economy.

The strategy that was crafted has been aptly described as resource-based industrialization. Its essential idea was to build the country's industry and its export activity on the basis of its abundant natural resource, natural gas. This was a notion that enjoyed considerable intellectual respectability.

In fact, the well-known Hecksher-Ohlin theory of international trade would seem to fit neatly into it.

Any casual assessment of Trinidad and Tobago's situation would undoubtedly have lent support to such a strategy as the way forward. Trinidad and Tobago was hardly a low-wage country by international standards. Its level of domestic technological development was low, and domestic productivity was not particularly high. Neither a strategy based on the export of low-cost, labour-intensive manufactures nor a strategy based on skill-intensive, innovative new products would a priori seem to have much chance of succeeding. With a small domestic market, inward-looking industrialisation seemed certain to fail. In fact, the country's experience with an import substitution strategy in the 1960s had already demonstrated this clearly.

The decline of the country's agricultural export staples in international markets (sugar, cocoa, coffee) plus its relatively high wage levels did not suggest a future as an exporter of agricultural products. What Trinidad and Tobago appeared to have was hydrocarbons -- oil and gas, and particularly, gas. Therefore, it seemed logical to predicate its development and industrialization on the export of energy-intensive really, gas-intensive products, since it was widely conceded that as a small country, Trinidad and Tobago would have to be an exporter.[2]

The apparent logic of this approach was buttressed in the mid-1970s by the events taking place in the international economy and the climate of opinion these events generated. The energy crisis of 1972-1974 seemed to many people at the time to mark a watershed in world history. For one thing the abrupt manifestation of OPEC's power seemed to suggest that developing countries were at long last managing to turn the tables on the developed, industrialized nations. It seemed that they were managing to reverse the inequities of an international economic order that had first colonized and then disadvantaged the Third World. They were doing so

---

[2] See Farrell (1982) for an articulation of the argument for the inescapability of an export-led strategy for small countries

moreover not by persuasion and moralistic arguments but by the exercise of countervailing power, and power through unity.

Suddenly, the vaunted multinational or transnational corporation did not seem quite so formidable. Suddenly, it seemed that Third World countries, if they had the strength, the unity and the gumption, could do things they had previously thought, and were told, were beyond them. This included the kinds of industries they could aspire to have within their borders, the exercise of control over production and prices of commodities and telling transnational corporations and their home governments just where to get off

Whether it was steel mills or aluminium smelters, supersonic jet fighters or international banking, the idea crystallized in Third World states that these were things they could actually acquire and build and use, not just dream about. Suddenly, the notion crystallized that the First World really and truly had no God-given monopoly over power or over technology.

Countries such as Nigeria and Venezuela or Trinidad and Tobago could now aspire to build steel mills, LNG plants, or petrochemical complexes. This change in perception was also influenced by perceptions about the nature of the energy crisis and what this supposed crisis implied. A lot of agitated discussion in metropolitan countries raised the spectre of an industrialized world, critically dependent on an energy lifeline plugged into the oil and gas reservoirs of the Third World.

Talk about the world 'running out of oil', of natural gas being too valuable to be burnt as a fuel was heady stuff for many a government in energy-rich Third World states. These states in general had neither the intellectual organisation, the wisdom, or the inclination to disregard the froth of international discourse and seriously examine the true energy situation and calculate what metropolitan responses would really be. As such, it was easy to believe that there was going to be a decisive shift in comparative advantage with respect to many industries in a new international economic order with a different distribution of power, and certain areas, of industrial production and the concomitant exports and wealth, would, it was thought swiftly and easily shift to the Third World.

On this basis, energy intensive industries such as steel, aluminium, petrochemicals, LNG and others, which were the activities thought to be synonymous with industrialisation and the developed world, now could and would be entered into by Third World states.

These notions were in fact encouraged by various agencies in the metropolitan countries, including and especially, multinational corporations. To some extent, these corporations genuinely feared the loss of markets and competitive advantage to others given higher and rising energy costs in their home countries as compared to energy-rich

Third World states. They consequently competed with each other to suggest projects to such countries.

However, the advantage in sophistication that many of these corporations possessed, in comparison to the states with which they dealt, enabled them to perceive that Third World aspirations could easily be exploited at considerable profit. Government bureaucrats with no experience to tell them what a service really cost, and with money to burn, could easily be persuaded to sign contracts at enormously inflated costs. Governments hungry for 'high-tech' industry, could easily be persuaded to invest hundreds of millions of dollars in plants and products destined soon to be obsolete. Consultants and contractors had incentives to push their wares in these suddenly wealthy, oil rich countries, given the slowdown in the OECD economies after 1974.

It must be noted that this set of events cannot truly be described as the exploitation by force of unwilling and resisting victims. Far from it. In the states involved, the MNC's, contractors and consultants, often found their 'victims' ready, willing, even begging to be ravished. To a not inconsiderable extent the game involved taking advantage of aspirations which were often naive, coupled with ignorance of the modern world, remnants of the colonial belief that (white) foreigners really *know*, and human ego which would deny indignantly that any of the above applied personally.

The strategy of resource-based industrialization, with natural gas as the critical resource, led logically enough in Trinidad and Tobago to the identification of a list of industries which had as their defining characteristic, high energy-intensity. While some of the ideas for projects pre-dated the 1973-74 oil boom (e.g., steel), several were generated in the first few years of the boom. In quite a few cases as well (e.g., fertilizer and methanol), the suggestions emanated directly or indirectly from foreign companies.

The list of projects grew with astounding rapidity. There were several reasons for this. The industrial projects identified often immediately implied others. For example, infrastructural projects such as ports, pipelines, electricity generation, and so on, were necessary if the large gas-intensive industrial projects identified were to successfully materialize. The pent-up social and other demands of the population were abruptly released, given the general awareness that the country now had money. This meant a spate of projects including housing, schools, health and sporting facilities, and so on.

The boom itself quickly created the need for yet more projects because of the impact that the sudden rise in income and expenditure had on the infrastructure and social services. For example, the rapid rise in incomes quickly led to an orgy of spending on cars. This in turn rapidly translated into tremendous traffic jams on what was now a glaringly inadequate road network. There was consequently an urgent need for several major highway construction projects.

About sixteen large industrial projects were considered between 1974 and 1977. Five of these were eventually undertaken. Major infrastructural projects were embarked on as well: highways, water, telephones, electricity generation (634mw which more than tripled previous capacity), a natural gas transmission system, and a major new industrial estate (which included a new port). Social projects included the creation of several new housing estates, a major new teaching hospital, a financial complex, a new Hall of Justice and a multi-storied new office building (Table 3.2).

The projects listed here are the major projects involving the construction of large, new facilities. In addition, the list includes only large industrial and infrastructural projects. There were a variety of other large projects that might be termed 'social/other'. These involved a school-building programme, a major medical complex (Mt Hope Teaching Hospital) and a variety of large public buildings including a Hall of Justice, a Financial Complex and another sky-scraper housing government offices.

As outlined in Chapter Two, estimates of project costs change and evolve over the various stages of project definition and planning. The figures for 'initial cost estimates' may be more of less meaningful depending on how much work has gone into the project definition and preliminary studies. This varies from project to project. The figures used here for 'initial estimate of cost' usually refer to the earliest figures for project costs that were given. However, in a few cases, other later figures are used, if for example, the scope of the project changed so radically from the initial conception that it was tantamount to defining a new project (e.g. iron and steel). In a few cases, the earliest available estimates were made around the start of construction (e.g. Fertrin Ammonia, Urea, Methanol). In cases such as those, the year in which the estimate was made is indicated.

Table 3.2

Public Sector Industrial and Infrastructural Projects Proposed and Undertaken After 1973

Major Industrial Projects Project	Aim/Objective	Implemented/ Not Implemented	Initial Cost Estimate (TT$)	Estimated Final Cost (TT$)	Special Features (if any)
Iron and Steel	Manufacture of Sponge iron: conversion into steel billets and rods	Implemented (on stream 1981)	$672 million (1977)	$1.2 billion (1981)	Rated Capacity: Iron -1million mt/yr Billets - 600,000 mt/yr Wire Rods – 500,000 mt/yr
Tringen Ammonia	Manufacture of ammonia from natural gas	Implemented (on stream, 1977)	$192 million	$281 million	Rated Capacity: 1090 mt/day; Joint venture with WR Grace
Fertrin Ammonia	Manufacture of ammonia from natural gas	Implemented (on stream 1981)	$619 million	$840 million	Rated Capacity: 2088 mt/day Joint Venture with Amoco
Urea	Manufacture of Urea from natural gas	Implemented (onstream 1984)	$355 million (1981)	$455 million	Rated Capacity: 1620mt/day 100% state-owned; managed by Fertrin
Methanol	Manufacture of Methanol	Implemented (onstream 1984)	$360 million (1981)	$430 million	Rated Capacity: 1200 mt/day 100% state-owned

Major Industrial Projects Project	Aim/Objective	Implemented/ Not Implemented	Initial Cost Estimate TT$	Estimated Final Cost TT$	Special Features (if any)
Petrochemical Complex	Olefins/Aromatics complex producing ethylene, propylene, chlorine, polyethylene, PVC, ethylene glycol, polypropylene, butadiene, butane, benzene, toluene, and five other petrochemical products	Not Implemented	$2 billion		
Polyester Fibre	Manufacture of synthetic textiles	Not Implemented	$185 million		
Furfural	Manufacture of furfural and acetic acid from bagasse	Not Implemented	$41 million		
Aluminium Smelter	To draw on alumina from Jamaica and Guyana and smelt into metal using natural gas	Not Implemented	$268 million to $662 million (depending on No. of pot lines)		Reportedly subjected to fierce metropolitan opposition from certain international agencies. Jamaica opened discussions with Mexico and Venezuela on smelter projects there.
Liquified Natural Gas (LNG)	To liquefy natural gas for direct export	Not Implemented	$2.1 billion		

Major Industrial Projects Project	Aim/Objective	Implemented/ Not Implemented	Initial Cost Estimate TT$	Estimated Final Cost TT$	Special Features (if any)
Cement I	Expansion of local cement plant	Implemented	$29 million	$123.6 million	
Cement II	Construction of a new cement plant	Implemented	$44 million	n.a.	No new cement plant was built in Trinidad. However, a new plant was built in Barbados as a JV between Trinidad and Tobago and Barbados.
Refractory Brick	Manufacture of refractory brick for use in the new steel mill	Not Implemented	Not Defined		
Glass	Production of sheet glass and glass for bottles	Not Implemented	Not Defined		
Single Cell Protein	Manufacture of Single Cell Protein from hydrocarbons	Not Implemented	Not Defined		
Pulp and Paper	Paper production	Not Implemented	Not Defined		

Infrastructure Projects Project	Aim/Objective	Implemented/ Not Implemented	Initial Cost Estimate (TT$)	Estimated Final Cost (TT$)	Special Features (if any)
Water I (Caroni – Arena)	To expand water production by 60 million gallons per day	Implemented	$200 million	$285 million	
Water II (Carlsen Field, North Oropouche, Other Waterworks)	To expand water production	Implemented	$101 million	$125 million	
Electricity	To increase electricity generation capacity by 634MW	Implemented	$288 million	n.a.	
Telephones	To increase the number of telephone lines	Implemented	$204 million (1974-1980)	n.a.	
Pt. Lisas Industrial Estate	To develop a site for several large industrial projects including plant facilities	Implemented	$105 million	(a) 63 million (b) 41 million	Cost split between two entities. The final cost figure of $63 million represents costs accruing to Plipdeco, the landlord and manager of the port. The harbour is owned by the NEC.
Natural Gas Pipeline system	Construction of pipelines to supply industrial projects	Implemented	$86 million	n.a.	In 1974, the system envisioned involved three 20" lines and one 24" line totalling 70 miles, plus compression facilities
Transportation	Major highway projects	Implemented	$437 million (1974-1980)	n.a.	

Notes:

The Iron and Steel project changed radically in scope from initial definition to final approval.

Re the cement project, another figure of $75 million in given in the 1977 Coordinating Task Force Report, as compared to the 1975 Report from which the two figures used in the text are extracted. See Coordinating Task Force 1975, Appendix 4. Here it is unclear whether and when the project definition changed.

Re Caroni-Arena Project: This figure represents the contract sums as of 1979. They do not include, however, certain costs such as project management fees. See Trintoplan, CH2M (69). The actual cost would be higher than the figure offered here.

Re Carlsen Field North Oropouche Water Project: This figure is drawn from the 1977 Budget Speech which gives cost estimates for various water projects. There are aggregated here to give the total cited in the text. See Minister of Finance (77) (66, p.73). The final figure estimate is an understatement of the actual final costs. The figure of $125 million is an estimated cost of contracts sum as of November 1980. It does not include certain other costs such as project management.

Re Natural Gas Pipeline Project: There is a different figure for the transmission systems offered in the same 1975 report. This alternative figure is quoted from a 1974 Amoco study and totals US$50.3 million (TT$120.7 million). There is no explanation for the discrepancies. See CTF 1975 (13, Exhibit V and Appendix XII)

Sources: Coordinating Task Force, Progress Reports (1975) and (1976-1980)
Government of Trinidad and Tobago, Ministry of Finance, *Budget Speeches* 1974 to 1985
National Energy Corporation, *Ten Year Plan 1981-1989* (1981)
Interviews
Trintoplan (1979) and (1980)

Organisational Arrangements

The organisational arrangements for handling this huge list of activities were noteworthy. In September 1975, the government set up an ad hoc body called the Coordinating Task Force. While some of the original project ideas (e.g., steel) had come out of the Industrial Development Corporation (IDC), a statutory body located under the aegis of the Ministry of Industry and Commerce, the IDC was not given the task of developing the projects. It could not have, since its mission was not the development of large-scale industrial projects

Some of the personnel who staffed the Coordinating Task Force were, however, moved over from the IDC. The Coordinating Task Force (CTF) was to report to Cabinet through the Ministry of Industry and Commerce. Subsequently, it reported directly to the Minister of Finance (who was the Prime Minister). Side by side with it was set up a four-person group called the Infrastructure Advisory Group. This was made up of representatives from the Ministry of Planning and Development, the Ministry of Works, the Electricity Commission and the Water and Sewerage Authority. Initially, this group sat jointly with the four-person Coordinating Task Force.

Table 3.3

Membership of the Coordinating Task Force 1975-1979:
(1975 Structure and Composition)

Dr. Kenneth S Julien	Chairman and Project Coordinator
Mr. E.G Warner	Ex-officio as General Manager of the IDC.
Mr. G Rampersad	
Mr. B. Ali	
Mr. S. Martin	Seconded from the Ministry of Finance
Mr. Carlos Hee Houng	Full time officer (formerly with the IDC; served from September 1975 to August 1978. Resigned to become Project Coordinator with the fertilizer joint venture undertaken with Amoco
Mr. R. Batchasingh	From September 1977
Mr. N. Thompson	From February 1977
Mr. R. Pollard	From April 1976
Mrs. C. Diaz	From March 1976
Source: Coordinating Task Force, Annual Reports 1975, 1977 Note: The professional staff approved by the Cabinet for the CTF were: 1 Project officer assigned from the IDC; 2 Senior professionals; 2 Junior professionals; 1 Administrative Assistant; Supporting staff were: 1 Clerk Typist, 1 Clerk/Stenographer, 1 Telephone Operator,1 Messenger, 1 Cleaner, 1 Education Officer and 1 Mechanical Engineer were also temporarily recruited for a short. term school building project for which the CTF was assigned responsibility.	

The CTF had as its professional staff (at peak) one project officer assigned from the IDC, two senior professionals and two junior professionals. This staff plus the five-member Board was by 1977 given responsibility for the overall coordination of the following projects:

- Tringen Ammonia
- Cement Expansion
- Furfural Polyester Fibre
- Iron and Steel
- Fertrin Ammonia
- Power Plant Installation
- Development of Carslen Field/ Las Lomas Water Supply
- Caroni Arena Water Project
- Natural Gas Pipeline System including the distribution system at Pt. Lisas (Phases I & II)
- Point Lisas Marine Facilities
- Point Lisas Industrial Estate
- Elements of the National Transportation System
- Aluminium Smelter
- Petrochemicals -Olefin/Aromatic Complex
- Liquefied Natural Cas
- Refractory Brick
- Methanol
- Pelletizing Operations
- Pulp and Paper
- Development of a Short Term School Building Programme
- National Agro-Chemicals Ltd. Apprenticeship Scheme for O Level Graduates
- Granular Fertilizer Plant
- Brighton Industrial Estate
- Stockpiling of Critical Commodities

All told, the projects being mooted were worth well over TT$8 billion (US$4.3 billion) on the basis of the initial estimates of their cost.

The Chairman of the Coordinating Task Force also had manifold other responsibilities including:

- Deputy Chairman (later Chairman) of the IDC
- Chairman, National Advisory Council
- Chairman, Trinidad and Tobago Electricity Commission
- Chairman of the Board of two industrial projects being built viz., ISCOTT, Fertrin

- Chairman of the Board of the Pt. Lisas Industrial Development Corporation (Plipdeco) up to 1981

In 1979, the Coordinating Task Force was transferred into a formal organisation, the National Energy Corporation, with the Chairman of the CTF becoming the Chairman of the new state-owned company. This was originally planned as a holding company that would serve as an overall corporate planning, control and coordination centre for the various 'line' companies that had been set up in steel, fertilizer, methanol, and so on. However, this arrangement never materialised. By the time the NEC was established in 1979, the majority of the large industrial projects which were eventually undertaken had already gotten underway. So it was really the Coordinating Task Force that played the key role in project planning in Trinidad and Tobago in the oil boom years.

The lack of local expertise in many of the critical areas of project planning and management, plus the lack of local experience and expertise with respect to most of the new industrial activities proposed, meant that a heavy reliance on imported foreign skills and services was inevitable. Foreign companies were brought in in a variety of roles -- project managers, financial advisers, the preparation of feasibility studies, engineering studies and financial plans, and as contractors, subcontractors and consulting engineers. Some found employment providing training plans and training, others were hired to find and recommend suitable expatriates for jobs; still others were able to sell plant, machinery and equipment, to say nothing of a wide variety of services.

Given the many foreign firms involved, the long list of projects, and the numerous activities entailed in planning and implementing these projects, the small number of people deployed in the CTF to plan and coordinate all these projects is a matter for wonder. However knowledgeable and talented individuals might be is clearly very difficult, if not impossible, for them to effectively fulfil such a mandate.

The organisational arrangements were deliberately designed to bypass the public service bureaucracy which was viewed by both the planners and the country's political leadership as moribund, inexpert and indeed, inert. While this was undoubtedly true to a large degree, it is reflective of the Trinidad political culture that the approach taken was not to shake up and reform the bureaucratic apparatus, but rather to bypass it.

The size and nature of the project planning team in the CTF reflected as well the country's inexperience with undertaking so many major projects at one time, and the consequent failure to understand what this really involved in terms of the size, composition, training and experience of the teams needed to properly plan and administer them.

The Projects and the Outcomes

Of the industrial projects listed in Table 3.2 above, most were never actually implemented. In fact, it is difficult to see how they could all have been during the decade of the boom. Up to 1984, five of the large industrial projects had been implemented and come onstream. By contrast, most of the infrastructural projects had been implemented as were several on the 'Other' and 'Social' category, notably the several new housing estates, the Mt. Hope Medical Complex (the Teaching Hospital), and the building programme. In terms of the number of projects which actually materialized, the achievement is impressive.

Our focus in this study is solely on the large industrial projects. Table 3.4 details the cost and organisational features of these projects. They basically cover three areas -- iron and steel, fertilizers, and methanol. All these projects were located at the Pt. Lisas industrial estate, located in the central region. This purpose-built estate, which incorporated a new port, was by 1984 valued at over TT$300 million.[15] It hosted not only the projects themselves, but also a large new electricity generating facility (634MW) and space for other industries. It was hoped that such spin-off industries would be located downstream of the projects themselves as forward linkages.

The five major projects cost a total of some TT$3.2 billon. They represented the major productive investment made by the government with the country's windfall oil wealth. Three of these were wholly state-owned. The other two were joint ventures with foreign transnationals as partners, but with the government nominally holding the majority of the shares.

Up to the end of 1983, none of these projects had managed to turn a profit. In every case, the actual experience turned out to be not at all what had been forecast during the planning stage. We can now attempt to understand what the reasons were for this, how the planning and execution of these projects implied a certain kind of technology and industrial policy and the actual results of these policies. We begin with the case of iron and steel.

---

[15] This figure is drawn from the valuation of the relevant assets given in Plipdeco's Annual Report 1983, plus an estimate of the harbour and its dredging given by an officer of Plipdeco during an interview. This latter cost was reported to be for the account of the National Energy Corporation and consequently not included on the Balance sheet of Plipdeco itself

Table 3.4

Major Industrial Projects Implemented in Trinidad & Tobago 1974-1984

Project	Ownership Status	Total Cost TT$ million	Permanent Employees	Organisational Arrangements
Iron and Steel (ISCOTT)	100% GOTT	1216.8	1200	Locally run up to 1985
Tringen	51% GOTT 49% WR Grace	267.4	90	Management and marketing contract with Grace
Fertrin	51% GOTT 49% Amoco	840.0	270	Management and marketing contract with Amoco
Methanol Co of Trinidad & Tobago	100% GOTT	430.0	190	Management contract with NEC (Government energy company)
Urea	100% GOTT	425.0	n.a.	Management contract with Fertrin; Marketing contract with Agrico Chemicals (US company)

4
ISCOTT: THE VENTURE INTO STEELMAKING 1975-1977

Introduction

Trinidad and Tobago's venture into iron and steel making was the largest single industrial project entered into at its Pt. Lisas industrial estate. In fact, with a price tag of some TT$1.2 billion (US$507 million) it represented the single most expensive project in the country's history. This wholly state-owned project has been an expensive failure. The new facility came on stream at the end of 1980 and was formally inaugurated in 1981. Within three years of start-up however, it was clear that the project, as configured, had failed to meet the objectives set for it. It quickly became a financial albatross around the neck of the country's government, requiring large subventions from the treasury to keep it afloat, and it consequently became an acute political embarrassment. By 1984, the government announced that it was planning to either find a foreign partner to invest in the plant, and take over its operations, or to close it down.

That the new company, Iron and Steel Company of Trinidad and Tobago (ISCOTT) has been objectively a failure is clear. This can be measured by (a) its inability, three years and more after start-up, to produce anywhere near the levels of design capacity; (b) its failure to meet financial targets set out beforehand; (c) technical inefficiencies in terms of plant operation, including poor maintenance of machinery and equipment.

In addition, when the project cycle prior to start-up is investigated, it turns out that the project suffered from substantial time and cost-overruns. In fact, the final estimate of TT$1,216.8 million in 1981 contrasts with an estimate of TT$672 million (US$280 million) in 1977 at the start of construction.

Even though the final figure includes the cost of an additional direct reduction facility not included in the 1977 cost estimate, the cost overrun involved is still very substantial. Given that the extra facilities cost some TT$216 million, the cost overrun on the plant runs to 49% of the initial cost.[16] The reasons advanced by the plant's management for the cost overruns were: (i) inflationary costs; (ii) local manhours during construction increasing from the originally estimated 7,000,000 to a projected figure of 8,356,000; (iii) higher wages demanded and received by construction workers during the period of construction; (iv) indirect costs that resulted from the initial poor performance of the original contractor (whose contract was terminated) ; (v) low estimate of the shipping costs.[17]

The plant went into operation overall about one year after the expected completion date (See Table 4.1). According to the plant's own management, the time overrun was directly responsible for a significant increase in the pre-operational costs or losses of TT$76.8 million "in part because of the need to fund some expenditures by short-term bank loans at comparatively higher costs".[18]

Since coming onstream, production levels in each of the three main areas of the plant have failed to exceed 40% of rated capacity (See Table 4:2). This is of great significance from the point of view of the effective acquisition of the technology to operate the plant. One widely used measure of the effectiveness with which a new plant is being operated is the time span required for production to meet and exceed design capacity levels.[19] New plants generally travel up a learning curve.

---

[16] Submission by ISCOTT to Minister of State Enterprises April 22, 1982, entitled "Financial Status Report and Request for Change in Capital Structure. For capital cost figures see ISCOTT (May 1977, pp. 19-21).
[17] Ibid. p.4
[18] Ibid. p.5
[19] See Baloff (1966), Hollander (1965) and Bell and Hoffman (1981)

Table 4.1
Time Overruns on the ISCOTT Project

Plant Facility	Scheduled Completion	Substantial Completion
Direct Reduction 1	March 1980	April 8, 1980
Melt shop	May 30, 1980	December 1, 1980
Rolling Mill	August 31, 1980	May 8, 1981
High Voltage Power Supply for DR and Melt shop	December 15, 1979	April 1, 1980
Overall	June 30, 1979	Oct. 30, 1980

Source: ISCOTT, Submission to Minister of State Enterprises, April, 1982

Three phases are distinguished by Bell and Hoffman:[20]

Phase 1   Start-up Improvement

Phase II   Post-Start up Improvements (I) "Disembodied efficiency Improvement" characterized by no or minor new investment in capital equipment.

Phase III   Post-Start up Improvement Il "Capital embodied Improvements" characterized by changes in operations involving new investments

Studies done on a wide variety of plants show that the first phase period (that required to reach to design capacity levels) varies widely. Maxwell's study of steel plants in Latin America showed that for seven green field plants examined, the duration of the start-up period varied between two and six years, with an average of 3.7 years.[21] Baloff's study of 28 manufacturing plants showed variations in the duration of the start-up period ranging from two to forty-three months.[22] After four years of operation, ISCOTT had still not completed this start-up period. At best therefore, ISCOTT will be one of those plants at the upper end of the duration scale, those which are the slow learners for one reason or another.

---

[20] Bell and Hoffman (1981, ch.4)
[21] For one plant it was two years, for four it was three years and for two, six years. See Maxwell (1980, p. 10)
[22] Bell and Hoffman (1981, p.120)

A new plant's failure to meet expected production targets may be due to insufficiency of demand for its output well as problems of technical efficiency. In the case of ISCOTT, while the former may at times have been a problem, detailed information on the state of the steel market since the end of the 1980-82 recession suggests that it would in fact have been feasible for the plant to successfully dispose of its full capacity output. Furthermore, other available evidence makes it clear that low productivity of the plant was due to technical and operating inefficiencies.[23]

A 1984 report by a special committee set up by the Trinidad and Tobago government to review the company's expenditure proposals and to find a suitable joint venture partner internationally provides detailed information on operating efficiency in the steel melting and casting area of operations. The report suggested that using various operating parameters related to input usage per tonne of output, ISCOTT's performance was some 20% below that of mini-mill operators with respect to consumables.[24] It also pinpointed excessive downtime for furnaces used in meltcast operations, poor repair and maintenance of plant and equipment and equipment breakdown or failures due to both inadequate maintenance and poor operating practices.[25]

Table 4.2

Production Levels at ISCOTT 1981-1984

Unit	Rated Capacity ('000 mt/yr)	Production Attained ('000 mt/year)			
		1981	1982	1983	1984
Direct Reduction Plants	990	179.5 (18.5%)	217.5 (21.8%)	302.5 (30.3%)	215.1 (21.5%)
Meltshop	600	53.1 (8.9%)	179.2 (29.9%)	209.6 (34.9%)	174.9 (29.2%)
Rodmill	500	29.1 (5.8%)	115.5 (23.1%)	164.2 (32.8%)	123.8 (24.8%)
Source: (a) Charles Labee, "First Caribbean Area Direct Reduction Plant-ISCOTT, Iron and Steel Engineer, October 1981; (b) Ronald Ramlogan (1984, p.189) (c) Point Lisas Courant, vol.2 no. 3, April 1985					
Notes: The melt shop capacity can be stretched to 700,000 tonnes per year with an increase in power supply from 40MW to 50MW					

---

[23] This judgment was concurred by executives of the steel plant in question during interviews conducted in February 1985.
[24] See Esau Committee (1984, Appendix 2)
[25] ibid. Appendix 5

The necessary concomitant of the poor performance of the plant has been larger than anticipated financial losses. Table 4.3 compares the early financial projections made at the start of construction in 1977 with later projections at the end of construction (plant start-up in 1980/81), and with the actual outturn for the first few years since the plant came into field operation. It can be seen from the data that ISCOTT's planners originally expected the plant to begin to show a profit by the third year of operation. The expectation at the end of 1980 when the plant began to come onstream was that by 1983 it would move to a positive profit situation. In fact, as column 3 in Table 4.3 shows, if 1980 is ignored, given that only a couple of months of production were involved, in the three years from 1981-1983, cumulative losses totaled more than TT$620 million.[26] This compares with the 1977 projection of cumulative losses of $50.8 million to 1983, and the 1981 projection of cumulative losses of $TT233.3 million to 1983.

Table 4.3

ISCOTT: Profit and Loss 1980-1985

(TT$ million)[1]

For Year Ending	Profit (+) and Loss (-) Projected at Start of Construction (1)	Profit (+)/ Loss (-) Projected in 1981 at plant startup (2)	Actual Outturn[2] Profit (+)/Loss (-) (3)
1980	-57.6	-112.6	-27.8[3]
1981	-18.2	-113.5	-164.7
1982	+4.1	-65.3	-195.3[4]
1983	+20.9	+58.1	-261.2
1984	+37.9	+116.4	-195.5
1985	+55.9	+166.3	

Source: (a) ISCOTT, Financial Status Report and Request for Change in Capital Structure, submission to Minister of State Enterprises, April 1982, p.3
(b) National Energy Corporation, Ten Year Plan 1981-1990, mimeo, 1981
(c) ISCOTT, op. cit., Attached submission to Ministry of State Enterprises dated June 1982, Appendix III
(d) ISCOTT, Draft Management Accounts, Income Statement for the period ended 30th April 1982

Notes: (1) TT$2.40= US$1
(2) For one year period ending July 31st
(3) Plant did not start up until October 1980
(4) For nine months ending April 1982

---

[26] The figure of TT$ -195.3 million shown as losses for 1982 in fact refer to just a nine month period ending April 1982. The losses for the last quarter of the 1981-1982 fiscal year would serve to increase the cumulative loss figure even further.

According to the 1977 projections, cumulative losses would have been wiped out by 1984 and a positive surplus would have begun to be shown from that year. The 1981 projections envisaged the same thing. However, by 1985 it was clear that these projections not only would not be realized, but that the date at which the cumulative losses would be wiped out and a positive surplus materialize was uncertain and possibly several more years into the future. In 1984, it was reported that ISCOTT's management own budgeted loss for that year was of the order of TT$145.1 million. The actual loss recorded turned out to be substantially greater TT$195.5 million.

The consequence of these much larger than expected losses has been the need for large infusions of fresh capital from the government. This came at a time when the decline in oil prices after 1983 had sharply reduced government revenues and the Trinidad and Tobago economy had sharply contracted. (Between 1982 and 1985, GDP contracted by some 21%).

The significance of this project, and the need to analyze carefully the reasons for its failure derives from at least three considerations. First, there was its sheer magnitude. As indicated earlier it was then the single most expensive project ever undertaken in the country's history. Second, it provides a most illuminating case study for students of technology policy. Here we have an operation that was totally new to the country; the successful acquisition of the technology to conduct it was clearly critical to its viability. The significance of this test case is heightened by the fact that steel-making is one of the premier industrial skills, in addition to which it opens the door to industrial development on a large scale simply because of the enormous number of linkages and spin-off skills it is capable of spawning.

Of concomitant interest, from the point of view of unravelling what went wrong, is the further consideration that Trinidad and Tobago while clearly a Third world country, is paradoxically an 'old' industrial country, with literally decades of experience with industrial operations in areas such as oil and sugar refining. Ironically, Trinidad and Tobago started off this experiment with far greater advantages than many other Third World nations (e.g., a largely literate work force, workers with some experience of industrial operations, etc.).

Third, we shall see that the approach to planning this steel project and the philosophy articulated for addressing the technological issues involved were in many ways progressive. Much of what was done would, on paper, appear to have been sensible and even sophisticated. The failure of ISCOTT challenges, or at least opens to question, much current conventional wisdom about strategies such as unbundling, acquiring technology through buying-in the skills of individual expatriates, the use of specialist foreign consultants, and the value of feasibility studies.

ISCOTT, for example, was not a 'turnkey' project. It attempted to involve locals and local organizations in the most intimate details of project planning and project management, and even to share formally in the project management function. Its planners consciously pursued a strategy of 'unpackaging'- sourcing equipment and systems from all over the world and then putting it all together. A similar strategy was attempted with respect to the recruitment of talent from around the world. Further, while the project ended up being wholly state-owned, it was originally conceived as a joint-venture, in which the foreign partners would contribute technology and markets as well as some equity. Some of the agreements for training workers to operate the various facilities incorporated features that are widely recommended today. Yet, despite all of this, the project has been to date a failure. Let us begin to explore this phenomenon by tracing through the project cycle and what happened. We shall begin with the background to the project.

Background: The Conception

The idea of steel making in Trinidad and Tobago goes back almost thirty years. As early as the 1950's, proposals were floated for setting up iron and steel manufacture in Trinidad and Tobago.[27] The interest at that time derived from what was thought to be a locational advantage that Trinidad and Tobago possessed, lying midway between North and South America. The latter region contained rich sources of iron ore, the former, potential markets.

The early ideas and proposals never got very far. However, at the turn of the 1970's several factors abruptly began to coalesce, and these led first, to the resurrection of the initial idea, and ultimately, to an iron and steel plant being built. The first of these factors was the discovery of large reserves of natural gas offshore Trinidad's East Coast. The second was the materialization of new technology in iron and steel making.

The advent of direct reduction and other innovations in steel-making technology meant (a) that the size of plant which could be technically and economically efficient was dramatically reduced; and (b) extensive use could be made of natural gas in iron and steel making. Natural gas could be used directly, as a reductant converting iron ore to sponge iron and indirectly, as an energy source for powering the various processes, i.e. through using natural gas for electricity generation. Around 1971-72 therefore, the possibility of an iron and steel project began to be

---

[27] Cf. Ramlogan (1984)

examined once again in Trinidad and Tobago's Industrial Development Corporation.

The 1973-74 oil crisis with the resulting dramatic rise in oil prices introduced a third, decisive factor into the gestation of the project. Suddenly, Trinidad and Tobago found itself with windfall financial resources. This seemed to open the door to the economic transformation sought since the 1950's. Furthermore, the very same events which offered this opportunity seemed simultaneously to confer an important advantage on Trinidad and Tobago and other energy-rich countries, a comparative advantage in energy-intensive production processes. It was felt that countries such as Trinidad had cheap energy while others, dependent upon now much more expensive imported energy were abruptly put at a relative disadvantage.

Speaking to his party's annual convention in 1978, the then Prime Minister of Trinidad and Tobago Dr. Eric Williams articulated his government's conception of this energy advantage in these words:

Our historical experience has been dominated by the prohibition of industry and manufacture – the slogan was, not a nail, not a horseshoe. They said, more pertinently, we had no coal, no iron, so energy, no industry. Today no coal, no iron, but gas, so we can buy iron ore. We no longer have to advertise in the New York Times, the Wall Street Journal or the Financial Times. Energy has become a precious commodity in the world and those who need it for survival as a country or as a business, come to us. The bankers who are necessary for this financing equally come to us. They know where the action is, and we don't need to go to them. It is a commodity on which we must build or not build at all. It is a commodity which can trigger off the industrialization programme which cheap labour and fiscal incentives could not hope to achieve. It is a commodity which makes us one of the no more than 10 countries in the entire world that have this precious commodity surplus to its need.[28]

Fourth, as the above quotation suggests, there was, arguably, another rather subtle factor that played a role in the gestation of the project idea. This factor was psychological. It was a set of perceptions about the world, Trinidad and Tobago's place in it, and what industrialization was about. It was shaped by a certain reading of the historical record with respect to industry and industrial development, and the significant role played by iron and steel in this history. It was coloured as well by the muted, faintly bitter memory of the role to which colonies such as Trinidad and Tobago were confined under imperial suzerainty, the role of plantation agriculture, with local industry stifled or forbidden. The

---

[28] Eric Williams (1978, pp. 9-10)

colonies were relegated to the backward status of "hewers of wood and drawers of water" with manufacturing, and even secondary processing of their own agricultural commodity exports, regarded as a metropolitan prerogative.[29]

These perceptions distilled into a set of notions including the idea that steel was almost synonymous with 'real' industrialization. It was argued that steel was "a basic building block of any modern industrialized nation".[30] Trinidad and Tobago's entry into this industry was therefore badge of its newfound status as an industrializing nation, and this was perceived in certain leadership circles as representing a decisive break with the colonial past. Back of these notions was the largely unconscious assumption that because iron and steel were the backbone of 19th century industrialization, they would necessarily play the same role in the future.

Finally, iron and steel making promised to confer enormous spin-off benefits such as increased employment through the variety of linkages it could spawn in the area of downstream manufacturing, and the improvement in the country's generalized technological capability. As a 1976 Report to the Trinidad and Tobago Minister of Industry and Commerce put it:

A steelmaking industry acts as a catalyst for the growth of the metalworking sector through numerous linkages that generate progressively greater employment opportunities. In addition, a local source of steel will reduce the price of steel products manufactured locally at present and in the future. A further benefit to Trinidad and Tobago was that the development of this industry would create invaluable new skills.[31]

Iron and Steel Production: A Layman's Primer[32]

Before going into the details of the project cycle out of which ISCOTT emerged, it would be perhaps useful to provide a brief overview of iron

---

[29] As late as the 1930s, West Indian aspirations to manufacturing and industry were regarded as little short of delusions in many quarters in the metropolis. It was in this context that Arthur Lewis suggestion in the 1950s that the West Indies could and should get into industry was, as the Trinidad economist Lloyd Best has pointed out, a revolutionary contribution. See Lewis (1951)

[30] See Government of Trinidad and Tobago, Report to the Minister of Industry and Commerce (1976, p. 1)

[31] ibid.

[32] The material in this section is drawn from UNIDO (1978), the US Office of Technology Assessment (1980), the Hatch Report (1974), and the American Iron and Steel Institute, Steel Processing Flow Lines (no date).

and steel production, so that the details of the story that follows may be put in better perspective.

The iron and steel making industry consists of a family of linked activities or processes. It is most convenient for our purposes here to think of the activities that go to make up the industry as occurring in a series of successive stages. In each stage however there are alternative processes that may be used for producing the output(s) of that stage.

Stage 1: The Processing of Iron-ore

At the very beginning, are the activities which are concerned with converting iron ore mined from mineral deposits into iron. Iron ore is really a mixture of oxides of iron and other substances (including other metals) which occur naturally in various minerals. Six of these iron-bearing materials are the important sources from which iron may be economically obtained. These are:

Mineral	Iron Content (%)
Haematite	69.9
Magnetite	74.2
Goethite	62.9
Chamosite	42.0
Siderite	48.2
Pyrite	46.6

The mined ores first go through a set of processes generically called beneficiation which basically do two things:(a) separates out some of the unwanted material thereby improving the metal content of what is left; (b) converts the iron-rich material remaining into a form suitable for further processing into iron. The processes employed depend upon the type of ore involved. The processed iron ore goes forward to the next stage in the form of lumps (after crushing to the desired size), sinter, or pellets. Both sinter and pellets are really agglomerations of ore that had previously been crushed and ground to talcum-fine particles (often termed 'fines'). Sinter may contain a wide variety of wastes from ore handling, iron and steel operations and environmental control equipment.

Stage 2: Ironmaking

The next stage involves the activities that process the iron ore into iron. Essentially, this involves removing oxygen from the iron ore. The older technologies for doing this revolved around progressively larger blast furnace operations in which processed iron ore was smelted into molten iron (termed 'pig iron') using crushed limestone and coke (produced from coal). In some furnaces charcoal is used instead of coke. The pig iron produced by the blast furnace method is then either fed into steelmaking operations or cast into iron for the merchant market.

There are several variations of the blast furnace process. These extend to electric furnaces of which about 100 exist throughout the world. Blast furnace operations are characterized, inter alia, by the enormous size necessary for achieving full economies of scale in the modern iron and steel making environment. Blast furnaces of over 2.5 million tons per annum capacity are not uncommon. In the USSR, recent blast furnaces have been designed and built with capacities of over 4 million tons per annum.

Dating from the mid to late 1950s, a new approach to iron production materialized and began to gain ground. This is the direct reduction method. Currently, there are about 20 different DR processes in use around the world, only two or three of which have so far been used on a wide scale, i.e., in more than four plants. The direct reduction processes convert iron ore (fines, pellets, sinter) into sponge iron and other forms of DRI. The term DRI (direct reduced iron) refers to the metallized iron which is produced in a solid state as a result of DR processes. This may be compared to the molten iron produced in the blast furnace. Sponge iron is a common form of DRI the name being derived from its appearance under the microscope. A major difference between sponge iron (and other forms of DRI), and pig iron is the metallic content of each.

The content of iron in pig iron is significantly less than DRI. Pig iron may contain about 90% iron, with the remaining material being composed of carbon (3.0 - 4.5%), manganese (0.15 - 2.5%), sulphur (up to 0.2%), silicon (0.5 - 4.0%), phosphorus (0.025 to 2.5%) and traces of other metals. Sponge iron by contrast, may contain 93% or 95% of metallized iron. This has a direct bearing on the subsequent processes needed to convert pig or sponge iron into steel.

Two important points may be noted here about direct reduction processes compared to blast furnace methods. The first is the significantly lower capital costs of DR processes (one-half to one-third of the traditional coke-oven-blast furnace method on a per ton basis when natural gas is used). The second is that the size of plant required to reap full economies of scale is significantly smaller than the older route.

The most notable of the DR processes developed to date have been the ones that employ natural gas as a reductant. Basically, these processes involve: (a) reforming methane rich natural gas into carbon monoxide using either steam or recycled carbon dioxide; (b) the carbon monoxide is then used together with hydrogen to reduce iron oxide into metallic iron in a solid state.

Stage 3: Steelmaking: Crude Steels

The next stage of activities involves the conversion of iron into steel. This essentially involves using oxygen to oxidize and remove most of the other elements present in metallized iron (e.g., sulphur, manganese, phosphorus, etc). Two main types of steel result (a) Carbon steels and (b) Alloy steels. Carbon steels are those containing 0.5 to 1.0 per cent of carbon and less than 1.5 per cent of other elements. Alloy steels are those containing more than a certain minimum (usually 0.05 to 1 per cent) of alloying metals.

There are a wide variety of different technologies available for converting pig or sponge iron into steel. At least five different processes may be identified: -

(1) Open-hearth

(2) Pneumatic (basic oxygen furnace, acid processes, Linz-Donawiz (LD) and several other variants are included here)

(3) Electric (electric arc method, resistance method)

(4) Continuous processes

(5) Atomic energy processes.

The first three are ones that have found the most widespread use to date. Of greatest significance for our purposes in this study is the third process, the use of electric furnaces, since this is the method of steelmaking that is generally utilized in conjunction with DR processes. Open hearth and pneumatic processes have been essentially associated with pig iron produced by the blast furnace method.

Steel smelted by one or other of these processes then has to be cast into solid form before it can be further worked. Traditionally, steel made by the open-hearth or pneumatic methods is first cast into ingots and then into one of three forms of semi-finished steel: (a) slabs; (b) billets; (c) blooms. More recently, continuous casting methods have been developed which allow molten steel to be cast directly into one or other of these three forms.

Stage 4: Steelmaking II: Semi finished and Finished Steels

From the three basic forms of cast steel – slabs, billets and blooms – a variety of semi-finished and then finished steels are produced in 'downstream' processing facilities such as rolling mills. A range of semi-finished and finished steel products result. From slabs are obtained galvanized products, tin mill products, welded pipe, and steel plates (used in automobiles, ships etc.) are produced, via intermediates such as hot-strip, skelp and plate. From billets are produced bars and light structurals, seamless pipe, rods, wire rods and other wire products. From blooms come a variety of structural shapes including heavy beams used in construction, and railway lines.

However, these are only the most basic members the family of steel products. There are in fact dozens of different steel products which may be produced with different specifications, some of them customized. There are several different alloy steels for example, to say nothing of various tool steels, stainless steels and specialty steels. With this brief sketch of the production processes involved, let us now return to the detailing of Trinidad and Tobago's experience as it attempted to enter iron and steel production.

The Approach to the Project and the Initial Definition

In December 1971, Trinidad and Tobago's Industrial Development Corporation (IDC) began analyzing seriously the prospects for making sponge iron in Trinidad and Tobago utilizing direct reduction technology. Nearly two years later, the IDC contracted a Canadian consulting engineering firm, Hatch Associates, to undertake a feasibility study on the development of an iron and steel complex. The initial project definition was concerned with a plant capable of producing 1,000,000 tons of sponge iron annually, and 500,000 tons of semi-finished steel.

The Hatch study was completed and submitted in March-April 1974, and the government agreed in July 1974 that the project be pursued further. The project was originally conceived of as a joint venture, to which the foreign partners would bring some equity capital, technology and very importantly, access to markets. The business of guaranteed markets was stressed by Hatch in the 1974 report, as well as the importance of gaining access to specialized technical and operating assistance.

Two factors which were later on to prove important were pointed out by Hatch in underlining the potential problem of markets. One was the difficulty of ensuring sales of steel in the open market during a business downturn, steel demand being notoriously cyclical. The second was that the products being planned for the new plant (at that time sponge iron, billets and ingots) would have to be oriented towards the industrialized world (Japan, Europe and North America) where finishing mills existed, since the products being planned were semi-finished steel.[33]

It is noteworthy that the project was conceived from the very beginning as export-oriented. Though the planners recognized at the outset the potential role of a steelmaking facility in generating linkages to downstream secondary manufacturing industries, and in stimulating domestic technological capabilities over a broad front, their emphasis was firmly placed on the project's role as an earner of foreign exchange.

No concrete plans were made for really exploiting the other potentialities of a steel-making facility. The recognition given to them turned out in the end to be lip service more than anything else. The official argument generally took the line that it would mainly be up to local private capital to take the initiative and embrace the opportunities the new complex would afford for generating downstream linkages. In fact, the record suggests that the planners really ended up so consumed with realizing the basic project as initially conceived, plus the other energy-based projects, that they had little time to devote to pursuing the other potentialities of the project in a serious way. There was some suggestion that there would be subsequent phases of the project where these other issues would be central. Thus the arguments for a steel project which pointed to the linkage potential and the spin-off benefits referred to above, did not have very much practical impact when it came to actually defining the scope and orientation of this project.

The Hatch report considered four options with respect to size of plant and products to be manufactured. As Table 4.4 shows, and as the report itself explicitly stated, the tonnages involved in all of the options, while not as large as in the traditional, large-scale metropolitan facilities, were nevertheless well in excess of what the domestic or regional market could absorb. Neither were the options delineated conceived in terms of what some potential downstream manufacturing industry might have absorbed. A perusal of the study shows that this consideration played no discernible part in the actual formulation of options with respect to plant size and output mix.[34]

---

[33] Later on however, the scope of the project was altered to include production of a finished steel item, wire rods. However, the imbalance in capacity between the various plants in the complex (i.e., direct reduction of 900,000 tpy, billet production of 700,000 tpy and wire rods 600,000 tpy) meant that supplies from prior stages of the production process would necessarily have to be oriented towards certain market areas where demand for these intermediates presumably existed.

[34] See, in particular, Hatch (1974, section 4)

The Joint Venture Partners

The IDC following upon its receipt of the Hatch study held discussions with some eleven firms from four different countries as potential partners in the project.[35] The list included:

Korf Industries	USA
Hoesch Estel	Germany/Holland
Nissho Iwai	Japan
Kawasaki Steel Corporation	Japan
Sumitomo	Japan
Mitsui & Co	Japan
Paul Stephens and Associates	USA
National Rolling Mills	USA
Ataka & Co	Japan
Amoco Oil Co	USA
IFC	USA

The IDC's view was that Trinidad and Tobago would be providing (a) a guaranteed long-term supply of gas; (b) supply of iron ore; and (c) a substantial part of the financing required. They decided to evaluate the prospective partners in terms of three factors. In order of importance, these were:

(a) A guaranteed long-term market for the semi-finished steel products to be produced;

(b) Know-how in the technologies of direct reduction and electric arc steelmaking.

(c) Contribution to the financing of the project.[36]

Because of the importance attached to (a) above, it was clearly indicated that, "all other things being equal, the IDC would recommend that in the choice of market partners preference be given to users ahead of traders",

---

[35] The firms with whom discussions were held and the IDC's evaluation of them are detailed in a 1974 report (IDC, 1974). A 1977 report (ISCOTT, 1977) claimed that 12 firms from six different countries were involved. No documentation to substantiate the involvement of a twelfth firm was found in the course of the research. Therefore the 1974 documentation is used as the more authoritative.

[36] IDC (1974), section on evaluation of potential participants

i.e., companies that would use semi-finished steel produced in Trinidad in their own captive rolling mills.[37]

In October 1974, four IDC officials including the then deputy Chairman (and later Chairman) of the Board held discussions with various potential partners. Hatch personnel sat in on these meetings with the IDC. A study of the minutes of these meetings, and of the IDC's own report evaluating the potential partners' submissions leads to the following conclusions.

First, there was a clear difference from the outset between what Trinidad and Tobago wanted to get from the project, and what the potential partners wanted, or said they wanted. Trinidad and Tobago wanted to produce not just iron, but steel. Semi-finished steel at first, with finished steels at some point later. Most of the potential partners, were not interested in seeing ISCOTT produce semi-finished steel. They indicated an interest in taking sponge iron, which they would then convert to steel in their own facilities.

Second, many of the potential partners were being deliberately vague about possible commitment to participate in the project. The tonnages they offered to offtake were generally accompanied by a caveat that it all depended on price, or on more information, upon Japanese government approvals, or on discussions with yet other firms, etc. However, they were quite explicit about wanting to examine the feasibility study. This would have given them access to the details of the plans being formulated by a plant that would be a competitor to them once built, including the cost of the natural gas and its consequent energy advantage, the price at which it would be obtaining its iron ore, and other important details.

Third, Korf's interest was basically in selling its direct reduction technology. To do this, it was willing to offer either to take an equity position, or to buy and dispose of output from the plant. Korf was involved in plants built using its technology in order to be in a better position to monitor the technology in an operational setting with a view to further developing it.[38]

Fourth, the Trinidad and Tobago representatives had little knowledge of, or information on, the foreign firms with whom they were negotiating, what these firms' situations really were, what strategies they were pursuing and why. The documents examined reveal nothing in the way of an in-depth assessment of the motivations of the firms and of the positions they took. Even if this was done informally, there is no evidence of it in the IDC's report evaluating the potential partners.

---

[37] ibid, p.3
[38] See Cooper and Maxwell (1975, p.50)

Fifth, it seems clear from a reading of the documentation in the light of the subsequent history of the project, that what the foreign firms were doing in most of the cases, was collecting information on a potential competitor.

At the end of the evaluation exercise, the Trinidad team shortlisted three firms as partners. They were: (1) Hoesch-Estel (Germany/Holland) (2) Kawasaki Steel (Japan), and (3) Mitsui & Co (Japan). Korf was deliberately excluded since it was a competitor for the choice of direct reduction (DR) technology. There was also concern expressed that its involvement in a number of other DR projects around the world meant that it was spread very thin with respect to personnel resources.

Table 4.4

Options for the Iron/ Steel Plant

Reduction	3 module Midrex	3 Module Midrex	2 Module HyL	2 Module Midrex
Steelmaking Furnaces		3-20'	3-18'	3-20'
Billets (mtpy)		200,000	200,000	230,000
Ingots (mtpy)		450,000	400,000	490,000
Metallized Briquettes (Iron) (mtpy)	1,200,000	475,000		
Source: Hatch Associates 1974, p.5				

Table 4.5

Summary of Offers/Positions Taken by Potential Joint-Venture Partners in ISCOTT 1974

Estel	Would take 500,000 tpy slabs or 300,000 tpy billets Interested in 500,000 tpy sponge iron Would market internationally 150,000 tpy billets and 200,000 tpy slabs Would be interested in 10-20% equity position No interest in selling plant and equipment, but could arrange such sales Foresee a cost-plus basis for product pricing
Ataka	Would commit only for sponge iron, not for semi-finished steel Would like to secure feasibility study and talk with friends in Japan about it Were talking with a couple other groups about a joint equity position
Korf-Mitsui	Interested in sponge iron production, not in semi-finished steel Under challenge from Trinidad representatives Korf and Mitsui divided: -
Korf	Would take total output of plant Willing to go it alone without Mitsui Flexible with respect to product mix Desirous of selling Midrex direct reduction technology even if not accepted as a partner
Mitsui	Would take 200,000 tpy sponge iron, 200,000 tpy billets Sponge iron is a condition for participation however
Nissho-Iwai	Would take total output of semi-finished steel 360,000 tpy of this will go to Kyoei steel. Rest would be sold on international market Would need to get Japanese government approval to put money in the project Interested in getting a copy of the feasibility study Together with Kyoei Steel willing to take up to 40% of equity
Sumitomo	Interested in sponge iron as a first stage Could not make any commitments without seeing the feasibility study

Source: IDC (1974).

Organizational Arrangements

In 1975, two important steps were taken with respect to organisational arrangements for the further pursuit of the project. It was decided to formally set up a company with the joint venture partners selected, and that this would be the vehicle that would be used for carrying out much of the subsequent details of the project planning exercise.

Accordingly, in June 1975, ISCOTT (the Iron and Steel Company of Trinidad and Tobago Ltd.) was registered with the following shareholding:

Government of Trinidad and Tobago	67.0%
Hoesch Estel	16.5%
Kawasaki Steel Corporation	11.5%
Mitsui & Co	5.0%

From the very beginning, the two Japanese companies approached the project on a joint basis, presenting a common front to the other partners and taking coordinated positions on all the issues.[39] A seven-man board of directors was set up on which Trinidad and Tobago had four seats including the chairmanship, and the other partners, one seat each. A Project Executive Group was set up to act on behalf of the Board between board meetings. The chief Trinidad negotiator, who was at that time Deputy Chairman of the Industrial Development Corporation, became chairman of both the Board of Directors and the Project Executive Group.

The planning for the project on the Trinidad and Tobago side, took place under the aegis of the Coordinating Task Force, an arrangement described earlier.[40]

The Collapse of the Joint Venture Approach

After the setting up of the joint venture company in June 1975, preliminary engineering work on the project began. A firm of investment bankers, First Boston Corporation of the USA was appointed to prepare a financing plan, tenders for 14 major pieces of equipment were invited, and plans drafted for fulfilling the complex of

---

[39] This is detailed in GORTT (1976). See above Chapter 3, and also Coordinating Task Force (1976-1980).
[40] See Coordinating Task Force Reports #1 (1975) and #4-7 (1976-1980)

infrastructural requirements --water, electricity, port and land facilities, etc.

Shortly thereafter however, the project ran into trouble as conflict surfaced between the partners. From the very outset, the foreign partners, like several others considered for selection, had indicated that they were not interested in seeing ISCOTT produce steel. They were willing to consider a plant which would produce sponge iron that would subsequently be converted into steel in their mills abroad. It was only at the insistence of the Trinidad and Tobago representatives, for whom steel production was the point of the whole project, that the partners reluctantly agreed to consider absorbing billets (semi-finished steel).

The Trinidad and Tobago representatives were interested in having their joint venture partners enter firm take-or-pay contracts for billets produced by the plant. In the original project contemplated by the joint venture partners, 1, 200, 000 tons of billets per year would be produced of which Kawasaki-Mitsui would take 600,000 tons, Estel 500,000 tons and 100, 000 tons would be destined for a local rolling mill. This production would have required a plant comprising three direct reduction modules, five electric arc furnaces, three continuous casters and a rolling mill. The estimated capital cost of this complex was US$392 million (TT$940.8 million). The operating cost per ton of billets was estimated at US$ 147.50 before financing charges.[41]

The Japanese companies, Kawasaki and Mitsui, put forward a joint position which was that they would only consider investing money in the proposed plant if the maximum price of billets was US$140 per ton fob Trinidad. To achieve this, they suggested the following financial arrangements to the partners: -

(a) No external borrowing.

(b) Suppliers' credit from Japan of US$108 million guaranteed by the government of Trinidad and Tobago;

(c) Equity of US$280 million, 67% of which would be contributed by Trinidad and Tobago

(d) The company would operate on a cost basis without profit for the first ten years.

---

[41] See GORTT (1976, p.5). Somewhat different figures for capital cost (US$364 million) and operating cost per ton (US$135) are given on pages 8-9 of this report. However the capital cost is stated to have excluded the rolling mill, hence the use of the more inclusive figure in the text.

(e) After the first ten years, an export allowance be made available to the company to allow taxation only on 50% of taxable income.[42]

Kawasaki and Mitsui insisted that a take or pay contract as required by Trinidad-Tobago was inseparable from the idea of a cost company. indicated explicitly that their objectives were two-fold: (1) To get a guaranteed source of billets at the minimum possible price to ensure production of finished steel in Japan aimed at both the home and export markets; (2) To obtain a substantial share of the equipment orders, as well as the construction activity *either for themselves or for other Japanese companies*.[43]

Estel's position was that they did not want to put equity into the project as defined having done their own analysis. They claimed in June 1976 that for billet offtake to be attractive for them, the fob Trinidad price would have to be US$150 per ton. The price at which return on equity would be zero would be US$175 per ton. Hence, they could not justify an equity investment in the project. They suggested that perhaps fiscal and financial incentives could be offered by the Trinidad government which might yet justify equity investment.

Thus, within one year of the joint-venture's formation, all the foreign partners had combined to put the Trinidad and Tobago government into a position in which they would now participate in the project only if the government agreed to operate it at a loss to the country.

The response of the government's representatives was naturally to refuse, as the Japanese and German companies probably calculated that they would. The Trinidad and Tobago representatives decided to investigate a smaller (reduced) project and to proceed on a 'Go-it alone' basis, if necessary. In May 1976, they met with the head of Korf Industries in New York, having decided even before a formal evaluation of the competing processes that Midrex was likely to be preferred.

Korf who had kept in close touch with developments on the project, quickly offered to provide information necessary for the planning of a reduced scale project. To this end, Korf arranged visits for two Trinidad and Tobago project officers to their new steel plant in Texas. They provided data on the capital and operating cost of this plant, and their already operating South Carolina steel mill. The project officers presented a report in June 1976 based on the data they had been given, indicating that a plant producing 450,000 tons per year of billets, with combination rod and bar rolling mill producing 150,000 tons per year of products would be feasible.

---

[42] ibid., p.15
[43] ibid.,p.13; my emphasis

They estimated that capital cost would be US$145 million (1976 prices), operating costs for billet production US$142.10 per ton and conversion costs into bars /rods, another US$14.00 per ton. At a sales price of $194/ton for billets, with another US$35/ton for rolled products, they calculated that the plant would yield a 9.5% return on equity with 100% equity financing and declared that it was "feasible and desirable for Trinidad & Tobago to proceed with the immediate establishment" of such an iron and steelmaking complex.[44] The Trinidad and Tobago directors took the line in dealing with Kawasaki, Mitsui and Estel that Trinidad was quite prepared to go it alone with such a reduced project, even though it would still welcome participation from its partners. It would have 300,000 tons of billets for sale.

Both the Japanese and the German companies made it clear in June 1976 that they were not really interested in investing even in the reduced project, stating however that they understood and accepted Trinidad and Tobago's interest in moving ahead. The Japanese further stated that they were very willing to cooperate in marketing as commercial agents, in supplying engineering services, hardware and equipment, and procurement of raw materials for a fee.

Estel, in a letter to ISCOTT's Chairman dated July 2, 1976, offered:

(a) to enter a long-term contract for the purchase of 300, 000 tons billets. ('Long-term' was to be 5 years); The price quoted was US$165 per ton, with a 2% a year escalation for labour costs and escalation in line with international prices for iron ore costs (at the time some 42% of operating costs);

(b) a marketing assistance contract for 150, 000 tons of mill products;

(c) basic and consulting engineering services;

(d) technical assistance including provision of training for ISCOTT personnel.

Estel made it clear that all this was an inseparable package

I would like to point out, however, that Estel is only interested in a combination of the above-mentioned points. With other words (sic) we cannot make a long-term contract for the billets without an essential part of the other assistance programs.[45]

The Trinidad and Tobago government decided in 1976 to go it alone with a reduced project. It is clear from a study of the experience that the

---

[44] Ibid., Appendix II, p. 11
[45] Ibid., Appendix IV, Letter from O.H.A. van Rojer, Managing Director, Estel.

foreign partners effectively outmanoeuvred their Trinidad and Tobago counterparts. They put themselves in a position from which whatever happened they could not lose: -

(1) If the Trinidad and Tobago government went along with their (deliberately?) ridiculous suggestion of a non-profit company, it would have meant that it would have literally been giving away its energy resources to the companies in question. They would have been able to capture and internalize in their own transnational operations, the comparative advantage that Trinidad and Tobago had in cheap natural gas, and appropriate it all for themselves.

(2) If Trinidad and Tobago rejected this suggestion, as it was pretty much bound to, and went ahead to become a competitor with these very same companies in international (third-country) markets, they would nevertheless have had the advantage of knowing all the details about the Trinidad project from the cockpit of the board of directors. They had had access to the basic feasibility study, they had information on the gas resources, costs, local capabilities, etc.

(3) They (and particularly the Japanese) were in an excellent position to set up themselves, (or brother companies in the case of the Japanese) as suppliers of equipment, engineering services, etc. This, as we shall later, in fact materialized.

(4) If Trinidad and Tobago backed away from steel production and contented itself with just iron production, they would reap pretty much the same economic advantages as in point (1) above and would as well block the emergence of a new competitor in steel production on the international market.

5
ISCOTT: FROM PLANNING TO CONSTRUCTION

The Reduced Project and the Project Cycle Post 1976

The decision of the Trinidad-Tobago government to go it alone with the reduced scope project in 1976 was to prove fateful. However, once the decision to proceed was taken, events moved rapidly. We will now look at the set of sequences in the project cycle under the following headings: Project Scope; Choice of Technology; Marketing Plan; Financial Planning/ Feasibility Analysis; Design; Project Management; Technology Planning; Procurement; Arrangement for Construction; Commissioning and Post-commissioning Experience.

Revised Project Scope

The revised project envisaged three process areas in the proposed complex. These were:

(1) Direct reduction - Single module 500,000 tonnes per annum capacity

(2) Melt/cast shop- Two electric arc furnaces; Two furnaces; Two four strand continuous casting machines for billets - 600, 000 tonnes per annum capacity (stretchable to 700,000 tons with an increased power supply)

(3) Rod mill including a reheat furnace - rated capacity 500,000 tonnes/year.

The original estimate of US$145 million provided by the two ISCOTT project officers who had sat down with Korf had grown to $US236 million by January 1977 and further to US$264 million by May 1977.[46]

The Choice of Technology

For students of technology and technology policy, the choice of technology in a project such as this is generally regarded as both important and fascinating. The technology chosen, first of all, may or may not be consonant with a country's factor proportions i.e., conditions of relative labour and capital availability. This issue has tended to be the focus of a lot of the literature on technology choice.[47]

More recently, the issue of technology choice has been viewed as significant because of the growing recognition of exactly how much can be determined by the choice of technology for a major project such as an iron and steel complex. The choice of a particular technology or technological route can automatically determine what raw materials can be used in a particular production process and from what possible sources they may be drawn. The decisions made can similarly determine what role, if any at all, local industry can play as suppliers of, or contractors for, suppliers and services to the project. This in turn can influence the development or retardation of local technological capabilities in a variety of areas.

The choice of technology, especially when we are dealing with sophisticated technologies, has enormous implications for the problems of acquiring and disseminating the necessary skills and capabilities for the conduct of the operations. It is not just the demands that a particular technological choice imposes upon local abilities in the context of a specific operation (e.g., whether the necessary number and quality of engineers or technicians can be found or produced). As Frances Stewart has pointed out, the complex of technologies that collectively constitute the capability to conduct a particular operation, do not exist in isolation. They have to be embedded in the necessary cultural and infrastructural matrix. This must exist if the activity is to be successfully carried out.[48]

For example, open heart surgery requires not just the medical team with the skills to carry out the operations and the equipment directly used in it. It also demands a certain kind and quality of blood bank, a reliable supply of electricity, and other ancillary systems, some of which are non-medical. Where these subtleties are not recognized, the choice of an

---

[46] See ISCOTT (1977, pp. 19-21).
[47] See for example, Beckerman (1978), Bhalla (1981) and Stewart and James (1982)
[48] Here see Frances Stewart (1977), Ch. 10

advanced technology, and its deployment in a developing country environment, can lead to poor results, and the failure of projects that would have seemed like a good idea at conception.

In the specific case of iron and steel, the issue of technology choice would seem to have heightened interest for students of both underdevelopment and technology policy for two reasons. The first is the fact that iron and steel production involves advanced technologies, the mastery of which promises to confer enormous benefits on a developing country concerned with building up industrial capability. Secondly, there is a wide variety of technological choices that can seemingly be made at each of the basic stages of the iron and steel production process. How then was the problem approached in this case? What factors were considered, and what decisions were made?

It turns out an analysis that the range of choice in this case was nowhere as wide as one might expect a priori. It also turns out to be the case that certain decisions, once made, virtually dictated several others. First, the traditional issue of labour versus capital intensity turns out to be moot in this case, and indeed in modern industry as a whole.

All of the modern, efficient processes are characterized by their relative high degree of capital intensity, though capital-output ratios do vary significantly. Technological development in both iron and steel making has resulted in a steady increase in the capital-labour ratios in all of the alternative processes. Any plant built that aims to be cost-efficient and competitive would necessarily have to be capital-intensive. It turns out however, that this does not mean that the complex of linked activities involved in iron and steel production may not be *employment intensive*, as opposed to labour intensive, that is, when the whole chain of activities is considered, reaching right downstream into the secondary manufacturing and fabricating plants which use finished steel products to turn out an array of consumer and capital goods, the total industry value chain may employ a large number of people. It seems to be the case however, that the bulk of employment creation is likely to be found downstream in the secondary industries, and not upstream in iron and steel production itself.

The choice of technology upstream is inevitably a choice among processes that are all capital intensive, though to varying degrees. In the case of the Trinidad and Tobago steel project, the actual choice of technology was in many ways dictated by the choice of direct reduction technology. Direct reduction technology itself dictated by (a) the fact that it used natural gas, in which the country was resource-rich; (b) the capital costs were significantly lower than the traditional, blast furnace methods (one-half to one-third according to some authorities); and (c) the levels of production that were economical were lower than in the traditional plants. This meant that plant significantly smaller than the norm need not be penalized on account of economies of scale. This rationale dictated not just the choice of direct reduction technology, but was the only basis on which it was possible to consider iron and steel production in Trinidad at all

Once direct reduction technology was chosen, the technology for steel production was automatically decided, that is, the logical route to steel making from DR is through electric furnace operations. This choice was further reinforced by the fact that the country's natural gas resources could also be used to generate, directly or indirectly, the large quantum of electricity needed for this operation. Similarly, continuous casting was virtually inevitable. It has been closely linked to the use of electric furnaces (though not confined to this method), and it is more modern and efficient than going through ingot casting.

The technological choices that really arose in the Trinidad and Tobago case then, were choices between DR processes and choices among alternative equipment suppliers. With respect to DR processes, once again the actual choice was not as wide as it would appear, a priori. However, one or two interesting curiosums do appear here.

While there are about twenty (20) DR processes catalogued, including those that are coal-based, the majority have not been widely used.[49] In fact, many have only been tried in one plant. Only five of these could have been considered at all. These were:

(1) Hyl process, developed in Mexico

(2) Midrex process, owned at the time by Korf Industries

(3) Armco process

(4) Purofer process (German)

(5) Fluidized Bed (a) Fior Process, developed by Exxon Corporation (b) HIB developed by US Steel.

Of these five, as the Hatch Report made clear, only the Hyl and the Midrex processes had been subjected to sufficient operational experience to be considered seriously for Trinidad and Tobago. By 1980, according to the US Office of Technology Assessment, the Hyl process had been installed in 14 plants going back to 1957, and Midrex in 17 going back to 1969. Armco had been tried in one plant, which was started up in 1972, Purofer, in four plants going back to 1980, HIB in one (1973), and FIOR, one (1976).[50] Thus the Hatch judgement seems quite sound in this regard.

The Hatch analysis of the two processes suggested that they were pretty much equal in terms of capital and operating costs overall. Operating

---

[49] See US Office of Technology Assessment (1980)
[50] Ibid. p.196

costs were put at Can$46.07 per metric ton (mt) for Midrex, using briquetted iron ore, and $46.01/mt if pellets were used. For the Hyl process, operating costs were projected as Can$46.96/mt using pellets. However, the slightly higher operating costs for Hyl was counterbalanced by lower expected royalty charges. For the Hyl process, one-time royalty of Can$2,500,000 was anticipated, while for Midrex, royalty costs were projected as Can$3,000,000 plus Can$2.00/mt product for five years.

What dictated the eventual choice of Midrex is not entirely clear. Two factors seemed to have played a role here. First, Korf executives stayed in very close touch with the Trinidad-Tobago planners throughout the planning and decision-making stages. When the original joint venture planners withdrew from the project, Korf moved swiftly into the breach, suggesting to ISCOTT that a reduced-scope project was indeed feasible. Korf was also willing to 'open the books' of its new Georgetown, Texas and its already operational, Georgetown, South Carolina plants, to ISCOTT personnel who were costing the reduced project. The company also outlined to the local negotiators a range of assistance it claimed to be willing to give to the project. Korf therefore worked hard, swiftly and adroitly to beat its competition and make the sale.

The second factor that seems to have played a role was the choice of an iron ore supplier for the plant. The DR process meant that feed unless it was decided to build a pelletizing plant as part of the complex, in which case the ore could be sourced in other forms (e.g., fines).[51]

Three supply sources were considered Brazil, Peru and Canada. In the case of Canada, the idea of buying into a Canadian mine to have a captive source of ore, was briefly considered. It was rejected on the grounds that management time was already completely tied up with the basic project. The Peruvian ore was the cheapest offered followed by the Brazilians.[52]

Ultimately, the Brazilian source was selected. This decision worked in favour of a Midrex plant, in that the argument was made that there had been no prior experience with using the Brazilian (CVRD) pellets in the Hyl process, whereas they had been successfully used with the Midrex. A decision to go with Hyl would probably have necessitated sourcing Mexican pellets as a matter of prudence.

---

[51] However, there might have been a third factor involved, though how much of a role it played is unclear. One of the project planners interviewed by the author indicated that he had personally argued for the Midrex process instead of Hyl on the grounds that the Midrex was a continuous process while the latter was at that time, a semi-batch operation. The equipment problems associated with the then new continuous process in Midrex could, he felt, have been ironed out by effective engineering. However, he stated that this view was rejected by his superiors who, he claimed, initially favoured the Hyl process. They subsequently changed their minds about the relative merits of the two processes
[52] See ISCOTT (May 1977, p. 34). In addition, several firms, including some of the erstwhile joint venture partners, indicated their interest in sourcing iron ore for a fee.

The Brazilians in their offer sought to negotiate for part of the pellets they would supply to be used to produce sponge iron for the Brazilian steel mills. This was an obvious attempt to take advantage of Trinidad-Tobago's comparative advantage in cheap energy to produce an intermediate product for the Brazilian steel industry. The Trinidad negotiators were very receptive to the idea, seeing the possibility of some profit from a tolling or processing fee arrangement in which they would produce sponge iron for the Brazilians.[53]

The decision to source iron ore from Brazil may well have led to a chain of unintended, and unexpected consequences, some of which we can only speculate about. One where speculation is all that is possible, is about what would have happened if Korf had not been involved in the project, and specifically if it would not have been more successful on start-up, in terms of production performance. As part of the deal with Korf-Midrex, Korf was contracted to provide considerable technical assistance to the new facility, pre- and post-start up. One of the crises that the plant faced when it came onstream however, was an anti-dumping suit by a Korf subsidiary, the very same Georgetown company to which ISCOTT's planners had been taken. This had the effect of paralyzing its US marketing efforts. As a response to this betrayal, the technical assistance arrangements with Korf for steel-milling were immediately and angrily terminated by ISCOTT's top management. However understandable in human terms, this reaction undoubtedly had repercussions in terms of the subsequent operating failures at the plant, since the new facility found itself shorn of much needed technical assistance, at a crucial time. Ironically, Korf's involvement with the project in terms of technical assistance was linked to the decision to buy its Midrex process and to accept other elements in the package it offered. Had Midrex not been bought, someone else might well have been chosen to provide technical assistance. A Korf suit would not then have led to a sharp discontinuity in the acquisition of technical assistance at a crucial time in the new plant's life.

One other consequence of the decision to use Brazilian pellets is equally interesting. ISCOTT's planners believed that it would have been possible to sell DRI abroad as an export commodity, taking advantage of Trinidad's cheap energy to add another string to its bow, so to speak. The Brazilian request seems to have played a role in convincing the planners that there would in fact be a possibly lucrative export market for DRI.

This, plus the request itself, led to discussions about creating a deliberate imbalance between the various stages of the complex. In other words, to produce surplus DRI to be returned to the Brazilians, the DR plant would have to be sized larger than was necessary to produce DRI just for the steel mill. The arguments in favour of doing this invoked the Brazilian

---

[53] IDC (1974, Appendix)

request (put forward as a condition of supplying the ore), the possibility of other export markets for DRI and the liberating of ISCOTT from a need to source scrap to charge into the furnaces along with the DRI. In fact, Korf itself also indicated in 1977 an interest in buying sponge iron from a plant in Trinidad.[54]

Ultimately the plant's configuration did include this imbalance (900,000 tpy DRI and 700,000 tpy steel), which meant that a market for surplus DRI would have to be found. The Brazilian deal fell through, reportedly because of the foreign exchange crisis in which Brazil found itself in the early 1980's.

However, a major technical problem arose in attempting to export DRI produced by the Midrex process. Since DRI is metallized iron, when exposed to air, under certain temperature conditions, and in the presence of moisture, it is susceptible to reoxidation i.e. back towards its natural state of iron oxide. In so doing, it is capable of spontaneous ignition (i.e. the material can begin to burn). The danger of this happening is obviously higher where the product is being transported over water (where the necessary moisture conditions can materialize quite easily).

There were therefore technical problems involved in shipping this form of DRI. At the time when ISCOTT came onstream, the techniques of coping with this problem had not won widespread acceptance.[55] In fact, interviewees told the author that some large insurance companies were refusing to insure cargoes of DRI.

The irony of this situation is that the Hyl product was supposedly not susceptible to this problem since the reduction temperature in the Hyl process was much higher than in the Midrex. Apparently, metallized iron which has been reduced at a relatively low temperature without melting, has a porous structure and a very large surface area. The Midrex process was characterized by a relatively low reducing temperature.[56]

When the time came to make a final decision between DR processes, Hyl, which had been recommended by the Hatch study as the only process along with Midrex worth serious consideration, was not asked to submit a bid. It was short listed along with Armco, Midrex and Tyssen, but only Midrex, and Armco were asked to submit bids in July 1976. A team was sent to hold talks with Purofer in Germany and ISCOTT's planners decided as a result that partly because of the 'untried nature of certain

---

[54] ISCOTT (1977, p. 12)
[55] The methods included (a) 'passivating' the DRI in a ship's hold, by keeping it covered with a layer of an inert gas such as nitrogen; (b) briquetting the iron -- converting it from pellets into larger pieces which are less reactive because there is less area exposed as surface area, and (c) passivation by covering the DRI with a layer of oxidized pellets. Contact with water could reportedly still pose a problem even with these measures.
[56] This point of difference between the two processes was explicitly articulated in the 1974 Hatch Report (Hatch 1974).

aspects' of Purofer's technology, it should not be considered. While Armco did submit a bid initially, it subsequently withdrew its process from the market. Midrex was then the automatic choice.[57]

Finally, one other aspect of the choice of technology for the complex is of interest here. This was the deliberate decision to 'unpackage' or 'unbundle' the plant technology, and to source the best equipment from the best suppliers around the world and put the plant together this way. In our discussion of purchasing and procurement, we shall see the actual implementation of this strategy, and in our detailing of the operating experience of the plant, post start-up, we shall see some of the results of it.

The Marketing Plan

ISCOTT engaged a US consulting firm, Booz, Allen and Hamilton, to do a marketing study.[58] Their report urged ISCOTT to go into the production of wire rods. They predicted that a 'window' for imported wire rods would open up in the U.S. market by 1980. They estimated that wire rod net imports would reach 1.6 million tons by that year and indicated that this market was both large and would continue to grow. They also projected that in 1980, Canada would be a net importer of wire rods to the tune of 200,000 tons declining to 150,000 tons by 1985.

The study also projected that supply and demand for steel internationally would be in balance or show some shortage by 1985 and stated that there was little likelihood of world steel over-capacity by 1985. With respect to the US market, they projected that in the 1980's there would be a need for substantial additional production capacity in the US. This, they stated, was unlikely to materialize due to capital access limitations, and the costs of pollution control and capacity expansion. They therefore indicated that the principal market opportunity for ISCOTT would likely be the United States, but that it would also be necessary for ISCOTT to achieve secondarily, a significant share of the wire rod markets in Canada and the Caribbean.

Based on these projections, the ISCOTT planners decided to emphasize the production of wire rods instead of billets (an intermediate steel product not widely traded in the merchant market at that time), and this marketing strategy focused principally on the US market.

---

[57] See Report to Minister of Industry and Commerce July 8, 1976 and also in the same document Report to PEG (GORTT, 1976, 7)

[58] See ISCOTT (1977)

Virtually every single projection and recommendation of the consultants was falsified by subsequent events. By the early 1980's, the world steel market was characterized by substantial excess capacity. US imports of wire rod in 1980 amounted to 800,000 tons, half of the 1.6 million tons projected. Canada, far from being a significant importer, became by the early 1980s an aggressive exporter of wire rod, aimed as well at the US market. By 1985, the evidence was clear. The steel mini-mills in the USA that were highly profitable, and which had stayed profitable throughout the recession of the early 1980s, were those that were producing stainless steels and other specialty steels, commodities which the consultants never mentioned at all as possibilities.

Ironically, in discussing the marketing problems likely to be encountered, the consultants placed no emphasis on protectionism apart from a brief caveat about the US market being realizable provided import restrictions were not applied. There is little doubt that this report and its recommendations, emanating from a prestigious foreign consultant, carried enormous weight with the decision-makers. These decision-makers were essentially inexperienced, both with respect to the steel industry and in dealing with foreign firms of this type, and at this level. There was a strong tendency to accord suggestions emanating from foreign sources an authority they did not always deserve. This was correlated with the failure to perceive the importance of setting up and training local teams to go out and analyze the world from a perspective that would accord better with local interests and extant reality (e.g., threats of protectionism). Both these failures owe much to the colonial heritage of the country.

It should be emphasized that the problem is not simply that the market projections turned out to be so spectacularly wrong. After all, many forecasts, equally in the developed as in the underdeveloped world, turn out to be egregiously in error. However, small countries have to be conscious of the fact that they cannot afford the mistakes that larger countries, or even large firms, can. A large entity, and particularly one possessed of large resources, can take advantage of the fact that of its many projects, some will go wrong and some will go right. Failures that would bankrupt a small entity can be shrugged off (up to a point) partly because of the size of the larger entity's war-chest and partly because the successes when they come along will compensate for the failures. In other words, the large entity can often afford to finance failure for a longer period, and wait longer for rewards, than the small. Also, the same (absolute) loss that would bankrupt the small entity, can be absorbed by the large without similarly destroying it. Therefore, a small country, or a small firm, for whom one project may represent a large chunk of its investment portfolio (i.e., many of its eggs in one basket) faces the imperative of being more thorough, utilizing superior methodologies, and being more accurate on average, than its larger, richer counterparts.

The understanding of this imperative, and the impetus derived from it, is perhaps more likely to be found in a well-trained local team, imbued with this consciousness, than in foreign consulting firms for whom a particular feasibility analysis may be essentially a routine, rather pedestrian, application of familiar methodologies to the stock of information that it possesses. A small country such as Trinidad and Tobago has to ensure that its success ratio with respect to forecasting is better than larger countries, simply because it can less afford to be wrong. This is not an impossible demand. Success in forecasting does vary. For example, it clearly varies with the effort invested in information, study, and accurate perception, as is evidenced by any comparison of the success of Japanese industrial strategy with British or US efforts when analysed over a variety of firms and sectors in the post-war world.

Financing

ISCOTT contracted First Boston Corporation, an investment banking firm to prepare and implement a financing plan. The plan, inter alia, sought (a) to maximize the use of long-term debt financing; (b) to utilize a 'project financing' approach rather than direct government borrowing; (c) simultaneously, to aid in the attainment of another, separate, government objective that was being pursued at the time. This was to introduce Trinidad and Tobago into international financial markets rather more fully.

The project was financed on the basis of a 60:40 debt-equity ratio. It was therefore highly leveraged. This of course is fine as long as a project does not run into trouble, since a high degree of leverage minimizes the owner's use of his own funds. More of the owner's pool of funds are left free for investment elsewhere in other activities. Another significant factor in project financing, which also became important in this case, relates to the arrangements made for financing cost overruns. Since a project is planned for completion within a certain time period and within a certain budget (inclusive of the usual contingency allowance), unexpected costs over and above budget have to be financed somehow. If long term financing has already been arranged on the basis of a budget, and adequate provision has not been made beforehand for dealing with most of any major cost overruns as part of this package, then serious problems could arise.

Overruns may have to be financed on a short-term basis which means significant financial charges in the early years of the project's life. This is precisely the point at which teething problems are being wrestled with in order to move up to design capacity, and inexperience in areas such as marketing and distribution may be contributing to lower than expected revenues.

Both problems subsequently arose to plague the ISCOTT project. Cost overruns at the plant ran to some 49% of the initial cost.[59] Apparently, two short-term bank loans totalling TT$96 million had to be obtained from the Bank of Tokyo to fund some of this, at significantly higher costs. Furthermore, the crisis experienced by the new company when it came on stream in terms of production problems, marketing difficulties and lower than expected prices made nonsense of the financing projections as far as revenues were concerned (see above Table 4.3). As a result, cash flows fell considerably below expectations, and the debt burden came to assume enormous proportions.

By April 1982, some eighteen months after start-up, the chairman of the ISCOTT Board of Directors was writing to the government seeking a change in the capital structure from 60:40 debt-equity to 30:70 debt-equity. This involved a massive new injection of capital by the state to retire prematurely a considerable amount of the debt incurred for the project, and since there was no perceived prospect of the plant being able to repay such an advance in the foreseeable future, the idea was that funding involved be simply converted into equity. The sums requested totalled US$257.8 million (TT$619 million) between 1982 and 1984.

One of the interesting features of the economic and financial planning that went into this project raises the question of why it was really undertaken. The long term capital borrowed for the project came at an average interest cost of 8.75 per cent per annum, with a maturity of 15 years. (This included a five-year grace period). However, the projections of the project's rate of return on equity were comparatively low. In 1977, when the final project definition was formulated, the projected internal rate of return over 20 years was only 10.4%, and over 25 years, 11.6%.[60] Given the risks and uncertainties involved and the size of the investment, a margin of 2-3% on capital invested certainly does not seem like very good economics.

Project and Technology Planning and Allocation of Functions

Early in 1977, the project got into full swing. ISCOTT received formal Cabinet authorization to proceed with the engineering work. The company quickly began formalizing its relationships with several foreign firms for the provision of basic and detailed engineering services, and for

---

[59] See Chapter 4 above.
[60] ISCOTT (1977, p. 24)

project management and other technical assistance functions. The company articulated an explicit technology strategy and this was reflected in the organizational structures it set up, and the way in which it proceeded.

ISCOTT's Technology Policy and the Project Management Function

The leadership of the new company explicitly recognized that Trinidad and Tobago had had no prior experience in steel production and would therefore necessarily have to rely on foreign technology for a considerable period into the future. However, a set of specific objectives were set out designed to ensure that nationals were trained, received exposure, maintained control over the operation and benefitted from a meaningful transfer of technology.

The chairman of ISCOTT's board listed seven objectives as 'needing priority attention'.[61] These included: (1) nationals taking a reasonable share of responsibility within the constraints of their qualifications and experience in steelmaking; (2) nationals to be given full exposure to all aspects of project management, engineering, commercial and other activities associated with the steelmaking industry; (3) local personnel to be given in-depth exposure to certain specialist activities as part of the process of transfer of technology. The management also explicitly and deliberately set out to 'unpackage' the technologies involved in the plant and were conscious as well of such issues as the impact of the project on the environment, and particularly on the geographical region where it was to be located. They were sensitive as well to the socio-cultural implications of the decisions made and the procedures adopted.

This was reflected in deliberate decisions made on the project management function, on the organizational structure set up and on the philosophy that underlay procurement and recruitment. First, ISCOTT was not a turnkey project. The Canadian company, Hatch, which had originally been employed in the role of consulting engineer, was given the responsibility subsequently for certain parts of the design engineering and the detailed engineering. Midrex, the Korf subsidiary, was given the contract for the major part of the direct reduction facility. However, Hatch was contracted to act as supervisor for the Midrex work (in its role as ISCOTT's Engineer), and simultaneously to have operational responsibility itself for the peripherals and the links between the DR facility and the melt shop. Korf itself was contracted to do some of the basic and process engineering work on the project, to provide technology in the area of steelmaking and rolled products and inter alia, to provide training.

---

[61] Ibid. p.52

The project management function itself was split three ways, among ISCOTT itself, Hatch, and Korf. A complicated organizational structure was set up around five work packages.[62] These were:

A. Overall project coordination, programming and Control
B. Planning, design and construction Direct Reduction Plant.
C. Planning Design and Construction -Steel mill
D. Planning Design and Construction – Rolling mill
E. Planning Design and Construction – Utilities, interfacing and peripheral systems

In addition, what was effectively a sixth work package was identified and entrusted to ISCOTT alone. This included: -

- Overall coordination of all ISCOTT's activities
- Liaison with the Central Government
- Marketing Planning
- Financial Planning
- Finalising negotiations for all major contracts
- Negotiations with technical assistance partners, consultants, major suppliers and general contractors
- Formulation of policies for training and industrial relations
- Appointment of all senior staff

ISCOTT's project management function was centralized in the office of the Chairman and exercised through a team operating out of that office headed by two coordinators. The management responsibility for five work packages was vested in a project executive group, headed by a Korf appointee and completed by the two coordinators from the Chairman's office (see Chart 5.1).

The Korf appointee was titled 'project director' and assigned responsibilities for all the work packages except B (direct reduction). However, the Project Executive Group just described, was to function as an overriding authority with respect to the Korf project director. This is how local control was to be effected. It was also stipulated that the ISCOTT Chairman could at his discretion summon meetings of the Project Executive Group under his chairmanship. A general contractor,

---

[62] 'Work Packages' are defined subsets of the complex of activities that have to be undertaken during the execution of a project. The subset of activities is usually viewed as concentrated and are consequently linked together and entrusted to a specific team or organization. The package may have its own time schedule and budget.

Rust International, a US firm was also hired to carry out the actual construction work.

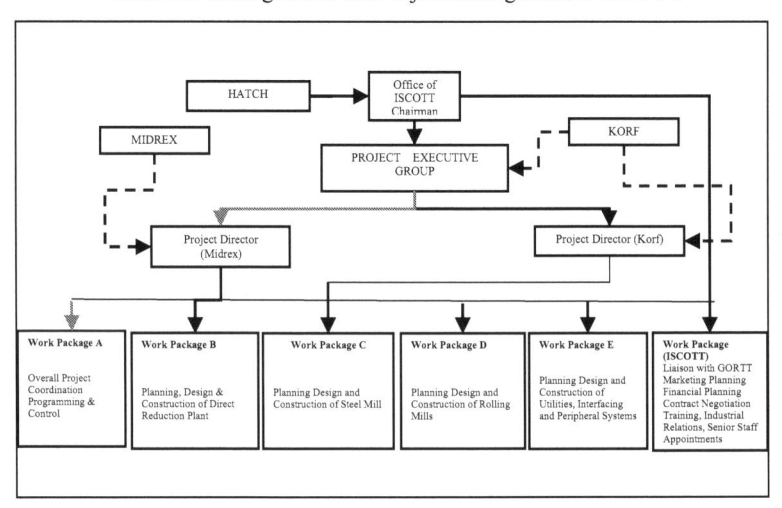

Chart 5.1: Arrangements for Project Management at ISCOTT

```
                    ┌─────────┐        ┌──────────────┐
                    │  HATCH  │───────▶│   Office of  │
                    └─────────┘        │    ISCOTT    │
      ┌─────────┐                      │   Chairman   │◀─────┐
      │ MIDREX  │                      └──────┬───────┘      │
      └────┬────┘                             ▼          ┌───┴───┐
           │              ┌──────────────────────┐       │ KORF  │
           │              │  PROJECT EXECUTIVE   │◀──┐   └───┬───┘
           │              │        GROUP         │   │       │
           │              └──────────┬───────────┘   │       │
           │                         │                       │
           ▼                         ▼                       ▼
    ┌──────────────┐                                  ┌──────────────────┐
    │ Project      │                                  │ Project Director │
    │ Director     │                                  │      (Korf)      │
    │ (Midrex)     │                                  └──────────────────┘
    └──────┬───────┘
           │
   ┌───────┴──────┬──────────────┬───────────────┬──────────────┬──────────────┐
   ▼              ▼              ▼               ▼              ▼              ▼
```

Work Package A	Work Package B	Work Package C	Work Package D	Work Package E	Work Package (ISCOTT)
Overall Project Coordination Programming & Control	Planning, Design & Construction of Direct Reduction Plant	Planning Design and Construction of Steel Mill	Planning Design and Construction of Rolling Mills	Planning Design and Construction of Utilities, Interfacing and Peripheral Systems	Liaison with GORTT Marketing Planning Financial Planning Contract Negotiation Training, Industrial Relations, Senior Staff Appointments

Procurement

Procurement for the plant was as disaggregated as the supply of engineering and project management services. In fact, it was reportedly an explicit objective of procurement process to source the best equipment and systems from all over the world.[63]

Initial tenders for fourteen major pieces of equipment in 1976 brought bids from a wide variety of firms from all over the industrialized world (Table 5.1). These 14 pieces of equipment accounted for 60% of the cost of the plant. The completed plant was composed of equipment sourced from several different firms and countries. Much of the electricals were sourced from the Japanese, as were the level-luffing cranes and the technology to erect the overhead cranes and install the high voltage switchgear (Toshiba, Kawaden and Mitsubishi). The billet casters were sourced from Concast (USA/Canada), the furnaces from Germany (Demag), and the reheat furnace from Canada (Salem).

Table 5. 1

Procurement of Major Items of Equipment

Item	Firms Bidding	Country of Origin	Price Tendered (US$ '000)	Basis
Billet Casting Machines	Concast	Canada/USA	15,281	f.o.b
	Demag	Spain/Germany	9,428	f.o.b
	Danielli	Italy	18,180	c.i.f
			16,680	f.o.b
	Mitsubishi	Japan	14,576	c.i.f
			12,960	f.o.b
Ship Bulker Unloader	GWS Krupp	Canada	4,865	f.o.b
	Fried Krupp	(West) Germany	3,984	f.o.b

Voest Alpine (Austria) designed and supplied the lime plant. Estel (Holland) provided consulting services on aspects of the harbour construction and designed the level-luffing cranes. These were manufactured by Kawaden of Japan and supplied by Mitsui. (Thus, the original joint venture partners largely succeeded in achieving their aim of getting some of the action as suppliers of equipment and services). The rod mill was sourced from Germany (Schloeman Siemag). Toshiba of Japan was hired to do some of the engineering with respect to the mill and to supervise its erection and commissioning.

---

[63] Interview with former executive of ISCOTT, February 11, 1985

It is not possible to say whether this approach resulted in significant cost savings or not. The lowest tender was not accepted in every case. In practice, there is sometimes good reason not to do so. Considerations such as reliability of the supplier, quality of equipment, financing terms available, delivery date, and the technological sophistication of the item in question may all legitimately sway a decision away from the supposedly lowest-cost supplier. What we see however, is that reportedly, this unbundling did create some unexpected technical problems.

It can also be said that the procurement process provided little opportunity for stimulating the development of local technological capabilities in supplier industries. The simple reason was that in a small, technologically backward country such as Trinidad and Tobago, there was no possibility of sourcing locally major bits of equipment and machinery, or technically sophisticated services. A study of the company's draft accounts for 1981 and 1982, which contained lists of contractors who provided management and technical services reinforced the conclusions derived from studying the source of the major items mostly minor services both in terms of type and in terms of comparative remuneration

Arrangements for Technical Services

Several contracts for the provision of technical services to the project were entered into by ISCOTT. Among these were the major contracts relating to the provision of various services by Midrex (the supplier of the direct reduction plant), Hatch (the supplier of consulting engineering, design engineering, project management, and other services), and Korf (supplier of project management, engineering and technical assistance services). There were other contracts for the provision of specific services, including the recruitment of expatriates on an individual basis to fill posts at both executive and operational level.

Several of these contracts were studied by the author including the major agreements with Hatch, Korf and Midrex. Certain points of interest emerge from the contracts.

First, the contracts were not licensing agreements with the set of clauses that students of technology policy have learned to look for over the last ten to fifteen years. In the case of Midrex, which involved proprietary technology for the direct reduction process, the contract really related to a package. This part of the plant was really built on what one might call a 'semi-turnkey' basis. That is, Midrex not only provided the technology, but was also responsible for the design, engineering, procurement of equipment, construction and start-up of the direct reduction module of the complex. The limits of what was Midrex's responsibility were carefully defined. Consequently, the interfacing necessary between the DR plant and the steel mill proper was Hatch's responsibility.

Midrex was also responsible for training the workers who would operate the DR plant.

The contract with Midrex's parent/affiliate, Korf, involved a range of services

(a)   Mobilization
(b)   Preliminary and Process engineering
(c)   Technical and Management Services
(d)   Project Management Services.

The same was true of the arrangements with Hatch. Here the range of services and know-how contracted for was even greater, and in fact grew steadily over time as Hatch's involvement in ISCOTT increased. Having started off, as we have seen, as ISCOTT's consulting engineer, Hatch moved on to play a wide variety of roles. The contract entered into in 1977 covered the provision of the following services: -

(a) Engineering - Preliminary basic and detailed engineering of certain areas of the complex.
(b) Project management (including procurement responsibilities, estimating and cost control, expediting, planning and scheduling)
(c) Construction supervision and inspection (both in the role normally assigned to a consulting engineer, as with respect to Midrex's construction, and in the role normally assigned to a project manager, where this function is carried out separately from that of the consulting engineer)
(d) Recruitment of personnel
(e) Technical assistance.

Second, the fact that the contracts entered into related to know-how, and specifically know-how expressed in a set of services, reflects an important phenomenon not always emphasized sufficiently. In many cases, the issue of the acquisition and cost of technology is not related to proprietary knowledge that is the subject of patents and therefore, legally protected. It is simply that someone, some organization, has in its possession a complex of skills and knowledge, which are valuable and which, if effectively acquired, would permit the acquirer to successfully carry out certain operations. The know-how may not be at all unique. There may be several individuals or organizations that possess it and would sell it. There may be little or no elements of it that are legally protected by patents.

In the instant case, there were, in 1976-77, several alternative sources of direct reduction technology. So that even where any particular process was still protected by patents, there were still alternatives readily available. Not only did no monopoly exist, but there were also alternatives available on which patent protection would have already expired. However, particularly for a newcomer to the steel industry, the particular process technology, even if acquired, would be of little use by itself. Successful operation of a plant required a package of know-how, of which the specific process technology was just one element.

This is even clearer when one looks at other areas of the complex, such as steelmaking, continuous casting, and the rolling mills. There are numerous competing suppliers of the necessary equipment. The technologies involved in, say, electric furnace operations are no longer either mysterious or closely held. Nevertheless, once again successful operation demands a complex of technologies and know-how which is possessed by certain organizations, and the acquisition of which, though it may not be legally protected by patents, can prove every bit as costly, as elusive, and paradoxically, as closely held, as legally proprietary knowledge.

Third, one of the characteristics of almost all the contracts examined was the intangibility of much of what was being purchased. This is of course, a point long noted in the literature. It bears renewed emphasis however, since it raises important issues about how developing countries should negotiate such contracts.

For example, Clause #5 of the agreement with Korf called for the payment by ISCOTT of a fee for 'technology transfer'. The clause reads: -

A technology transfer and know-how fee of US$500,000 was payable to KII in consideration of technology transferred and to be transferred to ISCOTT by KII in the course of its performance of preliminary and process engineering. ISCOTT agrees to pay the technology transfer and know-how fee to KII in three equal instalments of US$166,666 on the date of this contract, December 31,1978, and December 31, 1979, respectively.[64]

Nowhere in the agreement is there any definition of what exactly this know-how constitutes, over what time period it would be transferred, what would be the test of its being successfully 'received' or anything else that could be described as tangible. This was not unusual. In all of the contracts examined, even where the services to be performed were specified and itemized, there were several similar areas of vagueness. By contrast, the Midrex contract stands out as one in which there was great specificity as to exactly what equipment would be supplied, what activities the company would undertake, and, very unusually, a very detailed outline of its training program for tutoring staff in operating the new plant.

This program outline detailed three phases of training: classroom, on-the-job in a Midrex operating plant, and on-the-job in the client's plant. It specified the numbers to be trained, the length of training, the areas the workers would be exposed to, and the expectations at the end of their training ('a good, working knowledge of the plant at the time of initial start-up').[65]

Fourth, another characteristic of the agreements, that is probably a corollary to the previous point, is how little real control ISCOTT, as purchaser of the know-how and services, had over the provision of these services and know-how. These agreements never specified what would constitute adequate provision of a

---

[64] Contract between ISCOTT and Korf dated 2nd March, 1978, p.4
[65] Contract between ISCOTT and Midrex.

service or know-how. There was no requirement built in for a litmus test of effective acquisition, for example, that nationals would be able to perform some specific set of functions for some specified period at some defined level of performance. While this would obviously not be possible in all areas, it would certainly be possible in some technical areas of the operation.

Fifth, the agreements also turn out to contain little in the way of provisions to indemnify the buyer of the know-how and services against the failure to provide these adequately for the successful completion and start-up of the plant. This is a subtle difference from the previous point. There, the issues related most centrally to such areas as the provision of know-how for the operation of the plant. Here, it relates to the provision of say, engineering services, or the carrying out of a function such as construction supervision, or the preparation of manuals, or project management services.

The quality of performance of these services obviously bears on the successful completion of the plant within time and budget, and the post start-up functioning of the plant according to design specifications and the expectation of the owner. While some other agreements examined in other industries contain clauses that required performance bonds or guarantees by contractors that a new plant would operate successfully for a specified minimum time period, these agreements in the case of steel contained little protection for ISCOTT the purchaser.

The agreement with Korf did not contain a single clause that might be remotely construed as having that effect. The Hatch agreement contains a clause with nine sub-parts on the liability of Hatch as Consulting Engineer. The clauses specified that: -

1) Hatch was only liable for the consequences of errors and omissions arising from gross negligence. (Nothing indicates how this is to be defined or proven)
2) Any payments by Hatch with regard to any such liability as indicated in (1) was limited to Can$250,000.
3) The cost of Hatch's professional errors and omissions indemnity insurance in the amount $250,000 was to be paid for by ISCOTT.
4) Hatch accepted no liability for the violation of legal provisions, or the rights of third parties, unless ISCOTT had specifically brought these provisions or rights to its notice by prior written notice.
5) Hatch's liability to any third party for a tort claim related in any way to the project was to be limited to Can$250,000. This clause emphasized that the aggregate liability of Hatch under this and all previous clauses was limited to C$250,000
6) Hatch's liability specifically excluded any consequential damages.
7) Hatch's liability expired with the issue of the Maintenance Certificate.
8) Hatch had no liability for any part of the works not designed by Hatch, or constructed under its supervision.

9) Liability was also disclaimed where a contractor or a supplier had liability.[66]

In the context of a project costing over TT$1.2 billion (approximately CAN$600 million), and where Hatch's fees, as we shall see, were little short of astronomical, it is clear that the protection ISCOTT had against errors and failures due to negligence or incompetence on the part of Hatch was negligible.

ISCOTT had apparently hoped to include some protective clauses in its agreement with Korf. In its 1977 report to the Minister of Finance, it indicated that the Heads of Agreement specified clauses such as a retention clause whereby 10% of the management service fee would be paid upon completion, and a penalty clause whereby Korf would have to complete the provision of its services at no extra cost if the job took longer than the budgeted 30 months. Mild though these are, these clauses do not appear in the signed contract.

Sixth, by contrast, the agreements contained considerable detail on what the firms who were supplying services and know-how were to receive, what they were to be paid, and how they were to be paid.[67] Korf received payment under five headings:

1.	Mobilization	500,000
2.	Preliminary and Process Engineering	750,000
3.	Technical and Management Services Technology Transfer and Know-how	495,000
4.	Fee	500,000
5.	Project Management Services	2,005,000
	Total US$	4,250,000

The payment for project management services is noteworthy. This related to the services of eight individuals budgeted for 132.5 man-months. Having paid US$333,000 as an advance against the fee of $2,005,000 per the agreement (prior to the individuals' arrival in 1978), it turns out that the average payment for each of these individuals worked out as US$12,619 per month (TT$ 30,285). Such salaries were far in excess of anything these individuals received in their country of origin, and about double the daily consultant rates paid on some of the other contracts examined.[68]

Another firm, Pohlman International, was reportedly formed during the project by as Korf employee, seconded to ISCOTT to work on project management, who spotted a commercial opportunity in executive recruitment for ISCOTT.

---

[66] Contract between ISCOTT and Hatch Associates, Clause 2.4
[67] This excludes Midrex. I have not been able to ascertain a total figure for payments to Midrex from the available sources of information.
[68] Interview with former executive of ISCOTT. The figure cited is provided by the government appointed Esau Committee which reviewed ISCOTT's performance and undertook the search for a new joint venture partner (Esau 1984, p. 16)

This firm reportedly received fees totaling TT$29,057,000 (US$12,107,083) between 1979 and 1983.

Of great interest is the case of Hatch. Hatch entered into a 'joint venture' relationship with a local consulting engineering firm, Trintoplan. The motives to have included the perception that an alliance with this particular firm would lubricate doing business in Trinidad. The arrangements involved Trintoplan personnel spending time in Hatch's Toronto Office (the budget allocated man-months for this) and Hatch personnel operating in Trinidad, supposedly in conjunction with Trintoplan.

In fact, several interviewees reported that Trintoplan's role in the joint-venture was negligible.[69] Hatch had wide-ranging responsibilities on the project. The contract examined indicated the cost of the services provided by Hatch-Trintoplan was Can$5,143,490 broken down as follows:

	Can$
Project Management Services	1,570,000
Inspection	526,000
Engineering and Design	2,134,000
Sub-total Fees	4,230,000
Expenses	548,000
Relocation and Living Costs	365,490
Total	5,143,490

However, indications are that Hatch made a great deal more money from the project than this would indicate. It played a role as well in providing technical assistance, and in the recruitment of staff. This is apart from its initial involvement as Consulting Engineer. The government's own committee set up to review ISCOTT's 1984 expenditure proposals and to find a joint venture partner (Esau Committee) reported that Hatch's total receipts from ISCOTT from 1976 to 1983, in respect of the complex of services purportedly provided, totalled TT$143,613,000 (US$59,883,750).[70] If this is anywhere near correct, then it suggests that much of Hatch's money was made from providing technical personnel, doing recruitment, and providing other services not specified in the contract.

---

[69] Hatch- ISCOTT agreement (p. 42). It should be noted that there are different perceptions of the significance of the Hatch-Trintoplan joint venture in terms of technology transfer to Trintoplan and thereby to Trinidad. According to Cyril Solomon's interviews with Trintoplan's executives (1983, pp 93-107), these executives felt that they did benefit "immensely" from the joint venture in terms of experience gained. However, interviewees who had been involved in the ISCOTT project from the planning stage on, were unanimous in dismissing the suggestion that Trintoplan's role in the joint venture was anything other than marginal. The Esau committee's report [1984, p.15) also suggests that Trintoplan's role was not of great significance.
[70] Esau Committee Report (1984, p. 14)

We turn now to an evaluation of the commissioning and post start-up experience of this iron and steel project.

6
CONSTRUCTION, COMMISSIONING AND POST START-UP CRISIS

Introduction

The ISCOTT project ran into trouble virtually from right after the sod-turning ceremony. The general contractor that had been hired, Rust International of the USA, failed to even mobilize effectively. According to one interviewee, the company in question, Rust International was overextended at the time. Apparently, about half of all the people they sent to Trinidad to work had never worked with Rust before. They had been newly hired and promptly despatched to Trinidad.[71]

Rust International was, in consequence, soon fired. The decision was then taken not to tender for a new general contractor, and instead to break the work up and hire several individual contractors to do specific jobs. The arguments put forward were: (a) to hire a new general contractor would mean a long delay since the tendering and bidding procedure would require several months and consequently, a year or more could be lost; (b) it was also argued that any new contractor would likely be only willing to come in on a cost-plus basis; this could be extremely expensive; if a lump- sum contract was insisted on, the figure quoted would include such a large contingency that it might as well be cost-plus so that breaking up the job was likely to be cheaper.

As a result of this decision, ad hoc arrangements were made with several firms, including some already mobilized on site for particular jobs. According to respondents, a firm hired to do the landfill as part of the site preparation, was then asked to do piling as well. Then they were offered a job to do concrete

---

[71] Interview with former ISCOTT Vice-President, February 11, 1985

works as well. Another, hired to fabricate equipment was asked to do installation as well.

The problem that arose is familiar to every student of project planning and project management. On a large project, with hundreds of different activities to be carried out, careful and sophisticated planning and scheduling is necessary so that activities dovetail into each other, if enormous waste is to be avoided.

Without this, one finds the phenomenon of contractors being paid to be idle, because they are waiting on someone else to complete a job that is necessarily prior to their own. This problem arose, plus others. For example, with several contractors mobilized on site at the same time, problems of security multiplied. Pilferage became a headache. Also, with inadequate central coordination, workers appeared and reappeared on the payroll of different contractors. In the words of one respondent, "plumber for A today; carpenter for B tomorrow".[72]

The strategy of breaking up the project management function between three firms now proved to be a mistake. Whether it would have worked in the context of an efficient general contractor, it is impossible to say. However, in this situation, the division of the functions reportedly compounded the chaos.

A fundamental weakness proved to be entrusting a major aspect of the project management function to ISCOTT and the attempt to centralize control of things in the Chairman's office. ISCOTT simply did not have the staff with the requisite experience to carry out effectively the functions that it had assigned itself. One interviewee described his own experience. He indicated that he was an engineer by training but had had no previous experience in any aspect of the steel business. He was hired by ISCOTT, and within a couple of days was given the assignment of negotiating details of an important agreement with a team of experienced foreign executives.

Similarly, the centralized control was bound to flounder when the Chairman of the company was, as we have seen above, wearing so many different hats.[73] As the person who was in charge not just of the steel project, but chairman of the National Energy Corporation, the national electricity company (T&TEC), the Pt. Lisas Industrial Development Corporation, the fertilizer project and much else, it was clearly impossible for him to do an effective job of coordinating and controlling the project.

Not only did the project pay a price in terms of cost and time overruns, but there was a subtle effect on the arrangements for training which in turn affected the plant's post start-up operations and the assimilation of the necessary technologies. Reportedly, there was no effective overall plan and schedule for finding, choosing, recruiting, and training the people to operate such sensitive areas, as the melt-cast shop. Part of the problem was that in the frenetic set of activities being undertaken, it was difficult to determine long in advance

---

[72] ibid
[73] See above, Chapter 3

reasonably precise plant completion dates, against which proper training could be scheduled.

The argument was advanced that to bring in people and train them too early would result in a waste of money since they would have been hired, trained and be idle while waiting for plant start-up. This was advanced as a reason for deferring such planning. Other interviewees stressed the fact that the first Executive Vice-President hired with overall responsibility for Human Resource Development (a local) was inadequate for the job and never grasped it.

Moreover, as we have seen, there was considerable vagueness in respect of the precise responsibilities of some of the firms contracted to provide technical assistance. With little effective local expertise, and with weak central coordination, some of the firms were able to treat their contractual obligations cavalierly, and given the looseness of their contracts, were able to do so with impunity. Thus, one interviewee, a manager in the area of training, claimed that one of the key firms involved in the construction and the provision of services was able to demobilize and leave without providing certain critical manuals and technical drawings it was supposed to deliver.[74] This had a serious effect in terms of the employees' ability to operate and maintain certain parts of the plant.

The one reported exception to this was the direct reduction plant. Here, there was a good training program provided by Midrex. Furthermore, this was really a chemical process plant, and Trinidadians, because of the kind of industries the country possessed, had had considerable experience with process plant operations.

Start-Up and Operation

The Production Crisis

The plant came onstream at the end of 1980 and was formally commissioned in 1981. From the very beginning, there were several technical problems. Production as we have seen never came anywhere close to design capacity. As indicated at the start of this analysis, production in the first three years after start-up never crossed 35% of capacity in any of the plants in the complex. Operations have been plagued by low productivity, technical inefficiencies and poor maintenance and operating practices.[75] Financial losses have been much higher than expected. In fact, as early as June 1982, the Chairman of the Company indicated to his shareholder, the government that the company was in an "insolvent condition".[76]

The climax to the operating crises came in January 1984 when there was an explosion in the melt shop, the very heart of the complex and probably its most complex area technologically. The explosion put one of two furnaces out of

---

[74] Interview with ISCOTT manager, March 1984.
[75] See above Chapter 4
[76] Letter from ISCOTT's Chairman to Minister of State Enterprises June 2nd, 1982.

operation for four weeks. Inefficiencies in restarting it occasioned another two weeks of downtime. In the first quarter of 1984 in fact, production in the melt shop was barely above 20% of design capacity and fell some 30% below the modest production targets set by the plant's management.[77] One week after the explosion in the melt shop, there was a fatality in the melt shop. A worker was killed when a panel from one of the overhead cranes fell. This second issue spotlighted the problem of adequate safety measures, as well as the issue of proper maintenance practices. The first accident highlighted both the issue of maintenance and the competence of expatriate technical staff, one of whom had taken an erroneous technical decision on procedures to be adopted with respect to the furnace.

The government-appointed (Esau) committee which reviewed the plant's operation in 1984 was scathing in its condemnation of practices at the complex. Inter alia, the committee charged that:

- The complex was overmanned; staff of 1200 could be reduced to 900.
- The arrangements for provision of management and technical support services were "...unacceptable in every respect. The manning level and cost are excessive, transfer of skills is inadequate, services provided are not always appropriate to ISCOTT's needs, and existing arrangements are seen generally to be against the Company's best economic and operating interests". The committee recommended that the contracts with Hatch Associates Ltd. and Pohlman International Inc. "should be terminated as soon as possible".[78]
- The committee further stated that "ISCOTT's performance from commencement has been disastrous and cannot form the basis for any proposal to operate a viable steel industry in Trinidad and Tobago. In every area of activity, the Company has operated so inefficiently as to leave no doubt that a totally new outlook and management, competently directed on sound commercial principles is required if ISCOTT is to survive".[79]

The Personnel Crisis

The production problems ISCOTT confronted after start-up were partly due to, and partly accompanied by a set of personnel problems. The strategy had been to deal with the problem of technology acquisition partly by buying in technical assistance and training services, and partly by recruiting individual expatriates at both senior management and operating levels. In addition, efforts were made to recruit skilled nationals and more broadly, skilled West Indians who might have been living abroad. As we have seen, contracts were signed with firms such as Hatch of Canada, Korf and Pohlman of the USA, to provide technical and managerial assistance, and to recruit talent. The same approach was adopted with respect to sourcing people as was adopted with respect to sourcing

---

[77] Esau Committee (1984, Appendix 5)
[78] ibid. p.3 and 26
[79] ibid

equipment. The philosophy was to find the best people from all over the world and bring them in.

The expatriates who were hired on an individual basis generally came in at very high salaries. Interviewees from the plant's Personnel Department indicated that the salaries paid were generally much better than those received by those hired in the metropolitan (and other) countries from which they were drawn.

Initially, most of the top management posts were filled by expatriates. The company was set up using the American style of organization and titles, rather than the British. The top nine posts were: (a) President (b) Three Executive Vice Presidents in charge of Operations, Finance, and Human Resources; (c) Five Vice Presidents in charge of various functional areas. Initially, seven out of the top nine posts were held by expatriate staff. In addition, a wide variety of positions in the organization were staffed by expatriates, right down to Shift Supervisor level. One interviewee, a very senior executive in the Personnel Department indicated that initially, there were some sixty expatriates on the payroll, which did not include a host of other expatriates who functioned as consultants under technical assistance agreements.[80]

The operations quickly ran into a personnel crisis, so much so, that by 1984 the organization had virtually collapsed. There was an extremely high turnover among employees, particularly at managerial and at skilled professional level, and particularly among the expatriates. Many positions were unfilled. There were especially serious gaps in the top management structure due to unfilled vacancies, a function, in turn, of abrupt resignations. The organization reportedly degenerated into feuding baronies and cabals, with little effective central control and with executive authority often flouted. Morale plummeted, and there was little or no respect among the staff (both local and expatriate) for the two hapless locals who by 1984, were all that remained of the top management structure.

With respect to turnover of expatriate staff in the post start-up operations, one interviewee, an executive in the Personnel Department, reported that from a starting figure of 60, by February 1985 the number of expatriates left on the payroll was about 15, and that some 100 had passed through the plant.

Another indication comes from a study of the work permit records pertaining to ISCOTT. In Trinidad and Tobago, non-nationals entering the country to work are legally required to obtain work permits, making the analysis of work permits a useful channel for studying expatriate hiring in terms of numbers, country of origin, occupation and so on. Between 1980 and 1983, 267 work permits were issued in respect of expatriate hires. Of these, consultants and short-term hires (less than one year) were disregarded. Full time employment in general involved contracts of at least one year. Over the 1-, 2- and 3-year contracts, extensions were needed in just 25% of the cases overall. Table 6.1 shows that this ranged from 44% in the case of expatriates hired on 3-year contracts down

---

[80] A list of expatriates on staff at January 1984 lists 28, just one year earlier.

to 17% on 1-year contracts. This provides only a heuristic, and an indirect method of attempting to quantify expatriate turnover. However, it seems to support what several interviewees reported, and a phenomenon that has been widely commented upon by the Trinidad and Tobago public and the country's media.

The turnover began at the very top. The first president of ISCOTT, a Canadian hired through Hatch, left the company in 1983 after three years. He had been hired initially on a two year contract, and renewed it for just one further year. A 58-year-old, former executive at Sidbec in Canada, there was reportedly mutual dissatisfaction on both sides, his and the company's. The offices of Executive Vice-President, the next highest rung on the corporate ladder, bore all the resemblances to a revolving door with the added wrinkle that there were periods where vacancies at this level existed for considerable periods of time.

The turnover of staff was one problem. Another perhaps not unrelated, was the hiring of locals who had little prior training or experience for the jobs, into top positions in the company. There is evidence of nepotism and patronage in several appointments made. [81] The result was a management team which lacked competence and experience, and which was widely disrespected by both the expatriates it was nominally managing as well as the ordinary workers on the line.

Table 6. 1

Analysis of Expatriate Staff Turnover at ISCOTT 1980-1983

Category	Number	Extensions	%
Total Number of Work Permits Issued	267		
Consultants	12		
Non Consultants Of which:	255		
Over 3 years			
3 years	34	15	
2 years	56	19	44
1 year	136	23	34
Less than 1 year	29		
Notes: Expatriates were often brought in on service-type jobs Source: Unpublished Data			

---

[81] See Davan Maharaj, Square Pegs in Round Holes: A look into appointments at ISCOTT, *Trinidad Express*, July 19, 1984. This article details the story of an Executive Vice-President, Human Resources with a first degree in accounting and no experience in the area; a local, appointed President in place of the departed Canadian expatriate, who was a former economist in the Ministry of Finance with no prior steel industry experience and no technical background, and someone with a degree in Sociology who moved from the Personnel Department to act as a General Supervisor in the rod mill. The article also details the family relationships between several such local employees and government ministers and other ruling party supporters.

There were other problems which surfaced with respect to the expatriates hired. First, the sourcing of people from different countries, different cultures and different steel-making backgrounds created unexpected problems, especially in a context of weak and disrespected central management. Cabals developed on the basis of ethnicity and/or countries of origin. There were also clashes over how things should be done, since the expatriates hired came from different organisational and technical cultures. The result was infighting, lack of cooperation within and between departments, occasionally serious technical errors, and bad operating procedures.

Secondly, as interviewees reported, while the expatriates recruited often seemed to have excellent resumes on paper, it turned out in practice that people with 15 or 20 years of steel-making experience, might have had this experience in a different type of plant with a different type of technology. For some of them, the advanced technology of the ISCOTT complex was reportedly quite novel, in terms of their own prior experience. Instead of being experts therefore, they were themselves now learning.

Third, it was claimed by several interviewees, that many of the expatriates were uninterested in, or positively unwilling to train locals as understudies, or to pass on skills and knowledge to them. Some interviewees hypothesized that this, paradoxically, might have derived from the high salaries these people were making and a consequent unwillingness to make themselves redundant. This explanation however, is at variance with the fact of rapid turnover of expatriate staff. Another interesting suggestion put forward by very senior management personnel, was that the willingness or unwillingness to transfer skills and knowledge varied with country of origin.

It was claimed that the Americans hired were least willing to share their knowledge and the most difficult to manage. It was suggested that the Englishmen had the most positive attitude and adjusted best to the local culture, and that the Canadians did attempt to take the transfer of technology seriously.[82] How much merit any of this has is difficult to say. The respondents were quite clear about it, and it would obviously make an interesting area for further research. There has been little discussion of how such factors as race, culture, etc. may affect the transfer of skills and knowledge not just across international boundaries, but across racial and cultural ones as well.

A further problem which arose post start-up, with an important bearing on the issue of technology assimilation, was the inadequacy of the training that operating personnel had been exposed to. The failure to properly plan this area played a clear role in the poor operating performance.

In all of this, the company' s local board of directors played an essentially passive role. Its members had no knowledge or experience of the steel business. In several cases, a review of their backgrounds makes it very difficult to understand what would have qualified them for their appointments in the first

---

[82] Interview with ISCOTT executives, February 1985.

place. The result was that the rapid deterioration, and indeed, disintegration, of the company after start-up was presided over by a board of local directors that never took any forceful initiative to stem the tide of events. They never got on top of them.

The Marketing Crisis

As if these problems were not enough, the new company quickly ran into marketing difficulties. A contract had been entered into with an American firm, Atlantic Marketing and Management Services, to market ISCOTT's steel based on a commission of 2½ percent of sales. The company was not marketing ISCOTT's steel exclusively, and from all reports failed to do a good job. At the same time, ISCOTT's own marketing department staffed by locals was felt, by all the interviewees questioned, to lack the necessary experience, contacts and dynamism.

Amid the initial struggle to build sales, ISCOTT was in 1983 slapped with an anti-dumping suit, filed with the US Department of Commerce, by five US steel companies, Atlantic Steel, Continental Steel, Georgetown Steel, Georgetown Texas Steel and Raritan River Steel.

The suit alleged that ISCOTT received unfair bounties or grants (subsidies) from the Trinidad and Tobago government, citing, inter alia, the government's loan guarantees for the complex, preferential lease arrangements at its Pt. Lisas site, the fact that there was a marine terminal specially designed for ISCOTT, and that it received preferential prices for natural gas and preferential shipping. ISCOTT fell victim to both anti-dumping and countervailing duties as a result of this suit. Ironically, Korf who had sold ISCOTT the Direct Reduction plant, and sold it know-how and engineering services, was one of the companies behind the suit. Georgetown and Georgetown Texas were both Korf subsidiaries at the time, and in fact these were the two companies to which Korf had sent ISCOTT project officers to gather data recommending a reduced scope steel mill.

When the suit was filed, ISCOTT's Chairman, reportedly ordered Korf employees off the ISCOTT plant and abrogated the technical assistance arrangement.[83] As indicated earlier (Chapter 5), this decision may have also contributed to the subsequent technical problems in the plant's operations, since the planned technical assistance was now abruptly cut off. We have here then an interesting double irony.

The Denouement

The series of crises at the new company, and its large financial losses, led inevitably to severe public criticism and increasing political pressure on the

---

[83] Two interviewees indicated that the relationships between Korf and ISCOTT had begun to sour as far back as the construction phase. Apparently, ISCOTT's Chairman grew increasingly suspicious of Korf, and the perception of Korf as a competitor grew steadily. One can speculate how much of the detailed information used by the US, companies in bringing the suit, would have derived from intimate, inside knowledge of all the details of the project

government to do something about a project that had become something of a national scandal. However, nothing was done to change the management of the project. The exodus of the expatriate managers from the top positions in the company left a serious vacuum. This was filled by appointing two locals to the position of President and Executive Vice President, neither of whom had the training, the experience, or the technical background that would in a metropolitan company be regarded as a *sine qua non* for such high-level appointments.

The appointee to the post of President had been trained as an economist and had spent much of his prior career as a civil servant in the country's Ministry of Finance. Managerial inexperience plus the lack of a technical background especially in the context of a floundering company like ISCOTT, was clearly a major liability. The metropolitan counterparts of these people would generally be men who had spent 15, 20 or more years learning the business, in a variety of positions, and who more likely than not, would have had a background in engineering or a related technical field.

The government appointed a committee in February 1984 with a mandate to review the expenditure proposals for 1984 of the company with a view to effecting maximum savings in the shortest possible time, and secondly, to find a suitable international partner for the company. Emphasis was to be placed on a partner who would help with marketing, inject equity and provide technical support for the management.[84]

In March 1985, it was announced that an arrangement was being entered into with two US firms, Bechtel, a well-known engineering contractor, but not a steel producer, and Laclede, a Missouri based company. Laclede turned out to be substantially owned by another US firm called Ivaco. Ivaco was the parent company of Atlantic Steel Company. This company was one of those that brought the original anti-dumping suit against ISCOTT seeking to block it from entering the US market.[85] Following a public outcry, it was announced that the government had failed to reach agreement on a proposed joint venture with these two firms. However, in November 1985 a two-year contract to provide 936 man-months of management, technical assistance and marketing services was signed with two foreign companies. One of these was Austrian, Voest Alpine, and the other German, Neue Hamburger Stahlwerke. These events signified in a very real way an official admission that the ISCOTT experiment, as originally set up, had failed.

ISCOTT: The Anatomy of Failure and the Lessons of Experience

---

[84] Esau Committee (1984, p.1)
[85] US Department of Commerce (1983)

Trinidad and Tobago's initial venture into iron and steel making then, had in less than five years from its inception demonstrably failed. An enormous investment was made in state-of-the-art technology. The project was based on what would a priori, have seemed like the country's natural comparative advantage, cheap energy. The goal of diversifying the economy and getting into an activity capable of spawning such enormous linkages as steel production seemed to make sense. The philosophy outlined for acquiring the necessary technology and building a technological capability in the area would, in some areas at least, seem sensible and even progressive.

ISCOTT's planners recognized from the outset that they would need foreign assistance for technology and for marketing. They sought it through structuring a joint venture, in which they explicitly defined what their objectives were. They attempted to maintain local control over the venture and its direction. They explicitly recognized the importance of the complex of technologies that are involved in project planning and project management and sought to participate in these areas. They sought to implement a strategy of unpackaging the technology involved in the operations, and to source equipment and services from all over the world and put it together.

They explicitly recognized that technology skills and knowledge resided in people, and that it could be acquired by 'buying' the services of individuals, as opposed to accepting the primitive notion that vehicles such as foreign direct investment and the multinational corporation were necessary and/or sufficient to effect this acquisition. They had the tremendous advantage of capital availability, creditworthiness in the international financial markets, and consequently the lack of the kind of constraints that tied aid from multilateral institutions such as the World Bank implies. They were free to make their own decisions. Despite all of this, they failed. What were the reasons for the failure, and what lessons can students of technology policy and project planners distil from this experience? With the benefit of hindsight, we can identify at least six factors that arguably laid the foundation for the project's failure.

Errors in Conception

The first factor is the conception. There are two problems that can be identified here. The first is the supply-side trap or resource-based fallacy. This seductive notion suggests that what a country should produce are those commodities that are based on the resources it possesses. The trouble with this is that it can lead to a failure to properly appreciate the business of demand and where demand is going.

The fact that a resource is useful in terms of its intrinsic attributes need not mean that is it currently valuable or would be valuable in the future. Value is a function of demand. There may be no demand for a particular resource or commodity despite its intrinsic usefulness. Alternatively, an existing or prior demand may be eroded by a substitute, for example, the dethronement of guano as a fertilizer by chemical fertilizer. In addition, the areas where demand is burgeoning may not be the areas on which a particular resource, or commodities based on it, are centred. A not insignificant part of economic history, and the rise and fall of companies and countries, may really be read as shifts in the valuation of resources consequent upon demand shifts, and without any change occurring in the intrinsic utility of the resources in question.

It might be thought that this is something that everybody understands. In fact, it is not. It is only obvious once stated and bolstered by examples or experience. It might also be thought that surely feasibility studies would adequately take care of the need to recognize the demand side. Here there is another subtle trap. One of the fundamental weaknesses in the methodology customarily employed in doing project analysis, is that the methods used do not *organically* lead to the identification of structural changes taking place in the demand for a commodity. Neither do project analysis methods scan the entire horizon of possibilities and pick out the areas where demand is burgeoning. The method is applied to a particular project and an already identified commodity or set of commodities. The real opportunities may lie elsewhere.

The ISCOTT project is a classic example of this kind of problem. It was perfectly true that Trinidad and Tobago had lots of cheap natural gas. It was not necessarily true to go on to say that what Trinidad and Tobago should naturally and necessarily produce and export was either gas itself or commodities intensive in the use of gas, for example, steel. The choice of steel, (as of fertilizer or methanol) was in large part a simple derivative of the notion of cheap gas, since steel and Direct Reduced Iron were products intensive in the use of energy (read gas).

However, on international markets, steel in most of its variants, was a mature product. The demand for steel products was, and is, negatively affected by (1) the growth of substitutes (e.g., engineering plastics, composites, etc); (2) the shift in the economies of the industrialized countries away from the smokestack industries and towards services; (3) increasing saturation in the markets for some of the products that have historically used much of the steel produced (e.g., automobiles). The engineering study done by Hatch and the marketing study done by Booz, Allen and Hamilton, never dealt with the kind of structural changes taking place which would impact on the demand for steel. We have in these studies, classic examples of the way in which many feasibility studies are done, the weaknesses of this methodology, and the kinds of problems and mistakes that can result.

It is true that there are areas within the family of steel products where markets are good (e.g. stainless and specialty steels currently). It is also true that setting up a steel industry to produce finished steel to be utilized in a domestic market, or to be fabricated into metal products in domestic engineering industries might have been an idea that would contribute handsomely to the transformation of a Third World country such Trinidad and Tobago. However, it is doubtful, as experience has demonstrated, that there was merit in the idea to invest such large resources in producing a mature product for export, compared to identifying areas where demand was growing rapidly, (and which were no more technologically infeasible), and getting into those (e.g., a petroleum-based specialty plastics (rubbers and chemicals).

If the resource-based notion of what Trinidad and Tobago should produce was one problem, another was, apparently, the implicit assumptions and underlying psychological motivations of the key decision-makers, and especially the then Prime Minister, Eric Williams. It is of course, impossible to prove what people's implicit assumptions and psychological drivers might or might not have been. Asking them, even if it were possible, would be of doubtful utility. It may be hidden even from themselves. The best we can do is infer and speculate.

As suggested at the beginning of our study of the steel industry however, it seems that there was an implicit assumption that steel was somehow synonymous with industrialization. This emerges in certain speeches by the decision makers and in certain documents arguing the case for the project. It also seems that there was an unconscious assumption that because iron and steel were the basis of the First Industrial Revolution, they would continue to play a significant role in the future. There also seems to have been little or no recognition of the ways in which the economies of the metropolitan countries were evolving, and the implications of this in terms of where demand would grow, and where demand would decline. There was little understanding that the commodities of today and yesterday are the 'also-rans' are discards of tomorrow's world.

Conviction about the underlying soundness and desirability of a project generally play a very important role in decisions to proceed or not to proceed with it, whatever the numbers in the prospectus might say. From all indications this would seem to have happened in the ISCOTT project as well. Little else explains the decision to proceed with such an enormous investment (by local standards) when the promised rate of return was only 10-11%. It must be remembered as well that ISCOTT was paying an average 8.75% for its long-term debt capital. Given the risks involved, from an economic point of view such a project should probably have been rejected on this ground alone.

Here we may underscore the significance of this business of errors in conception. Projects virtually never turn out exactly as planned. If however, the underlying conception is sound (e.g. the choice of a commodity for which demand is genuinely booming), then there is often a cushion against mistakes and errors (except the most egregious). By contrast, a marginal project based on an infirm conception is often doomed by the first bad roll of the dice against it.

Failures in Planning

The second factor that arguably underlies the failure of ISCOTT is a failure in the planning of the project. Three aspects of this failure can be highlighted here. The first is the failure to undertake a detailed, strategic analysis of the international steel industry (as opposed to feasibility studies). This is the sort of analysis which (1) incorporates the lessons of product cycle theory, (2) focuses attention on possible substitutes, (3) analyzes the spread of technological capability in the industry internationally, the consequent rise of new suppliers and the implications for market structure, prices, etc., and (4) pays attention to structural changes taking place which can influence the prospects of an industry.

The second failure in planning was the product planning and marketing strategy adopted. One aspect of this is the failure to foresee the rise of protectionism in the target markets. This was in turn related to the failure to undertake the kind of strategic analysis outlined above, plus misperceptions about the world, and specifically about the reactions of metropolitan firms and governments to severe competition and the loss of domestic market share to foreign producers. A small country with little or no countervailing power is uniquely vulnerable to foreign protectionist policies. It is interesting to note that neither the Hatch Report nor the feasibility study undertaken by Booz, Allen and Hamilton flagged the threat of protectionism. Had this been anticipated, the arrangements to benefit or subsidize ISCOTT could have been structured in alternative ways so as to ward off anti-dumping and countervailing duties and the consequent disruption of the new company's efforts to penetrate international markets.

The failure to appreciate the protectionist response in metropolitan markets is really part of a generally ill-conceived marketing strategy. The planners may be faulted both in terms of choice of products and choice of target markets, quite apart from the merits of a decision to go into steel at all. The fastest-growing markets in steel internationally are the developing country markets, not the metropolitan markets. Similarly, if metropolitan markets were being targeted, the products for which markets were most promising were stainless steel and specialty steel products. ISCOTT was, with hindsight, badly advised with respect to its marketing strategy.

A third aspect of this business of product planning was the decision taken to add a second direct reduction plant in the belief that there was a market opening up for direct reduced iron. While this may indeed have been true, the decision really represented an unnecessary and risky over-extension of the project in the light of (a) how new and uncertain this market was, and (b) the unresolved technical problems with respect to shipping DRI from the Midrex process. It is often much wiser in industrial development to proceed rather cautiously into new markets and new technologies. In fact, some of the most successful firms aim not at pioneering new technologies into product innovations, or being the first to open up a new market, but to be second or third in. The pioneers are the ones who often pay the highest costs of learning by experience. Suitably positioned followers have the benefit of much cheaper learning from the pioneer's stumbles. (The case of IBM in the personal computer market in the early 1980's is one example of this kind of strategy).

The decision to add the second DR module and to create a deliberate imbalance between the different stages of the production stream from iron through semi-finished to finished steel products seemed attractive at the time. It seemed to give ISCOTT more strings to its bow, i.e., to give it the flexibility of taking advantage of marketing opportunities in three product areas as opposed to one. However, what it also meant was multiplying the headaches of marketing if all stages of the plant were operating at capacity It is interesting to observe by contrast the product strategies of the Japanese steelmakers. These have generally gone to great lengths to integrate and balance the successive phases of their steel operations and to minimize imbalances.

Failures in Reaction-Decisions

The third general area that we can point to in this anatomy of failure is the taking of certain decisions which were later to prove crucial in terms of their impact on the success of the project. What is interesting about these decisions is that they were what we might call reaction-decisions, that is, they were taken in response to some, usually unexpected, and usually untoward event. It is often exactly these decisions that measure the sophistication and experience of policy makers. It is these decisions that separate the excellent managers and organizations from the second-raters, and that separate developed countries and systems from underdeveloped ones.

Two of these decisions may be noted and regarded as fateful. The first was the decision to go it alone after the betrayal in 1976 by the joint-venture partners. When that decision is analyzed, it turns out that the set of sensible reasons put forward initially as to why a joint venture partner was needed, were abruptly discarded. If a joint venture partner was seen as necessary before for technical assistance and marketing, it is not at all clear why this should suddenly become unnecessary and going-it-alone become feasible. The evidence points to a reaction that seemed to involve pique, anger, and a determination to demonstrate that Trinidad and Tobago would achieve its objectives regardless.

The decision seemed to convert what before was a leaning towards Korf-Midrex, into a quick acceptance of that company. Korf was however, (as was later belatedly recognized) a competitor in the very market being targeted. Korf's subsequent suing of ISCOTT after selling it the DR technology and providing it with steel-making assistance is therefore, in some ways no surprise. The choice of the Korf process also created a ripple of consequences, e.g., the sourcing of Brazilian ore, the technical problems with shipping Midrex DRI and the crisis in operating the plant and acquiring the technology, when the relationship with Korf was abrogated following the lawsuit.

A second such fateful reaction-decision was the one made after the failure of Rust International to perform adequately as general contractor. The decision not to hire a new general contractor but to sub-divide the work was a bad one, especially in the context of a three-way split in the project management function. The ripple of consequences here includes the chaos during construction, the failure to plan recruitment and training properly (with consequent devastating effects on the effective acquisition of operating technology), and the large cost and time overruns. This last played an important role in the failure of the complex financially, given the use of short-term, high-cost debt to finance the overruns, and the financial crisis this precipitated.

Mistakes re Foreign Companies

Fourthly, the planners made mistakes with respect to the foreign companies they dealt with and how they utilized them. It was most probably a mistake to utilize Hatch in such a wide variety of roles: consulting engineer, project manager construction supervisor, technical assistance, managerial assistance, and so on. This arrangement not only involved the payment of an inordinate amount of money to one firm, but it clearly created conflicts of interests with respect to that firm's operations.

ISCOTT needed an expert that was paid simply to provide it with dispassionate, unbiased advice and information. When the same firm that was supposed to act as advisor was simultaneously involved in various operational roles, its power and influence over the project became too great, its opportunities for manipulation multiplied, and its advice was hardly consistently disinterested.

When we analyze the history of ISCOTT's relationship with Korf, with its original joint-venture partners (Kawasaki, Mitsui and Estel) and with other firms such as Rust International that were contracted to provide it with services of one kind or another, ISCOTT lacked the ability to generate the necessary information on these firms and their strategies. It might be questioned whether the planners ever perceived the necessity to do so. It also is clear that in at least some areas, ISCOTT was charged exorbitant fees for services provided, (e.g., Korf's project management services, and the cost of expatriates hired as individuals). This raises the question of information on what a fair return for services rendered was, and how a small, developing country, inexperienced in a particular activity, sources that kind of information.

Yet another area of weakness lies in the contracts entered into for the provision of technical assistance and other related services such as training. We have seen above the issue of the vagueness of the clauses detailing the contracting firm's obligations to ISCOTT. The lack of any measures of effective delivery of the services contracted for, and the lack of a system of rewards/penalties related to such measures permitted situations to arise where despite large expenditures, the services contracted for were provided inadequately or with specific services not provided at all.

Over-centralization and Ineffectual Local Management

A fifth source of the project's failure can be found in the local management of the project at both political and technocratic levels. The original organization set up to plan the project (the Coordinating Task Force) was incredibly overloaded having regard to both the numbers and the experience of its personnel. The Chairman of the Board as we saw wore numerous hats. It was obviously impossible for someone charged with the management and operationalizing of the largest project in the country's history to be effective in overseeing it, while carrying such a range of other responsibilities. The predictable result was bad management and ineffectual management. The attempt to centralize control over the project in the Chairman's office in such a context was doomed to failure. The large cost overruns on the project and the confusion during the construction phase demonstrates the weakness of this arrangement.

It is also interesting to observe how ineffectual Cabinet's control over the project was. The special relationship that existed between the Chairman of ISCOTT's Board and the then Prime Minister played a role here. Agreement between these two men on any matter sufficed to ensure that whatever it was they agreed on would be effected. The central bureaucracy and Cabinet itself had little knowledge of or control over much of what went on in the project. It must also be stressed however, that neither of these institutions possessed expertise or capacities which would either have provided an effective check on the mistakes that were being made or an alternative technical input that would have improved the planning and management of the project.

While Cabinet control of the project was touted, this control was largely nominal for these reasons. The same can be said for the Board of Directors of ISCOTT during and after construction of the plant. The Board never played any role other than that of a rubber stamp of the wishes of the Chairman and Prime Minister.

In other words, we have here a project which to a very great extent was dominated by the perceptions and personalities of two men. It is not that this is necessarily unusual or a bad thing. If everything goes well, the elimination of bureaucratic red tape and internecine institutional warfare is probably a good thing. The problem arises when the dominant leadership makes bad decisions and there is no effective check. Regrettably, it may be very difficult to have it both ways i.e. clear, decisive, activist leadership and checks on their (bad) decisions.

Poor Choice of People

The sixth fundamental problem we may identify in many ways derives from the fifth. In several areas, poor personnel decisions were made. These decisions applied both to the recruitment of expatriates and to the recruitment of locals. A study of the persons appointed to ISCOTT's Board of Directors shows that none of the members appointed had the kind of knowledge or experience of steel or related businesses which would automatically suggest them as a candidate for inclusion.

Similarly, several locals appointed to managerial positions within the company, including the top positions, were clearly unsuitable. The mistakes here, and the choice of top expatriates meant that ISCOTT began life with a poor-quality management team. Inevitably, there was a ripple of consequences from this which spelt the doom of the initial venture.

Technology Planning

Of special interest to us is the technology planning that went into ISCOTT. Critical to the overall failure of the project was the failure to acquire the necessary technology effectively. This is one dimension of technology planning.

There is a second dimension to the failures in technology planning to which we might draw attention. This is the issue of whether the complex of objectives that was established was what was really desirable or possible. These two dimensions or 'issue-areas' are explored below.

The arrangements for acquisition of the necessary technologies for successfully operating the new plant seemed a priori, sensible and even sophisticated in some areas. There was a clear recognition that foreign technical assistance was needed and would be required for several years. The initial idea was to acquire the necessary technology through a joint venture arrangement. This seems sensible enough.

The plans also sought to allow nationals to keep control over the overall direction of the venture, to insist on their being exposed to critical areas of technology, and to split the project management function among three entities Korf, Hatch and ISCOTT itself so as to ensure that nationals participated in this critical knowledge area and learned from their participation. With the breakdown of the joint venture and the decision to go it alone with a reduced project, plans were formulated to buy in the necessary technical assistance and necessary training of nationals to operate the plant.

It was also decided to hire expatriates on an individual basis and that skilled expatriates would be hired to fill the top executive positions. Elaborate understudy arrangements were proposed with the aim of ensuring that a transfer of technology took place from expatriates on contracts to locals who would ultimately take their place. Most of this sounds fine. However, it did not work as planned.

Arguably, there was little wrong with the plans themselves. The one area that is perhaps subject to criticism is the notion of splitting the project management function into three, so that ISCOTT could maintain effective control and its people could participate and thereby learn. ISCOTT did not have at its disposal the necessary experienced local staff to adequately discharge the responsibilities it allocated to itself. Its leadership's time was also distracted by involvement in numerous other activities, a problem we shall return to below. It may be then that its plans in this regard were over-ambitious.

The real problem seems to have been in implementation. The absorption of needed technology through technical assistance contracts, and the hiring of skilled expatriates, all turn out to depend crucially on the top management of an operation, and their own knowledge, skills and capabilities The capture of the necessary technologies depends in the final analysis on the systems set up, the arrangements made, the ability to choose people correctly, motivate and manage them so that they fulfil the objectives set for them. It depends on what is insisted on, at a very detailed level, under technical assistance contracts, and the ability to determine whether what is wanted is being received.

Here, the top management chosen, including the expatriates chosen to head the company initially, were deficient. One might argue that the plans for technology acquisition do not seem to have recognized adequately enough exactly how critical the choice of the top management would be. However, this may be expecting a little too much from a planning process.

Interviews with executives at ISCOTT brought forward the suggestion on more than one occasion that the Canadian expatriate chosen for the Presidency was the wrong man for the job. One interviewee argued for example, that he was the kind of executive that might succeed at running an organization that was already a well-functioning going concern. He was neither the entrepreneurial-type executive nor the organization and systems builder that creates an organization. There is also the issue of how highly motivated the expatriate top management was to have ISCOTT succeed. Whether the mechanisms had been set up so as to really intertwine the success of the new company with their own career goals and their own success is a very real question. What is not in doubt however is that the failure to manage the operation so as to acquire the necessary operational technologies, owed a great deal to managerial failure at the topmost levels.

When we turn to the technology planning that went into the project more broadly, the mistakes are rather clearer. The most useful way to approach the overall technology policy and planning that went into the project is to set up a framework of what the desirable and feasible objectives could have been, utilizing the conception of the set of technology policy issues that arise for developing countries in conjunction with the set of activities involved in the project cycle.

The six technology policy issues that arise for developing countries such as Trinidad and Tobago may be summarised as follows:

(1) Technology Policy and its link with overall development strategy;
(2) Building Technological Capability;
(3) The Acquisition of Imported Technology;
(4) The commercialization of technology (costs, terms, channels of payment for imported technology; patents, licensing and other agreements);
(5) Technological Functionality/Dysfunctionality i.e., the impact of technology utilized; (of particular significance is the impact of current new metropolitan technologies on developing countries;
(6) Technology and Institution-building.

In Table 6.2 the possible objectives that might be distilled in each of these six areas from the specific iron and steel project are outlined. In Table 6.3 we utilize the specific objectives identified in Table 6.2 in conjunction with the specific areas of activity in the project cycle where they may be thought to arise. We next indicate whether the particular objective seemed, in our judgement to have emerged clearly, partially or not at all, in ISCOTT's planning for, and approach to each activity area in the project cycle. This does not attempt to indicate whether the planning in relation to the potential objective was good or bad, or whether it was achieved or not achieved. The issue treated as prior is whether it was recognized and addressed at all. (The issues of the effectiveness of whatever planning was done emerges in the discussion of the experience as a whole).

This analysis allows us to draw four (4) conclusions in respect of the technology planning that went into ISCOTT. First, it recognized the need to plan to build a technological capability for iron and steel operations. Second, it did not address the utilization of the project to build capability in other areas such as the engineering industries, metal-working and downstream secondary manufacturing industry. The issue of the linkages ISCOTT could create was explicitly recognized and explicitly recognized as important. However, the actual planning of the project never seriously addressed the creation of these linkages and the building of the set of capabilities involved. Rather the planners contented themselves with the suggestion that it would be up to local private entrepreneurs to come forward, identify the opportunities and capitalize on them. While this may sound good enough in theory, it was not good enough in practice. The local capitalist class, experience suggests, was not by itself equal to the task of creating the necessary complex of linkages required to generate the real benefits of the steel project. So far however, one new downstream mill has been set up utilizing ISCOTT's products and another existing operation has been drawing on it. The reality though is that there is little option but the state playing a lead role in generating the necessary activities.

Table 6.2
Technology Policy Issues and Possible Planning Objectives

Issue	Possible Objectives
Building Technological Capability	(i) Building capability in iron and steel making. (ii) Utilising Iron and steel production to stimulate the development of capabilities downstream in the engineering industries, in areas such as metal—working, design, the utilization of machine tools and the manufacture of simple machinery and equipment
Technology Policy Development strategy -the implications of the choice of development strategy for technology policy	(i) Related to (ii) above, the utilization of iron and steel to build a base for a range of secondary manufacturing industry (e.g. in the area of (metal) furniture manufacture, steel products needles, pins, paper clips, nails, etc.).
Acquisition of Technology from abroad. (This is a critical component of (1) above)	(i) Acquisition of Technology for iron and steel making. (ii) Acquisition of technologies in selected areas of project planning and management (e.g., generating information on foreign firms, procurement, negotiating contracts etc.)
Commercialization Technology (defined here in terms of the cost and terms on which foreign technology is acquired)	(i) Minimizing the payments for foreign technologies. (ii) Sourcing the best technologies internationally on the best terms (apart from cost such issues as genuine transfer, least restrictions on use, etc.) (iii) Development of skills for negotiating and bargaining including such areas as information on foreign technologies, foreign firms, patents, etc.
Technological Functionality/ Dysfunctionality (defined in terms of the positive/ negative Impact of technology utilized on variables such as the economy, particular sectors, culture, society and environment)	(i) Minimizing negative environmental effects as a result of the project. (ii) Maximising the diffusion of skills/technologies arising out of the project into the wider society. (iii) Ensuring that the sociocultural impact of the project maximized net benefit.
Technology and Institution Building (This policy goal relates to the setting up and functioning of the complex of institutions needed for coordinating, monitoring and managing a country's technology policy)	(i) Ensuring that skills, knowledge and competencies acquired during the project are not be dissipated or lost.

Table 6.3
Activities in the Project Cycle, Areas of Possible Fit with Technology Policy And ISCOTT's Planning Response

POSSIBLE TECHNOLOGY POLICY OBJECTIVES	Conception	Engineering Marketing Financial	Organisation of Project	Project Management Arrangements	Design	Detailed Engineering	Procurement (Plant and Equipment)	Acquisition Of Technology	Construction and Commissioning	Training	Other

Technological Capability
  Capability in Iron & Steel making
  Capability in other areas
	Y
	P
			N	Y	Y			Y
								N
										Y
										N	

Technology Policy and Development Strategy Economic Diversification	Y										

Acquisition of Imported Technology
  Acquiring Technology for Iron and Steel making
  Acquiring Technology in Project planning and management
			Y	Y
				Y
					Y			Y		Y	

Commercialization
  Minimizing Payments
  Sourcing
  Negotiation
				Y
				P
							Y
							Y
								Y
								P			

Technological Functionality/ Dysfunctionality
  Environmental Impact
  Diffusion
  Socio-cultural Impact
	Y	N	N			Y		N		N	Y

Technology Policy and Institution Building Plans for Retaining Pooling and Building on Knowledge and Experience Gained			N							Y	N

Y: Recognised in ISCOTT's planning for particular activity area; N: Not recognised in ISCOTT's planning for activity area; P: Partially recognised in ISCOTT's planning for activity area

It is also important to note that when the final decisions were taken on ISCOTT's product slate, the decisions were based on finding export markets primarily and not on the use of ISCOTT as a base for the development of local industry.

Third, there was limited recognition given in the technology planning that went into the project of the need to plan carefully the negotiations with foreign firms for services and technology. Fourth, there was also little planning for promoting the diffusion of the technologies being acquired, for preventing its dissipation, or for infusing the experience gained int͏ͬ institutions charged with technology policy formulation and management.

Lessons of Experience

We can now conclude this lengthy examination by articulating a few lessons of experience that arguably can be distilled from our study.

Lesson One: The Importance of Experienced Technical Management at Top Levels

The first lesson that we can draw is that experienced, technically competent management at the top is critical at all stages of a large industrial project such as this: planning, project management and operations. If a country does not have such people, then it may really find it is necessary to use turnkey and joint venture strategies initially while it produces them, even if there is an initial opportunity cost to so doing. If a way can be found to hire such management and have them operate in the genuine interests of the project and the country then this would probably be preferable. The ISCOTT experience however shows that this is not simple and straightforward.

High salaries and lavish perks are not enough. Regrettably perhaps, there seems to be some circularity in the problem. To effectively find, choose and motivate good top management may itself require good top management. This is precisely what may be missing in the first case.

Producing experienced, first-class managers capable of setting up and running large projects takes many years. The ISCOTT experience seems to suggest that there is no short cut. Consequently, it might be necessary to be patient both with respect to the need to use foreign technical assistance in certain forms at the start, and to spend the necessary years preparing one's people.

Lesson Two: Domestic Receptivity Conditions

The second lesson we may perhaps draw is related to the first As Frances Stewart has pointed out, introducing advanced technology into developing countries is not simply a matter of putting in a plant and operating it. Success demands surrounding cultural and infrastructural matrix of supporting services, skills, values and institutions. ISCOTT provides a good example of the truth of this. The domestic receptivity conditions in terms of local political and technocratic management, local capabilities with respect to generating information on the external environment and local understanding of that environment just did not exist in as developed a form as was necessary. It is for these subtle reasons that suggestions for Science Parks in underdeveloped Caribbean countries intent on aping the metropole are likely to lead to frustration. The build-up of a country's technological capabilities has to proceed on a broad front. It is both direct (in terms of actual projects) and indirect (in terms of ideas, the training of people, the exposure they receive, the infrastructure set up including here information systems and the values created).

Lesson Three: Risk, Project Analysis and Size of Projects

The ISCOTT experience raises the issue of risk and the size of projects undertaken in the light of the clear methodological problems in project analysis methodologies. The long gestation period of projects, the hazards of projecting future prices and market conditions, and the problems of large errors in cost estimates consequent upon the timing of 'Go/No Go' decisions on projects, all combine to make traditional project analysis fraught with the possibility of error.

Three lessons are derivable in this regard from the ISCOTT experience. One is the absolute importance of strategic analysis of the industries or activities being entered into. The second is the importance of a sound conception based on a good strategic understanding of the current and future international environment (Directions of change are of great value, even where specific numbers cannot be provided as for example in terms of precise future prices). The third is the desirability of spreading the risks over several activities (i.e., using the law of large numbers). One of the problems with the ISCOTT project was that in terms of its cost, it was simply too large in relation to the risks, and the spread between the projected rates of return and the cost of capital was far too narrow. Trinidad and Tobago would have probably done much better to start with a smaller, cheaper project, expanding it later if necessary and investing (over time) in several other different projects.

Lesson Four: Problems of Unbundling

The ISCOTT experience raises questions about the strategy of unbundling. While we cannot say that unbundling will not in fact achieve the objectives it is popularly supposed to, there can be some unexpected problems. Engineers pointed to the fact that equipment was generally designed with a particular operating environment assumed, in terms of what other equipment and systems it would be interfacing with, or a part of. This interfacing requirement can cause severe problems when operations commence, if adequate care has not been taken.

Other engineers pointed out yet another subtle problem. This was the problem of lack of standardization of certain kinds of equipment (e.g., pumps, valves, compressors, turbines) not just in a given plant, *but across industry* in a country. The argument here can be perhaps encapsulated as economies of skill, i.e. the development of a corps of technicians and service people who build skills in dealing with a particular kind of equipment or system. The introduction of completely different equipment or systems as part of an unbundling strategy can, it was pointed out, stymie the development of local technical skills and reinforce dependence on foreign service crews. Where this multiplies over a variety of makes of the same equipment (e.g., turbines) the suggestion is that the costs to the country may be not inconsiderable.

The suggestion here is that in sourcing equipment and systems in a small country, this issue of the value of 'standardization' may provide another consideration to oppose the considerations of sourcing the best and the cheapest worldwide for a particular plant.

Lesson Five: Organizing the Project Management Function

Fifth, ISCOTT's experience strongly suggests the unwisdom of project arrangements which combine the role of consulting engineer with too many other roles. It may be fine to hire a firm as project manager under a turnkey contract to design and build. However, the consulting engineer, if there is one, should not be in a position where conflicts of interest are not minimized.

It is also doubtful whether ISCOTT's splitting of the project management function was wise Certainly in the absence of a general contractor, it proved disastrous. It is clearly of great importance to set up these relationships on a project with a great deal of circumspection and with proper dovetailing of responsibility with authority.

Lesson Six: Technical Assistance Contracts

We can also clearly see the need for a better system for negotiating and entering into contracts for 'intangibles' such as training and technical assistance. Two points stand out. The first is the undesirability for developing countries to negotiate contracts based on someone else's draft. The second is the clear need introduce stipulations which provide for performance tests.

It may be quite true that the knowledge a person acquires may not be a tangible commodity in the way that a pump is. However, knowledge can be tested (as every university student knows). It can for example be tested operationally e.g., in someone being able to successfully perform a certain function.

This obviously cannot apply in every circumstance (the training of people to be top managers, for example). But there are many in which it can. It is in principle possible to insist that the technical assistance or training that a firm contracts to provide, be tested by the successful performance of the trainees for a predetermined period and in a specified set of circumstances.

Lesson Seven: Information on Foreign Firms

ISCOTT suffered greatly from its unwillingness and/or inability to read the strategies of the foreign firms with which it was dealing. It is also instructive to note how many different foreign firms it had to deal with. There were all told well over a score of them. One lesson of experience is the need for mechanisms that can provide a certain amount of basic information on foreign firms. Often basic information available through legal reporting requirements, features in the ordinary press and in the trade press, information provided by brokerage houses and market analysts can prove invaluable in deducing the motivations of companies and their strategic imperatives. A mechanism that simply provided such a service would undoubtedly be of great value to small, information poor developing countries.

Lesson Eight: Domestic Organization

The ISCOTT experience demonstrates the weakness of Trinidad and Tobago's domestic organizational systems. There was inadequate oversight of the project, little check on the errors being made by a chairman wearing too many hats, and a lack of any alternative technical capacity elsewhere in the country with respect to the steel business, project planning or the other dimensions of the ISCOTT project.

The existence of a corps of technocrats located elsewhere in the system would be a necessary (though not sufficient) condition for providing the requisite balance to the not infrequent tendency towards runaway projects in countries such as this.

This list hardly exhausts the lessons that can be distilled from this experience. These eight are however, arguably among the more important. Since however any individual case study is, from a methodological point of view, necessarily limited as a source of valid generalizations, the conclusions drawn here need to be tested against other project experiences. It would be useful for example, to study other failures to see whether the factors identified here emerged in those cases, or what other factors that could be identified as sources of failures might have emerged in those cases. Another useful kind of comparison would be with projects which succeeded in some sense or other. One may attempt to identify for example, whether conditions identified here, and held responsible for ISCOTT's failure, can be found to exist in other successful projects without any manifestations of the ill-effects detailed here. One may relatedly attempt to define a set of necessary and/or sufficient conditions for successful project management and technology acquisition by studying a set of successfully executed projects with effective technology acquisition to see what, if anything, they had in common with respect to the arrangements made.

Let us make a first step in this direction by turning now to an examination of three other large industrial projects, which can be held to have succeeded in certain areas where ISCOTT failed for example, effective acquisition of operational technologies, successful operation post start-up. These projects however, as we shall see have so far turned out to be below expectations in certain other, crucial dimensions.

7
THE FERTILIZER STORY: PART 1

Introduction

Apart from steel, Trinidad and Tobago invested a significant amount of its foreign exchange windfall from the oil-boom years in several other major, export-oriented projects, in fertilizer and methanol. Of the three fertilizer projects, two were ammonia plants, and one urea. The fourth project that may be mentioned was a methanol project.[86] The experience with these four projects offers certain interesting points of contrast with the iron and steel project, in terms of approach, organization and results.

As we have seen, the iron and steel project was undertaken as a wholly state-owned venture. Responsibility for such project cycle activities as design, project management, construction and training was distributed among several different organizations, with the state-owned company, ISCOTT, attempting to play an overarching role with respect to control and coordination. The two ammonia projects, by contrast, were both joint ventures with foreign multinationals. Both projects, in addition, were undertaken on what might be called a 'semi-turnkey' basis, with major engineering firms carrying out the projects under Design-Build type of arrangement, with the client participating to some extent in project planning and project management.

---

[86] As indicated in Chapter Three, there have been certain other projects set up at the same Point Lisas industrial estate apart from fertilizer, steel and methanol. These however we do not treat with here. Some of these have been necessary ancillaries to the industrial projects, infrastructural projects such as port construction, electricity generation and road works. A couple of others have been either small plants to provide certain inputs to the major projects (oxygen-nitrogen) or privately owned downstream plants such as Centrin, set up downstream of Iron and Steel to manufacture various finished steel products from billets produced at ISCOTT.

The methanol and urea plants were set up as wholly state-owned companies, but with management farmed out under management contracts to other entities. In the case of the urea plant, a management contract was set up with the joint venture firm running one of the new ammonia plants. In the case of the methanol plant, another state-owned company was given the formal responsibility for management. Both the methanol and urea plants were constructed under more or less classic turnkey arrangements.

While in all four of these projects the final price tag was rather more than initially projected, none of the four experienced the particularly difficult birth of the iron and steel project. There were rather minor time overruns and initial teething problems with the two ammonia projects. After a successful start-up, the methanol plant ran into some comparatively minor technical snags. However, none of these four, up to the time of writing, had yet lived up to the (financial) expectations initially held for them. Neither of the ammonia projects, which came on stream in 1977 and 1981 respectively, had shown a net profit up to 1984, or even met the financial targets projected for them when they were planned.

By 1985, neither methanol nor urea had yet accumulated sufficient operational experience for their profit performance to be properly assessed. However, in both cases, prices for their output at start-up in 1984 and in the months thereafter, were below expectations, suggesting that these projects as well would have some difficulty in immediately achieving their planned financial targets.

In the next two chapters, we shall concentrate on the ammonia projects, essentially because of their somewhat longer post start-up experience compared to urea and methanol. These projects as well offer some special interest to the analyst because of the impact of the involvement of foreign multinationals as joint-venture partners.

Ammonia Projects: Background, Conception and Genesis

The first of the two ammonia projects to be undertaken was really the expansion of an existing facility, Federation Chemicals (Fedchem). The plant in question was a wholly-owned subsidiary of a foreign multinational corporation, W.R. Grace of the United States. Grace had begun commercial production of fertilizer in Trinidad in 1960. Its entry had initially been aimed at utilizing cheap local natural gas, to produce fertilizer for the planned West Indian Federation on an import substitution basis. The name Federation Chemicals owes everything to this initial concept.

The idea of a tariff-hopping, import-substitution type plant died with the short-lived West Indian Federation, which lasted only four years (1958-62). The demise of the Federation led to a rethinking of the concept by Grace, and the eventual revamping of the facility into a world-scale export-oriented facility. This proved to be an extremely profitable tactical manoeuvre by Grace. Its Fedchem subsidiary enjoyed the benefit of such cheap gas that it was the envy of many in the international fertilizer industry. It also enjoyed the benefit of extraordinarily generous tax incentives, granted under a specially designed legislative regime, custom-built just for Grace.

The incentives were granted by a young government (full internal self-government and a national government having come only in 1956). The government's anxiety for jobs and for development was matched only by its innocence about the fertilizer business, multinational corporations in general, and Grace more specifically. Where the usual incentive regime provided for a five-year tax holiday, Grace was given ten years. This was allied with extended depreciation allowances, ten-year waiver of customs duty, and other incentives.

So generous were these incentives that up to 1975, no corporate income tax was ever received from Grace. Commercial production began in 1960. A detailed study of the data for the second half of the 1960's shows that no more than 13% of the value added in the industry accrued to the local economy. In addition, employment up to 1975 never crossed 610 workers or 0.16% of the country's labour force.[87] As far as we know, the Trinidad and Tobago government never conducted an in-depth examination of its experience with Grace and fertilizer or attempted to measure the actual benefits that accrued to the country from the Fedchem operation. However, in the early 1970's there was great enthusiasm for more fertilizer production in government circles.

This enthusiasm was kindled by four factors:-

(1) The discovery of large reserves of natural gas and the embrace of the resource—based strategy of industrialization. This strategy was based on the identification of activities which would utilize natural gas intensively.

(2) The rise in oil prices, and as a derivative the expected upward pressure on gas prices (and energy prices generally) in the metropolitan countries This promised to give countries such as Trinidad and Tobago with apparently abundant reserves of cheap gas a significant competitive advantage in gas intensive industries.

---

[87] See Parsan, (1981, pp. 144-151 and Tables 6.4, 6.5)

(3) The widespread predictions around 1974 of an imminent world food crisis. It was presumed that to relieve the projected shortages and unavailability of food, agricultural expansion would be critical and therefore, there would be increased demand for fertilizers.

(4) As with steel, windfall foreign exchange earnings after 1973-74 made it possible to concretize the ideas about gas utilization in actual projects, including fertilizer.

The interest in government circles in fertilizer and other similar energy-based projects was quickly taken advantage of by both Grace and Amoco, the latter being one of the major oil companies operating in the Trinidad oil industry. Both companies responded to some general prodding by Trinidad's then Prime Minister Dr. Eric Williams, by proposing fertilizer projects.

In 1974, in the wake of the first oil price hike Williams undertook a visit to the United States. During this visit, he indicated that his government expected foreign companies operating in Trinidad to demonstrate a tangible commitment to participate with the government in its strategy of building and diversifying the local economy using its energy resources. While Williams's prodding was apparently rather general, the proposals of Grace and Amoco were quite specific. Both companies suggested fertilizer projects and joint-venture arrangements.[88] In fact, the projects that finally materialized owe a great deal in terms of both conception and detail, to the multinational joint-venture partners.

The Projects: An Overview

The first of these plants to be agreed on, designed and built was the W.R. Grace/Government of Trinidad and Tobago plant called Trinidad Nitrogen (Tringen). This plant was nominally a 51:49 joint venture between government (majority shareholder) and Grace. It took just three years from initial conception and agreement in 1974 to completion in July 1977 and start-up in October of that year.

The new facility was designed and built by the large US engineering firm, Fluor. It had a capacity of 1090 metric tons per day of ammonia (358,000 metric tons per year). This was the standard size of large capacity

---

[88] See speech by Errol Mahabir, then Minister of Energy on Grace's role in Tringen proposal, (1981, p. 2) and Amoco's role in the Fertrin proposal (1979, p.3). Mahabir candidly stated that Tringen was established on the initiative and promotional activity of W.R. Grace & Co.

ammonia plants built in the 1970's. It was located on 108 acres of land adjacent to Grace's Fedchem plant which itself abutted Trinidad's Pt. Lisas Industrial Estate, and the new plant shares several common services with the older facility. In fact, Tringen really worked out as an extension of Fedchem and a mechanism whereby the Trinidad and Tobago government obtained some equity in that operation.

While Tringen was formally incorporated as a separate company (it was formed in June 1974), with a board of directors and a President, in fact Grace ran the show through Fedchem. Fedchem obtained a management contract for the new plant, and a marketing contract for all its output. The first President, a local, reportedly quit in disgust after a relatively short time in the job. He had little to do, and no real executive authority.

The Tringen facility was originally slated to cost TT$192 million. The final cost was by one official estimate TT$281 million, though a slightly lower figure of TT$267.4 million has been given by another official source.[89] However, whether the true figure is $267 million or $281 million, there was some degree of cost overrun of at least 39%. The percentage figure is quite high but the absolute amount, either TT$75 million or TT$93 million depending on which final cost figure is used, is not as large as the overruns experienced on some of the country's other projects in the oil boom years. Also, the overrun involved, though sizeable, is not particularly startling when analyzed in the context of other large industrial projects internationally.

Not uncommon in projects of this kind in developing countries, the local contribution to the project during construction was not particularly large. About TT$65 million of the sums expended was spent on local materials and services, about 25% of the total project cost if the lower of the two capital cost figures is used. There was little local input into the procurement of such services as design engineering and project management. Nor was there significant local participation in the areas of detailed engineering and the fabrication and supply of machinery, equipment, vessels, piping, and so on. The virtual absence of a local engineering services and supply industry automatically precluded the possibility of any such participation.

At peak of construction, the project employed some 900 persons. Permanent employment was provided for 90 employees.[90] In keeping

---

[89] See Coordinating Task Force (1975, Appendix 8), Progress Report #1. Also see Minister Errol Mahabir's speech to Parliament of 9th March 1979. The slightly lower final figure of $267.4 million appears in the Minister of Finance's Budget Speech of 1980 and also in the valuation of the new company's assets in its accounts for the year 1977.

[90] See Mahabir (1979. The Coordinating Task Force Report #6 of 1978 (sec.3, p.1) gives a figure of 90 with another 50 Fedchem employees providing services to Tringen.

with this type of industrial project, the capital cost per job provided was extremely high, over TT$2.0 million.

With respect to actual operations, the major inputs required by the new plant were natural gas, water and electricity. Of these, natural gas is key. Ammonia production from natural gas involves reforming the hydrocarbons that constitute natural gas, (mainly methane, CH_4, and ethane, C_2H_6), to generate hydrogen which can be combined with nitrogen obtained from the air to produce ammonia (NH_3). Carbon dioxide is a by-product. This can subsequently be combined with ammonia to produce urea.

The Tringen plant was projected to utilize 51 million scf/day of natural gas from 1982. Gas costs in 1982 were 43.4% of the Tringen plant's cost of production of ammonia. The plant also required some 800,000 imperial gallons of water per day and over 5 megawatts of electricity per day.

Fertrin

The Fertrin plant (Fertilizers of Trinidad and Tobago) came on stream in 1981/1982. Like Tringen it was a 51:49 joint venture. In this case the partnership linked Amoco Oil Company with the Government of Trinidad and Tobago. As in the Tringen case, the government was the majority shareholder. Amoco had other involvements in Trinidad apart from this fertilizer project. It was the largest oil producer on the island, accounting for over 50% of the country's crude production from its offshore fields on the East Coast of Trinidad. It was also the country's major producer of natural gas and the owner of a substantial portion of the natural gas reserves.[91]

Fertrin comprised two ammonia plants, each with a capacity of 1044 metric tons per day of ammonia. The first plant came on stream in November 1981, the second in August 1982. Total completion can be put at September 1982. As in the case of Tringen, the new plants were very much in line with what had become standard size for large-scale new ammonia plants in the 1970s. The Fertrin plants were not purpose-built for Fertrin. They were actually two units bought from two North American companies, Pan Canadian Petroleum Limited, and Agrico Chemicals Company. These units had been built for these companies but had not been put into use. They had been built by Kellogg, and this company was hired by Fertrin to be the general contractor on Engineering Design and Construction for the Fertrin facilities. The major agreements for the Fertrin complex were concluded in the second half of 1978, and construction of the plant began in 1979. At the start of construction in 1979, the cost of the complex was put at TT$618.9 million (US$288

---

[91] The term 'substantial portion' is taken from the White Paper on Natural Gas (1981, p. 8). The document does not offer an actual figure.

million).[92] Actual cost on completion in 1981-82 was put at TT$840.0 million.[93] The time overrun on this project was approximately one year and the cost overrun about 36%.[94]

Fertrin approximately doubled Trinidad and Tobago's ammonia production capacity. The new facility when operated at capacity requires some 71-72 million scf/day of natural gas, 1 million gallons per day of fresh water and 14 megawatts per day of electricity.[95] Like Tringen therefore, the Fertrin project had major infrastructural implications in terms of the demand for water, electricity and of course the natural gas which was the ultimate raison d'etre of the whole exercise. Like Tringen, the new facility employs relatively little labour, about 270 persons.[96] This implies a figure of TT$3.1 million per job created. Since the Fedchem/Tringen complex has an installed capacity of 635,000 metric tonnes of ammonia a year, the addition of Fertrin meant that Trinidad and Tobago acquired an ammonia capacity of over 1.3 million metric tonnes a year. (Assuming 330 operating days per year, Fertrin would have an annual capacity of some 689,000 metric tonnes.) As Table 7.1 shows, fertilizer production more than tripled between 1977 and 1983 due to the Tringen and Fertrin projects.

Urea

In 1984, a new urea plant was commissioned as well. This plant has a capacity of 1620 metric tons per day and came on stream at a reported cost of TT$425 million. The design and construction work was carried out by the Italian firm, Snamprogetti, under a turnkey contract. The technology utilized was that developed by Snamprogetti themselves. This firm is a major multinational with an internationally recognized capability in the urea business.

---

[92] See Budget Speech 1980
[93] See speech at formal commissioning of Fertrin by Minister Errol Mahabir (1981)
[94] According to the 7th Progress Report of the Coordinating Task Force dated December 1978, the entire project was due to be completed in May 1981, with the first ammonia shipment in September 1981. However, the one year figure may rather overstate the extent of the time overrun. Part of the delay in getting the second plant started was lack of sufficient gas. While technically this still means that there was a one-year time overrun, it was not all due to construction delays. Such delays only accounted for part of the one-year time overrun.
[95] NEC (1981)
[96] ibid.

Table 7.1

Fertilizer Production in Trinidad and Tobago 1975-1984

Year	Fertilizer Production ('000 tonnes)	Export ('000 tonnes)
1977	342.1	272.1
1978	631.9	519.4
1979	604.9	541.5
1980	687.0	613.6
1981	559.4	494.1
1982	939.7	850.6
1983	1274.3	1213.9
1984	1458.1	1281.6
Source: Central Bank of Trinidad and Tobago, *Annual Report* 1984, Table 1.9		

The main raw materials for the manufacture of urea are ammonia and carbon dioxide. The urea plant is projected to use 940 tons/day ammonia and 1240 tons/day of carbon dioxide. Sited next to Fertrin, the idea was that it would draw its feedstocks from Fertrin's ammonia production and the carbon dioxide that it generates as a by-product of ammonia manufacture. This would mean there that there is trade-off between producing ammonia and producing urea. Like the ammonia plants, the new urea plant requires large amounts of water and electricity (950,000 gallons/day of the former and 7.4 MW/day of the latter). Direct natural gas utilization is much lower (7.2 million scf per day) given the fact that ammonia is the major feedstock. Project employment is likewise small with 103 persons projected as direct employment.[97]

The Fertilizer Projects: Organisation and Rationale

Urea

It had been envisaged originally by the government's planners that the Fertrin ammonia and the urea plants would have been one integrated complex not just physically but in terms of ownership and management as well. During the preliminary study phase however, Amoco argued that the projections suggested that urea manufacture would not be

---

[97] ibid.

economically justifiable and that it should be excluded from the project.[98] While the Trinidad and Tobago planners seem to have acquiesced in this judgement initially, they soon changed their minds and the urea project then went ahead, but as a wholly state-owned venture.

It was however, physically integrated with the Fertrin plant, relied on it for its feedstocks, and in addition, Fertrin was asked to manage it under a management contract. A marketing contract was entered into with an American company, Agrico Chemicals, for marketing the output of the plant.

Ammonia

Turning now to the two joint ventures for ammonia production, three features stand out. First, while the Trinidad and Tobago government wholeheartedly entered into these projects and indeed saw them as fulfilling its objectives, the foreign partners were able to shape the choice, design and scope of the actual projects so that they fitted their own corporate strategies much more successfully than they realized the state's objectives. As we shall see below, neither of these two ammonia projects has so far met the state's expectations with respect to prices, earnings and foreign exchange contribution.

Secondly, in both joint ventures, the arrangements set up have effectively meant that control over the operations rested essentially with the MNC joint venture partners. Thirdly, in contrast to the steel project both ammonia projects were efficiently organized, with respect to construction and post-start-up operation, though to date they have not been as profitable as expected. This greater efficiency can be traced to three factors: (a) the impact of the involvement of the MNCs; (b) the arrangements for design and construction, and (c) the fact that Trinidad and Tobago had accumulated several years of experience with ammonia production prior to these new projects.

Technology and Fertilizer Production: A Synoptic Sketch

Trinidad and Tobago's experience with respect to the construction and operation of new fertilizer plants in the 1970's is probably best understood if we first grasp certain key features of technology and technological arrangements in the international fertilizer industry. It is useful firstly to separate the relevant technologies into two broad areas (a)

---

[98] Interview held with Amoco executive in July 1983 also Coordinating Task Force Report #6 (1974-1980)

those involved in the construction of fertilizer; and (b) those involved in the operation of plants post start-up.

The technologies involved in building these plants can in turn usefully be divided into five:

(i) Those process technologies related to various key stages in the manufacture of ammonia and urea.
(ii) Those related to basic engineering, such as the design of plants, incorporating the various chemical processes that have been developed, for specific locations, with specified inputs (e.g., the chemical composition of the natural gas that would actually be utilized, the kind and quality of water available, and so on).
(iii) Those related to detailed engineering the actual fabrication of items of machinery and equipment to specification. This includes here such items as pressure vessels, heat exchangers, boilers, compressors, piping, furnaces, etc.
(iv) Those technologies related to such software type activities as procurement, project management and activity scheduling, market studies, etc.
(v) Those related to erection, site preparation, plant start up and commissioning.

There are essentially six basic processes involved in the manufacture of ammonia:

1. Desulphurization, the removal of harmful sulphur components from the natural gas feedstock.
2. Catalytic steam reformation.
3. Catalytic shift conversion.
4. Carbon dioxide removal and regeneration.
5. Methanation
6. Synthesis and refrigeration.

Critical to the reformation process is catalysis and furnace design.[99] The catalysts used play an enormous role in not only determining the temperatures and pressures at which reformation takes place but also in determining the cost and efficiency of the whole process. For example, the need to utilize more elevated temperatures and pressures would impact on cost through the demand for energy and the kind of equipment design that would be called for.

Features of Technology Supplying the Fertilizer Industry

The first noteworthy feature of technology arrangements in the modern fertilizer industry that stands out is the way in which the critical process technologies are the province of a handful of large firms in the developed

---

[99] See UNCTC (1982, p. 42) and UNCTAD (1985, Ch. 2 and Appendix 1)

countries. It is reported that "the commercially proven processes in current use utilize almost exclusively the catalysts from three sources and sometimes from a fourth as well".[100] The four sources are Denmark, [West] Germany, the USA and the United Kingdom. Five firms are important here :- Haldor Topsoe (Denmark), ICI (United Kingdom), United Catalysts (USA), BASF and Girdler ([West] Germany).

The second feature that may be noted is that the set of technologies related to the basic engineering of fertilizer plants is similarly dominated by a handful of large multinational firms. These include:

Kellogg	USA
Fluor	USA
Braun	USA
Foster Wheeler	USA
Snamprogetti	Italy
Technimont	Italy
Stamicarbon	Netherlands
Unde	Germany
Heurtey	France
Creusot Loire	France
Toyo Engineering (associated with Mitsui Toatsu)	Japan
Mitsubishi Heavy Industries	Japan
Sumitomo	Japan

There are as well a few others that have concentrated on certain aspects of plant engineering. These include Haldor Topsoe (Denmark), Humphrey and Glasglow (UK) and Davey Power Gas (UK).

Thirdly, there is a close link between the firms that dominate the process technologies and those that dominate the basic engineering of fertilizer plants worldwide. The latter utilize the processes developed by the former, generally under special licensing agreements.

The fourth point to note is that the large multinational engineering firms that dominate the basic engineering end of the business, are very active in the areas of erection, procurement, and project management as well. However, in these areas they have rather more actual or potential competition since there are many other firms capable of undertaking those activities.

However, the virtual stranglehold that the major engineering firms have on the basic engineering end of the business and the advantages that they possess as a result of their (mutually) beneficial links with those firms who dominate the process technologies, tends to ensure that they get the

---

[100] UNCTAD (1985, p.21)

lion's share of business with respect to overall plant engineering and construction. Kellogg for example, has had its process incorporated into half of the world's ammonia expansions of the late 1960's and the 1970's. It is also interesting to observe that the same firms that dominate process technology and basic engineering in the Western World play roles that are just as key in building fertilizer capacity in the socialist world. It needs also to be observed that the process technologies and basic designs of fertilizer plant are kept closely guarded secrets. Patents play a part in the maintenance of secrecy, but only a part. Much of the know-how is not patented, and even non-patentable.

Fifth, we may note that the manufacture and supply of standard bits of equipment, e.g. blowers, pumps some compressors valves etc. can be produced by many firms in several countries. Some items may even be literally bought 'off-the-shelf'. Some developing countries have increased their share of the supply of equipment and services going into the construction of fertilizer plants by developing and drawing upon their capability in these areas. It is also true that some of the more advanced of the developing countries (such India and Brazil) have been increasing their domestic technological capabilities for the supply of certain items of specialized equipment. They have also been able to undertake the actual erection of entire plants, though still dependent on the transnationals for process technology and basic engineering.

Sixth, some of the technologies going into fertilizer plant construction, just like some items of (standard) equipment are fungible, that is, they can be utilized in other industries and other activities outside of the fertilizer business. Included here would be some of the detailed engineering (fabrication to specs of items of equipment), some aspects of construction, such as site preparation, installation of utilities such as water, power and waste disposal, and some of the 'software' type activities involved in procurement and overall project management.

The significance of this point lies in the strategy for technological development open to a small country which may be only building one or two of a particular type of plant, but at the same time, is building a great many plants overall. For such a country, there may be little hope of and little sense in, trying to develop a comprehensive technological capability in the design and construction of a particular type of plant, unless it proposes to export this capability. There may however be scope to build certain aspects of capability which can be described as 'lateral'. The skills involved can find 'full employment' but deployed over a variety of different industries and activities rather than just one.

The seventh and final point we may usefully note here in this synopsis of some of the key technological features of the fertilizer industry, relates to the skills involved in actually operating the plants. The skill demands of the large, sophisticated modern plants are not as great as one might think initially. This is not to say that unskilled labour runs these plants. Far from it. The point rather is that much of the sophisticated technology is, literally, *built into* the plant.

The modern plants for example are highly automated. The application of electronic technology permits not only much of the information required for operational decision-making to be generated automatically, but a significant number of operational decisions are actually taken and implemented automatically, without troubling the intellectual capacities of the human minders of the machines. It is therefore quite normal to walk around the large areas covered by a modern fertilizer plant and see no more than ten workers, with most of these engaged in monitoring operations in the highly sophisticated control room. It is perhaps not too much of an exaggeration to say that to a large extent these highly automated plants run themselves.

Human skill, knowledge and intervention are particularly called for in such operations when something untoward happens. Also, certain routines must be religiously pursued, most notably with respect to maintenance schedules and quality control. Apart from this, it is the areas of repairs, and modification and adaptation, which can be most demanding and technologically complex, and which in several areas can long remain dependent on foreign expertise. Routine operations in the modern plants however, can be observed to be largely following the book i.e. the conduct by well—drilled operators of precisely laid out procedures and practices in the various manuals. This is in marked contrast to the 'pan—boiler' operations that are at the heart of sugar manufacture, or the melt shop in a steel mill, or machine—shop operations to cite just a few examples. It is important to note that the acquisition of a capability to run these plants does not simultaneously confer the ability to build them. In fact one may go further and say that to a not insignificant degree, the technological sophistication built into these plants through customized electronics, to say nothing of the secrecy shrouding many of the key processes, makes even modification and adaptation in a developing country far more difficult than certain older industrial activities.

Implications of Technology Arrangements in Fertilizer

The first implication of the set of features outlined above is that a developing country seeking to build fertilizer capacity is confronted with a dilemma, which it is very tempting to resolve in just one way. The dilemma may be stated as follows: the quickest, most reliable, and possibly the cheapest way to build a new ammonia or urea plant is under a turnkey contract with one of the large internationally recognized engineering firms that dominate the fertilizer construction business.

The firm chosen would be one that either has designated access under licence to the relevant process technologies that are desired for the fertilizer plant under consideration, or possesses its own. If the process technologies are obtained under licence, it would be in most cases sourced from one of the multinational firms specializing in the process technology or some aspect thereof. A country that chooses this route however, is probably doomed to remain technologically dependent 'forever' as far as fertilizer manufacture is concerned.

It is also likely to find that unless it has and can maintain, a significant cost advantage with respect to feedstock (say natural gas), it will eventually be defeated by new competitors with lower costs of production if for no other reason than that the continual improvements in plant technology will both favour newer plants and be only available on a non-exclusive basis. There would be little scope to win out over time in the marketplace because of the possession of some 'unique' proprietary process technology.

On the other hand, an effort to develop a comprehensive domestic technological capability in the fertilizer business is likely to be more expensive than 'buying in'. Locally designed and produced plants are likely to cost far more initially, assuming this can be done at all. The risks of failure are far higher at the initial stages and there is also the sense of 're-inventing the wheel'. For a large country that is looking forward to several plants, it may however, be correctly seen as wise to accept the costs of learning and pursue a strategy which involves steadily increasing local content up to and including the acquisition or development of the process technologies, a design capability and an R&D capacity.[101]

The benefits would include not only the chance of a greater competitive ability over the long term, but perhaps more importantly, the development of a broad range of industrial capabilities which will have repercussive effects on the transformation of the entire economic system.

For a small country that may build just one or two or three fertilizer plants, the investment in 'learning' with respect to fertilizer plant construction may not be anywhere as promising. Design skills for example need to be applied to designing plants. Procurement skills are to some extent specific, or at least benefit from the intimate knowledge of a particular business and the actors in it. This type of knowledge also becomes obsolete in a few years unless continually updated. Unless therefore the country (or the specific local organization involved) has ambitions to enter the international arena in this area, the temptation to avoid the risks and costs of trying to develop a technological capability in

---

[101] See Sercovitch (1980) on the Brazilian petrochemical industry.

this area and to settle for turnkey plants or semi-turnkey plants, is difficult to resist.

The Trinidad and Tobago Case

In the case of Trinidad and Tobago's fertilizer plants, the route taken was that of turnkey plants designed and constructed by one or other of the large engineering firms with international reputations in the fertilizer business (Fluor and Kellogg in ammonia, Snamprogetti in urea) This was a sharp contrast to the approach taken in steel.

What were the reasons for this difference in approach, especially when it was not only the same government involved, but the same state agency (Coordinating Task Force/National Energy Corporation), and even the same leadership? As in steel, the paramount interest of the government's planners lay in the concept of an industry that would be highly intensive in the use of natural gas and one which would be a foreign exchange generator. Little priority was attached to the concept of utilizing any of these projects as a vehicle for building a broad-based technological capability based on the notion of the fungibility of certain skills and certain hardware. In fact, there is some doubt that there was any official recognition of the feasibility and/or desirability of such an industrial and technological strategy, or that such an option was debated at all. The main interest of the planners as far as technological development was concerned, lay in being able to operate the plants effectively and efficiently.

In the case of steel however, an important factor that led to a series of technology policy decisions being taken which led down quite a different path from fertilizers was simply the unravelling of the initial plans for a joint venture arrangement with the multinationals with whom discussions were held. Another factor that may be identified was the more closely held nature of the key technologies in fertiliser plant construction, and the way in which the logic of the technological arrangements almost dictated a turnkey approach. Far more so at any rate, than in the case of steel with the exception of direct reduction technology, a process plant operation, which as far as technological arrangements go, has many features similar to fertilizer plant construction.

Another factor that dictated the choice of technological arrangements, at least with respect to the ammonia plants, was the impact of the joint venture partners, Grace and Amoco. Both multinationals were very concerned with the speed, efficiency, and cost at which construction could take place. The business of building up local technological capabilities and investing in learning played no part in their approach to the projects.

Both partners had important influences on the way in which their respective ammonia projects proceeded. On the other hand, it must be noted that local professionals employed in one or other of the two fertilizer operations did say in interviews that the systems and procedures the multinationals put in place, both before and after construction did improve significantly the efficiency with which the plants were run after start-up, as well as impacting positively on the project planning and management stages. Thus, while the involvement of the MNC joint-venture partners and the approach they favoured led away from, rather than towards the kind of technological developments the projects might have been aimed at, yet at the same time it had an apparently positive effect on the efficiency with which both the project cycle and post-start-up operations were conducted.

Another factor that played a role in the greater efficiency with which the fertilizer plants were brought on stream and operated post start-up was the fact that Trinidad and Tobago had had nearly twenty years of experience with fertilizer production prior to the new plants of the 1970s and 1980s. Grace's Fedchem operations proved to be a seed bed from which experienced personnel here drawn to staff all levels of operation of the fertilizer plants, to say nothing of steel and methanol as well. For example, when Fertrin came on stream in 1981 three of the nine senior managers were Fedchem alumni (two, the managing director and the plant manager were expatriates on secondment from Amoco). Former Fedchem employees occupied critical positions such as Technical Manager, Maintenance Manager and Marketing Manager. Similarly, at least four of the eight plant superintendents had previously worked at Fedchem.

Locals, who held senior positions in the project planning team, stated in interviews that there were several occasions during the design stage when they were able to identify and argue for changes in Kellogg's design of the facilities based on their years of experience with operating ammonia units.

One final factor that played a role in the technological route taken for building the new ammonia and urea plants is the fact that the virtual non-existence of a local engineering industry meant that there was little chance of Trinidad and Tobago having a major input at even the level of the detailed engineering. Local contractors could play a role in some areas such as site preparation, tank construction, some of the utilities and some of the construction and structural work. The absence of a sophisticated local capability meant that the much greater participation in plant design and construction that one sees in developing countries such as India and Brazil was hardly possible in the case of Trinidad and Tobago.

All of these factors contributed to the use of the turnkey plant option. There was none of the 'experimentation' that we saw in the case of the steel plant. The results of the choices made are easy to summarize. While the ammonia plants did experience some degree of cost and the time overruns, these were hardly abnormal judged by the standards of large industrial projects internationally. Put more directly, the results may not have been what project planners would ideally like to see, but they were no worse than many similar projects.

Post start-up, neither of the ammonia plants had the type of difficulty steel had in physically exceeding design capacity In fact, Fertrin produced some 714,000 tons of ammonia in 1983, the first full year with both its plants in operation, as compared to the 689,000 tons that would theoretically be expected based on 330 operating days a year at full capacity production.[102]

It is equally clear however, that these projects did not have the kind of impact on the development of local technological capabilities they might have been geared to have. This would have meant going the route of a semi-turnkey operation, with a prior careful disaggregation of the technologies involved, directly and indirectly, at each stage of the project cycle, the identification of those areas that were (a) fungible across projects (b) fitted in with an overall strategy for the development of industrial capabilities and attempting to utilize the projects to develop such areas. We need be under no illusion, however, of the cost and risks attached such a strategy. Equally, we need be under no illusion about the long-term price the country would pay for not pursuing it.

---

[102] Interview with Plant Superintendent, February 21, 1984.

8
THE FERTILIZER STORY: PART 2

Introduction

Trinidad and Tobago's experience with fertilizer throws light however, not just on the problems of technology policy formulation in a small country but also illuminates several subtleties in successful project planning. An examination of the joint venture arrangements set up for the two ammonia plants, and the management and marketing arrangements for the urea plant provides useful insights into the whole business of joint ventures between the state in developing countries and foreign multinationals, and the distribution of benefits from these arrangements. The project financing arrangements offers additional insights into the techniques of project financing and the strategies of the multinationals.

There are useful implications to be drawn from a study of these areas for strategies centred around the presumed benefits of foreign direct investment and for strategies centred around the presumed utility of joint ventures. These fertilizer projects also provide valuable lessons in the perils and pitfalls of feasibility studies and contemporary project analysis techniques.

As outlined earlier, by contrast with Trinidad and Tobago's steel venture, the design and construction of the fertilizer projects was overall, rather smoothly accomplished as was plant commissioning, start-up and post start-up operations. This we have seen can be attributed to (a) large specialist engineering firms with proven reputations in the business of fertilizer plant construction were used to design and build the plants; (b) the systems and procedures of the MNC joint venture partners contributed significantly to effective project planning and project management, and (c) locals had had not inconsiderable experience with fertilizer plant operation.

However, an examination of the financial outturn shows that in the first few years at least, the expectations of financial success were not met. In addition, when the financial outturn is evaluated in the framework of the project financing arrangements set up, and what can be distilled of the strategies of the MNC joint-venture partners, it appears that the losses that materialized did not affect both partners in the respective ventures equally.

Financial Performance of Tringen: 1977-1983:

It is well known that very often new plants fail to show a profit for some time after they come on stream. This period is variable. It can last for a few months or for several years. Therefore, simply highlighting the financial losses of an industrial project in the first few years is methodologically inadequate for properly evaluating its financial success. Similarly, a plant may in some circumstances not be expected to make a profit, and consequently, none may be planned. For example, an operation may be set up as a tax avoidance device, or to satisfy some social need or political expediency. Therefore, the best way of evaluating success or failure is by comparing expectations to actual outcomes and analyzing the reasons for any variances between the two.

The Tringen plant came on stream in 1977 and Fertrin in 1981-82. Up to the end of 1983, neither of these operations had shown a profit (Latest data available at time of writing [1985]). However, Tringen had been projected to turn a profit after 1980 and Fertrin by 1983. The actual losses for the years for which losses were projected also turned to be larger than projected as Table 8.1 shows.

Table 8.1
Actual and Projected Profit/Loss for Fertrin and Tringen Plants 1979-1983 (TT$ million)

Year	Projected Profit/Loss	Actual Profit/Loss	Projected Profit/Loss	Actual Profit/Loss
	TRINGEN		FERTRIN	
1978	-	(22.7)		
1979	(7.6)	(16.5)		
1980	(1.4)	(3.8)		
1981	1.0	(3.5)	(72.5)*	(6.4)**
1982	2.4	(0.8)	(21.6)	(86.8)
1983	2.7	(3.9)	8.5	(32.2)
1984	4.9		33.5	

Source: National Energy Corporation, Ten Year Plan 1981-1990. Unpublished Company Accounts for Tringen, Fertrin (various years)
Notes: * - 12 months;   ** - 2 months

The available evidence suggests that a major reason for the poorer than expected financial performance lies in much weaker prices for ammonia than had been forecast when the projects were planned. According to the NEC's 10-year plan, the price assumptions used for forecasting the financial performance for Tringen and Fertrin were as follows: "Tringen starts at $235 per short ton in 1981 and escalates at 42% 1981-1985 and 2% thereafter to arrive at $310 per short ton in 1990. Fertrin starts at $399 per short ton in 1981 and escalates at 11% 1981-1985 and 7.3% thereafter to arrive at $829 per short ton in 1990".

The plan document does not indicate what currency the prices cited are denominated in. It is clear however that just by examining the projected percentage price increases and comparing with the course of actual prices (see Table 8.2), that actual price movements in no way accorded with the planners' optimistic expectations.

Table 8.2

Ammonia Prices Gulf Coast)
1981-1983 (US$/mt)

Period	Range
1981-1	155 -160
1981-2	155 -160
1981-3	175 -185
1981-4	175 -185
1982-1	150
1982-2	150 -160
1982-3	135 -160
1982-4	135 -160
1983-1	120 -130
1983-2	140 -145
Source: Chemical Marketing Reporter (Various Issues)	

In fact, the entire set of assumptions about the fertilizer business and its prognosis that were made in the 1970's have been proven by subsequent events to have been infirm.[103] The projected world food crisis has not

---

[103] See NEC (1981, p. 4-2). Major forecasts about the fertilizer market emanate on a regular basis from a joint World Bank/ FAO/UNIDO group of experts. See for example FAO (1981, p. 8). This forecast suggested that for ammonia, there would be worldwide "a marginal deficit appearing in 1982/83 with it becoming larger in subsequent years". In practice, however supply and demand will balance and any apparent deficit will be reflected in higher prices. Thus, the tables suggest that some additional capacity will be needed if an excessive price rise, by the mid 1980's is to be avoided. This forecast is quoted and echoed by the US

materialized in the way that many thought it would in the 1970s. While there is indeed starvation, most notably in Africa, the need for food has not been translated into a demand for fertilizer in the relevant food-producing countries. Where food needs have been strongest, effective demand has been weak due to economic distress and lack of foreign exchange to pay either for food or for inputs such as fertilizer that are needed to produce it.

In many food-short nations whose economic situation has not been quite as grim as the Sahel region in Africa, over the last decade there have been surprisingly successful efforts to reduce and even eliminate their deficits (notably India and China). India is now reportedly not just self-sufficient, but even beginning to produce a surplus. Furthermore, agricultural productivity has grown significantly in such countries as Argentina, and the result has been challenges to such traditional major food exporters as the USA and Canada in third country markets.

The continuing surges in productivity in major food producers such as the USA has led to a paradoxical sort of embarrassment of riches. Food surpluses plus greater competition internationally on the supply side has meant lower prices on average. This in turn has led to the taking of land out of production on the one hand, and depressed farm incomes on the other. Both factors operate to *reduce* demand for fertilizer in a major market area such as the USA.

The forecasts of the fertilizer market also tended to commit the classic error of failing to incorporate the likely response of various actors to the forecasts themselves. Thus, many gas-rich developing countries, seeing the same forecasts as the Trinidad and Tobago planners did, proceeded to respond in the same way to the projections, and build fertilizer plants anticipating a fertilizer shortage. The impact of their aggregated investment decisions was the falsification of the assumptions on which the decisions were made. The experience underlines once again that the smartest forecasts are the ones which incorporate the responses of other actors to the data they are all seeing.

Also, in the first half of the 1980-85 period, the international economic recession impacted directly on the fertilizer market through the effect of lower real incomes on the demand for food and the sharp reduction in price inflation in the USA. It is also likely that the weakness in the fertilizer market may well be long-term, and that the international market may come to be affected by protectionism if the fertilizer plants in

---

Department of Agriculture (1981, p. 19 and 21). The USDA forecast in 1981 that North America and Western Europe would become net importers of nitrogenous fertilizers. It is on the basis of forecasts such as these that countries Trinidad and Tobago hurried to build and expand fertilizer plants.

developing countries do seriously threaten to put their competitors in the metropolitan countries out of business based on their cheaper gas.

In the long term (post 1995), a confluence of technological developments in the areas of biotechnology and genetic engineering are also likely to impact both directly and indirectly on the demand for fertilizer. Directly, through the genetic engineering of bacteria to fix nitrogen for certain plants or to improve the nitrogen-fixing ability of bacteria which already have such a capability (e. g. Rhizobia in legumes). Indirectly, through the impact of increased agricultural productivity on the amount of land, and the quantity of fertilizer needed to produce a given quantum of food supplies.

Joint Ventures and the Distribution of Gains and Losses

The forecasts on which Trinidad and Tobago's investment decisions were made were produced by prestigious metropolitan organizations whose technical competence is widely conceded. The situation points up, therefore, the fundamental weakness of current forecasting methodologies -weakness that cuts across the question of who develops the forecast. It is obvious that in cases such as this, there are costs to the investors whose decision throws up results that are not as good as had been anticipated. However, the available evidence strongly suggests that in the instant case of joint venture investment decisions the two partners have not paid quite the same price for the gap between initial projections and subsequent reality. This is due to the arrangements made for setting up and running the projects and for financing them. The project financing also has interesting implications for strategies of development predicated on the notion that foreign direct investment means foreign equity investment.

When we look at the actual financing of the joint ventures, both 51:49, the first striking feature is the degree of leverage of both projects and what this implies about the actual capital injection of the MNC partners. The Tringen plant cost by one estimate TT$267.4 million. Actual equity injected by the two partners was only TT$60 million. Loans accounted for 77.6% of the project's cost, an extremely high degree of leverage.

A study of the loan financing shows that of the TT$198.9 million of loans that are specifically identified by source, loans from the shareholders amounted to $99.8 million. Medium term loans totaled TT$89.5 million, of which TT$41.5 million was provided by local banks and TT$48 million borrowed on the Eurodollar market. There was also an externally sourced long-term loan of TT$9.6 million. Total funds provided by the shareholders was TT$159.8 million or just about 60% of the project's cost. Grace's share was TT$78.2 million or 29% of the total project cost. The device of providing part of the shareholders' capital injection as a loan to the project rather than as equity investment is interesting.

The loans are 'subordinated' meaning that in satisfying creditors, there would be prior liens on the company's assets e.g. priority liens in favour of other commercial lenders such as the banks. What this device does do however, is to reduce the tax revenues that would be derivable from the operation, since interest expense is deductible for tax purposes. This has clear implications for the distribution of benefits between the partners since one of the partners is the state.

Table 8.3

The Financing of Tringen

	Locally Sourced	Externally Sourced	Total (TT$ Million)
Equity			
Government of T&T	30.7		30.7
W R Grace		29.3	29.3
Sub-total	30.7	29.3	60.0
Loans			
Shareholders (Subordinated)	50.9	48.9	99.8
Total Funds from Shareholders	81.6	78.2	159.8
Medium-term Loans			
Eurodollar		48.0	
Local Banks	41.5		
Sub-total Medium-term	41.5	48.0	89.5
Long-term Loans		9.6	9.6
Total Debt and Equity	123.1	135.8	258.9
Unspecified			8.5
Grand Total			267.4

Detailed accounts available for 1982 give an indication of the size of the advantage this mode of financing affords to the foreign joint venture partner. Interest payments charged to the account of the shareholders in 1982 totalled TT$9,982,685. Had the loan funds related to this been provided in the form of equity, it would have it would have converted the loss of TT$808,896 posted for that year into net profits of TT$9,174,788 on which the tax liability would have been TT$4,586,394 (ceteris paribus). If, to go further, the new income resulting had been distributed as dividends to the shareholders, the government's share or the resulting net profits after tax would have amounted to TT$2,339,571. This would bring the total distribution in favour of the state to TT$6,926,965 and to Grace, TT$2,247,823. By contrast, with the mode of financing set by Grace, interest payments to the government amounted to TT$5,088,311 and to Grace $4,895,374. Factoring in the loss posted of $808,896 as being shared by the partners, at some point, in proportion to their equity, the government loses an amount of TT$2,251,193 and Grace gains by the same amount, purely as a result of the mode of financing (see Table 8.4).

Table 8.4

Comparison of the Effects of the Mode of Financing Tringen Using Part Loan (TT$99.8 million) compared to Equivalent Equity Injection

(1) Actual Using Loan Financing	
Posted Profit/ Loss for 1982 of which:	(808,897)
GORTT Share	(412,537)
GRACE Share	(396,359)
Interest Charged to Shareholders Account of which:	9,983,685
GORTT Share	5,088,331
GRACE Share	4,895,374
Net Funds Attributable (Interest earned net of share of Loss)	
GORTT	4,675,774
GRACE	4,499,015
(2) Hypothetical: Assuming Equity Injection of TT$99.8 million	
Profit/Loss	9,174,788
Tax (@ 50%)	4,587,394
After Tax Profit Of which:	4,587,394
GORTT Share	2,339,570
GRACE Share	2,247,823
Total Funds to GORTT (Tax and Dividend)	6,926,967
Total Funds to GRACE	2,247,823
(3) Difference between (1) and (2)	
GORTT	(2,251,193)
GRACE	2,251,193
Source: Calculated from Trinidad Nitrogen Co. Ltd., Financial Statements for year ended December 31, 1982.	

It is also noteworthy that in this project, at least 45% of the financing was locally derived. When this is considered in conjunction with the fact that Grace with 49% of the equity of the project injected only 29% of the capital invested, as well as the high degree of leverage in the project financing it is clear that the widespread belief that foreign direct investment necessarily means that foreign capital is actually providing all or most of the financing, and bringing in capital and foreign exchange, is, at least some of the time, both exaggerated and misleading compared to what actually transpires.

It should also be noted that even though the Trinidad and Tobago government is nominally the majority shareholder, nevertheless, a management and technical services agreement, plus a marketing contract, gives Grace virtually complete *de facto* control over the Tringen operations. As pointed out earlier, Tringen is little more than an expansion of Grace's wholly owned Fedchem plant. There is thus considerable asymmetry between the foreign MNC's actual capital contribution, its formal minority shareholding, and its informal domination of the project. The joint venture arrangements are not just farcical with respect to Trinidad and Tobago's supposed majority shareholding implying control. They also provide another mechanism whereby the distribution of gains or losses from the operation are not what they may superficially appear to be. Grace receives a management fee, as well as a marketing fee. The output of the plant is 'technically' sold to a Grace subsidiary, Aruba Chemicals Industries, incorporated in the Netherlands Antilles, a tax haven.

A study of the prices at which product nominally moves out of Tringen suggests that the transfer prices set are designed to work to the advantage of Grace. The prices fob Trinidad are significantly lower than the netback prices one would expect using spot prices in the US Gulf and allowing for freight charges. For example, a detailed study of prices for 1982 showed that whereas spot prices in the US Gulf ranged around US$150-$160 per ton for most of the year (they declined towards the end of the year), the average price per Tringen's accounts was only $113 per ton. Allowing for freight costs of US$10-$12 per ton, one would have expected an fob Trinidad price rather higher than Grace claimed. The usual argument that is offered in this kind of situation is that long-term contracts generally involve lower prices than spot market prices.

It is rather more likely that the prices used are transfer prices which allow profits to be nominally accumulated in the tax haven of Aruba, protected both from Trinidad and Tobago taxes, and to some extent, from US taxation as well. The transfer pricing phenomenon is one factor impacting significantly on the distribution of benefits from the joint venture. Another factor is the actual fees received by Grace for management and marketing. The Tringen accounts for 1979-1983 reveal the following sums:

	TT$
1979	4,228,756
1980	n.a.
1981	7,377,168
1982	10,096,611
1983	8,855,008

The conclusion therefore is that the actual distribution of benefits and losses from this joint venture are not at all what they appear. They are skewed significantly in favour of Grace.

Fertrin

In the case of Fertrin, the joint venture between the government and Amoco, one finds several elements similarity with the Tringen case. The Fertrin project like Tringen was very highly leveraged. Of the capital cost of TT$840.7 million, only TT$166.9 million (19.9%) was equity financing while TT$673.8 million represented loans. In this project however, local financing (whether equity or loans) played a minor part. Most of the financing was external (82%). The high degree of external loan financing implies a heavy debt burden on the project in the first several years of its life. In a situation where price projections have not materialized as expected, the heavier than expected losses in the first couple of years owes a great deal to the classic problem of highly levered projects where either prices or output goals failed to be met.

Table 8.5

The Financing of Fertrin (TT$ million)

	Locally Sourced	Externally Sourced	Total
Equity			
GORTT	85.1		
Amoco		81.8	
Sub-total	85.1	81.8	166.9
Loans			
Pan Canadian Petroleum		68.9	
US Ex-Im Bank		117.3	
Commercial Banks		102.6	
Credit Line Commercial Banks		275.6	
Sub-total		564.4	564.4
Loans from Shareholders			
GORTT	69.9		
Amoco		67.1	
Sub-total	69.9	67.1	137.0
Total	155.0	713.3	868.3

Notes: The total figure is rather more ($28 million) than the figure given for the capital cost of the project. There is nothing in the accounts from which these figures are derived which explains this discrepancy. It could conceivably be injections of working capital post start-up, but this cannot be confirmed from the data available.

Source: Fertrin, Financial Statements, 1981, 1983

In the case of Fertrin, it can also be observed how significant supplier's credits and Ex-Im Bank type financing have become as countries and companies seek to boost their export sales. Again, as in the Tringen case, the joint venture MNC partner with 49% of the equity and day to day operational control of the project, turns out to have contributed a minority of the financing from its own funds (just 17%). Again, as in the case of Tringen, we observe that a significant proportion (45%) of the funds supplied by the shareholders took the form of subordinated loans. This as we have seen has an important impact on the distribution of the financial benefits from the project, where the state is the joint-venture partner.

With the larger than anticipated losses the shareholders found it necessary to increase their financial stake in the joint venture. This was also done by providing loans rather than 'fresh equity. (The loan agreement with the commercial lenders permits this to be done up to a stipulated ceiling). The amount owing to the shareholders had therefore reached TT$251,732,929 by 1983. Amoco's total financial commitment at the end of 1983 had risen to TT$201,552,373 in terms of its own capital injection. The government's stake had increased to TT $209.8 million.

However, in the case of this project, the benefits to Amoco include as in the case of Tringen, the fees it receives through its designated subsidiaries for providing management and marketing services. These were as follows from 1981-1983:

	Dividends	Management	Marketing
1981	-	5,319,831	571,656
1982	-	2,296,293	3,801,633
1983	-	2,528,461	6,409,136

Also, the gas that is the principal feedstock for the manufacture of ammonia ultimately derives from Amoco's offshore production. This gas serves not just Fertrin but several other industries as well. While the necessary information that would permit us to compute Amoco's true profit and loss from its operations taken as a whole, is not available, it is clear, as in the case of Tringen, that the actual distribution of benefits and losses from these projects, are not what they may superficially appear.

Summary, Conclusions and Some Lessons of Experience

The experience with fertilizer stands out in sharp contrast to that with steel, and the contrast highlights the role of irony and paradox in human affairs. We see finely drawn here what can be called the 'duality of phenomena', the way in which something can be both good and bad simultaneously, strong and weak simultaneously, and it can be difficult, if not impossible, to have one without the other.

In the case of ISCOTT, the strategy of going it alone, unbundling the technology package, involving locals intimately in project management activities, hiring individual expatriate skills, failed comprehensively. In the case of fertilizer, turnkey or semi -turnkey operations, under multinational control and with subsequent multinational domination of post start—up operations, succeeded in the sense of producing plants that operated effectively. Ironically, the more conservative, philosophically more 'backward' strategy was pursued in the industry where there was greater local experience. The more sophisticated, 'modern' strategy was attempted in the industry where locals had no prior experience at all.

Paradoxically, the ultimate learning from the failures with steel may perhaps turn out to be greater and have a broader impact on the development of the country's capabilities, than the operational successes of fertilizer. Much depends on whether the lessons are learnt and applied to subsequent projects.

In the fertilizer projects, certain 'external' factors operated to constrain local choices: (1) the technological features of the modern industry and its close control by a handful of metropolitan firms; and (2) the dominance of the MNC joint-venture partners, their methods and procedures, and their definition of their own interests. While these factors, together with prior local experience in the industry, played a key role in the successful construction and start-up of the plants, the very same factors helped prevent the realization of the potential that inhered in these projects for developing local technological capabilities. These same factors operated as well to skew distribution of material benefits, knowledge (learning) and power, in favour of the multinationals involved.

The experience with fertilizer also highlights the dilemmas confronting technology policy in small, developing countries. The unavoidable (though 'minimizable'), costs of learning are easier to bear where policymakers can foresee a succession of projects in which the acquired capabilities will be deployed. This materializes much more easily in a large country like China, India or Brazil, which envisages needing half-a-dozen or a dozen plants to satisfy domestic demand. Where half-a-dozen or a dozen plants means, as in many a small country, three or four or more different industries, the benefits from mastering the technologies involved in the project cycle for each type, may just not appear to outweigh the costs of learning.

The resolution of these paradoxes and this duality can only be achieved by highly sophisticated planning based on a broad conception of how a country's technological capability needs to be built. It is only such detailed, sophisticated planning that permits the identification of those technologies that are fungible across a set of seemingly, disparate activities, and hope to enjoy scale economies. It is only sophisticated domestic organization that would permit the matching of the MNC's methods and procedures, their information systems and their experience in project planning and project management. It clearly requires an intimate understanding of modern industry and its dynamic, for the planners of a small, developing country to grasp what areas they must learn, master and be able to do for themselves, and what they will have to concede to others, building in these latter areas, their capability in the art and science of choice. Even the much-discussed strategy of finding niches and building strength in them as part of an export-based strategy, involves articulating and implementing this kind of conception.

The fertilizer projects also, as in the case of steel, demonstrate both the methodological weaknesses that affect current techniques of forecasting, and the consequences of the resultant failures for small, developing countries which are often limited to having just a few eggs in their basket. We can see too the consequence of the often-blind faith in, and reliance on, metropolitan analyses and projections which blinker planners and policy makers in the ex-colonial countries of the Third World. The counterpart of this faith is of course a rejection of locally-produced analyses and warnings, and a failure to think things through for oneself.

Though not guaranteed to produce unerringly successful forecasts, and a consistently better performance than the metropolitan firms, a different perspective based on a different world view lead, not infrequently, to different projections. Japanese as compared to American projections in a variety of industries in the post-war world are a case in point. The failure to project protectionism and its consequences by metropolitan consulting firms, in situations where a different awareness of the historical record would predict it, is another case in point. Most importantly however, just an understanding of the weaknesses of current methodologies, plus an awareness of the sociology of metropolitan forecasting (e.g., the follow-the-leader or 'herd' phenomenon so often observed) would induce greater scepticism and a more critical approach among Third World policymakers.

Finally, the fertilizer projects provide insights with respect to current MNC behaviour and its implication for development strategy. We see quite clearly for example, that joint ventures as a mechanism for sharing control or sharing investment costs can easily be farcical. This is an 'old' phenomenon, which the Trinidad and Tobago fertilizer projects merely re-affirms.

Looking at how little of their own capital foreign multinationals may actually bring to a joint venture, and how the project financing may be so organized as to rely heavily on loans, it can be easily seen, in microcosm, how the link between foreign direct investment and the international debt crisis has been forged. It is in many quarters little realized, to how large an extent the heavy indebtedness of Third World countries to the multinational commercial banks, is linked to foreign direct investment. MNC strategies of financing their ventures in developing countries, with the maximum use of loans as opposed to equity capital, has played a role in precipitating the debt crisis of the 1980's, and has also meant the blurring in practice of the distinction between portfolio capital and foreign direct investment.

The notion of the two as alternatives is increasingly not justified in many cases. So too is the notion that bringing in the multinational means bringing in foreign equity capital and shifting the risks to the investor. Foreign direct investment, as can be clearly seen in the case of Trinidad and Tobago's fertilizer joint ventures, does not necessarily mean foreign equity capital on a significant scale. The advocates of foreign direct investment, who claim for it advantages on this score, often end up, wittingly or unwittingly, deluding themselves and others.

The experience with the joint venture partners in fertilizer also underscores another frequently discussed trend among the multinationals, that is, the strategy of segregating, pricing separately and selling a firm's assets, and especially its intangible, non-balance sheet assets such as its management capability, its marketing know-how, its 'name', etc. This leads to the appropriation of benefits from a venture through several different channels other than profits and dividends e.g., management, marketing and technical assistance fees, royalties, payments for know-how and the use of trademarks, brand names, or the use of the corporate name in raising finance, and so on. In the case of the fertilizer projects examined, it was quite clear how this approach could result in the skewing of benefits (or losses) from a venture in proportions far removed from the distribution of equity shareholding between the partners.

The Trinidad and Tobago planners and policy makers suffered from at least two weaknesses in their dealings with the foreign multinationals involved in the fertilizer projects. First, local strategy was focussed quite narrowly on just building and operating energy-intensive fertilizer plants that would earn foreign exchange. While occasional genuflections were made in the direction of other goals and considerations, these were largely ritual, and had little impact in the final analysis on what was done, and how.

Secondly, the Trinidad and Tobago government had just never built a team of professionals who were trained to understand and deal effectively with foreign multinational corporations. Local dealings with foreign companies have been and remain at the level of the amateur. Inevitably, there is a price to be paid for this.

Let us turn our attention however, to yet another experience with large, industrial projects. This involves an almost classic turnkey type of project, but with the plant, as in the case of steel, wholly state-owned and state-run. This is the case of methanol.

9
THE METHANOL EXPERIENCE

Introduction

In May 1984, Trinidad and Tobago's new methanol plant was brought on stream. This plant has a capacity of 1,200 metric tons of methanol per day (396,000 tons per year on the assumption of 330 onstream days a year). Construction costs were put at TT$430 million (US$179 million).[104] Construction began in March 1981 with mechanical completion scheduled for March 1984. In fact, though formal acceptance came in August 1984, mechanical completion was substantially achieved by January 1984, some three months earlier than projected. The actual project approval by the country's National Energy Corporation came in November 1980, and formal governmental approval in early 1981. At the time of these approvals, the project was expected to cost TT$359.7 million (exclusive of working capital). The final figure of TT$430 million thus represents an overrun of about 19%. Most of this overrun can be traced to certain items of cost omitted in the original budget.[105]

This project then was completed with comparatively minor cost overruns and well within its time budget. From the point of view of smoothness and efficiency in planning and execution, this project would rank as one of the most successful of the large industrial projects undertaken by

---

[104] Minister of Finance, Budget Speech 1980
[105] The NEC's November 1982 report on the state of the project explained 2% of the variance between the original budget and the then projected final cost as due to minor differences in the exchange rate used for calculations, 30% as due to a higher estimate of erection man-hours given by a German sub-contractor hired by Toyo, the main contractor, and 57% as due to costs omitted in the preparation of the original budget. There is no explanation of whether omission was inadvertent or otherwise. The rest of the variance is explained as increases in various contingencies.

Trinidad and Tobago in the 1970s and early 1980s. It was carried out under essentially classic turnkey/ semi-turnkey arrangements. The actual arrangements deserve to be looked at in some detail both because of the lessons that they may offer when compared to the country's other experiences with its projects and because of some of the modern features they incorporated.

While the actual project cycle was conducted with relative efficiency, we find that post start-up, this plant like the others, failed nevertheless to quite measure up to its planners' financial expectations. Like fertilizer, and unlike steel, the problems at start-up were less operational than financial. The forecasts upon which the plant was built and which provided the basis for the expectations of its viability turned out to be very much wide of the mark. This too needs to be examined in some detail. Our analysis of this project will therefore focus on two areas. First the technology arrangements and secondly, the role of the forecasts.

The Methanol Project Cycle and Technological Policy

Methanol is one of the well-known basic chemicals. Several chemical intermediates and final products are derived from it. It is manufactured by the steam reforming of methane-rich natural gas with carbon dioxide, under conditions of elevated temperatures and pressures. There are two basic processes in use. One (older) process is a high-pressure process. This is associated with such names as Haldor Topsoe, the large Danish firm which we earlier saw as playing a major role in certain areas of the fertilizer plant engineering business. It is also associated with names such as ICI (England), Lurgi (West Germany) and Mitsubishi (Japan). Of these three, the ICI process is probably the leading process today.

There are several similarities with the fertilizer case examined earlier. In methanol production, as in fertilizer manufacture, catalysis is critical to the economics of production, and consequently to the success of rival processes and the plants that incorporate them. The catalyst employed plays a key role not only in the conversion efficiency of the process, but in the costs associated with it, especially energy costs. The ability to carry out a process at a given efficiency level, but at lower temperatures and/or pressures than a rival process can mean considerable savings in energy costs and in material costs. One example of this is the difference in the kind and cost of materials needed for vessels that must withstand high temperatures and pressures as compared to the materials that would perform satisfactorily in vessels where the stress demands are not as great. Both capital costs and operating costs can therefore be affected by the catalysts employed and the particular processes in which they are incorporated. In the case of methanol, the high-pressure process may mean production costs some 10% higher than in the low-pressure process.

Again, as in the case of fertilizer plant engineering, we find a handful of large metropolitan firms dominating the basic process technology. These firms license the use of their process to specified large, engineering contractors (also metropolitan based). These large engineering firms in turn build many of the plants. Construction often takes place, under Design-Build, semi-turnkey, or full turnkey arrangements.

In methanol, as in fertilizer, much of the technology is really built into the plant. The modern plants are highly automated requiring relatively few workers to operate them. The actual operations, except for certain aspects of repair and maintenance are not highly demanding. Less day to day skill is required than in older chemical operations or in other types of production processes. As in the case of fertilizer however, it is important not to construe this as meaning that unskilled workers are enough to run this type of plant.

Traditionally, much of methanol production (over 50%) was absorbed in the manufacture of formaldehyde. Formaldehyde in conjunction with various other chemicals such as urea, phenol and melamine is the basis for the manufacture of a variety of products - various types of resins, coatings, moulding compounds and binders. These are employed in turn in the manufacture of wood and paper products laminates, plastics, and so on. Methanol has also been traditionally used in the production of Dimethyl Terephthalate (DMT), an input into polyester fibres, as well as acetic acid. Over the last few years however, new uses have been proposed for methanol including the production of Methyl Tertiary Butyl Ether (MTBE), an octane raising agent used in unleaded gasolines. It had also been proposed to use methanol as a blending component into gasoline, and to actually convert methanol into gasoline. Methanol was also identified as the most desirable feedstock for the manufacture of single cell protein, for which great hopes were entertained a decade or so ago. It was envisaged as animal feedstuff, or even as a direct nutritional supplement for humans.

The Attraction of Methanol

The attraction of methanol production to Trinidad and Tobago as to several other hydrocarbon rich developing countries lay first and foremost in the fact that natural gas-based methanol production had become in the 1970s the most efficient and economical source of methanol. This was in comparison to other routes using feedstocks such as naphtha, LPG, or the partial oxidation of heavy fuel oil. Increasingly, methanol production was natural-gas intensive, and as such was especially attractive for low-cost gas producers with large reserves of methane-rich natural gas.

Secondly, not only was methanol a natural choice in a resource-based industrialization strategy, where abundant supplies of low-cost natural gas was the resource, but in the mid to late 1970s, metropolitan forecasts suggested that by the mid-1980s, methanol prices would be both high and rising. A tight supply-demand balance was forecast. This forecast was in essence a derivative of other forecasts predicting high and rising oil prices. High and rising oil prices meant high and rising gasoline prices. This meant increased demand for methanol as a cost-reducing blending component with gasoline. Methanol can be used in a similar fashion to ethanol, which can be blended with gasoline to give 'gasohol'. This is a cheaper form of fuel than gasoline because of the lower cost of the ethanol component. The requirement for gasoline to be unleaded, due to environmental concerns also promised to open up a large market for MTBE as an octane booster.[106]

High and rising prices also promised to give countries with abundant reserves of cheap natural gas a major competitive advantage in methanol production just as in ammonia and urea production. The reasoning here was based on the link that developed in the 1970s between oil prices and natural gas prices in the OECD countries. Rising natural gas prices here were forecast partly because of the assumption of a general energy shortage in these countries a shortage which would include natural gas.

In addition, in the Trinidad and Tobago case, the fact that the major inputs into methanol production were natural gas and carbon dioxide made a methanol plant seem an even more attractive proposition. This followed from the fact that carbon dioxide was a by-product of ammonia production. So not only could the country make further use of its cheap and abundant natural gas reserves, but by siting the methanol plant next door to the Fertrin ammonia plant, use could be made of a by-product which would be wasted, if it were not employed in this, or some other industrial venture. For these reasons therefore, methanol production seemed, a priori, to make a great deal of sense.

The Planning of the Methanol Project

While the Trinidad and Tobago government had considered going into a methanol project as far back as 1970, official interest in methanol

---

[106] The reduction or elimination of tetra ethyl lead from gasoline has been deemed necessary in order to deal with harmful emissions into the air from vehicle exhausts. However, such a reduction reduces the anti-knock qualities of the gasoline. MTBE, an octane booster, helps to compensate for this.

production after 1973-74 was really stimulated by certain multinational companies. Several American and Japanese companies expressed interest in a methanol venture in Trinidad. These expressions of interest can be traced back to 1974 when the Japanese company, Mitsui, expressed an interest in both equity and offtake in a methanol plant. Between 1975 and 1977, four of the fourteen companies that dominate methanol manufacture also expressed some form of interest. These four were Tenneco, Georgia-Pacific, Hercufina and Borden.

In early 1978, therefore, Trinidad and Tobago's Coordinating Task Force (the forerunner of its National Energy Corporation) decided to engage with Borden in a pre-feasibility study. It was felt, as in the case of steel, that a joint venture with a foreign partner was desirable since the project would have to be export-oriented and there would be a need to secure markets. By mid-1978, however, Borden was found to be undertaking an alternative methanol project in the USA and was no longer interested in a project in Trinidad. However, given that other companies such as Tenneco were still expressing interest in buying products from a Trinidad and Tobago facility, the Coordinating Task Force continued to press ahead with project development work.

In 1979, though Tenneco reduced its proposals for product offtake from 80 million gallons per year to 30 million, URBK of West Germany and Air Products having dropped out, negotiations were pursued with two other companies. The contracted volumes were for a 10-year period and the prices involved represented substantial discounts off the spot prices ruling at any given point in the contract period. For one firm the discount was 13% off a specific spot price, for another 9% and for the third 8% off on a computed price that was generated by using a particular formula.

Following the receipt of updated forecasts of prices and economics from Chem-Systems Inc. in October 1980, the NEC's board approved the project as a 100% state-owned venture and formal governmental approval followed early in 1981. Three firms, First Boston Corporation, Morgan Grenfell (UK) and Schroders International (UK) were engaged to prepare a financing plan for the project. Toyo Engineering was hired to supply the plant and the engineering services and to undertake construction.

Project Management, Construction and Technology Acquisition

As in the case of the fertilizer plants, the emphasis in the arrangements made for the execution of the methanol project, was on bringing a plant onstream that would utilize the country's natural gas reserves and earn foreign exchange through exports. As far as technology policy went, there was little explicit technology policy planning that went into the project apart from the basic concerns of having a plant built that would operate efficiently, and which nationals would be able to run effectively. There was little concern that could be discerned with other issues such as unbundling the technology package or using the plant as part of an overall, long-term strategy of building technological capabilities in defined areas either through the downstream activities that could be based on it, or through the set of activities involved in the project cycle itself.

It might be averred that the planners did make explicit mention of the possibilities of urea formaldehyde production being developed downstream of methanol. While this is certainly true, there was little concrete action taken during the planning of the methanol plant to operationalize such a downstream facility. One can find no plans that related such a downstream facility, nor can one find any plans that related such a downstream activity to an overall technological strategy. Post start-up however, there has been expressions of renewed interest in going downstream into urea formaldehyde. What will materialize this time around remains to be seen.

In the circumstances therefore given what were the dominant concerns of the planners, Toyo Engineering was contracted to build the plant under what was a semi-turnkey arrangement.[107] Two separate contracts were let. One was a contract covering the supply of equipment, materials, and related services, including training and detailed engineering. The other covered construction, commissioning and start-up services.

The plant was based on ICI's low-pressure process. Toyo Engineering was one of the firms having arrangements with ICI to build plants incorporating this process technology. Under the contracts, Toyo provided the critical inputs of design engineering, procurement of equipment materials and spares, choice of subcontractors (subject however to owner's approval) delivery, installation and inspection of equipment, construction, commissioning and start-up, plus training and provision of know-how and a license to use the ICI process.

It is noteworthy that as in the case of fertilizer plant engineering, the provision of the necessary licensed technology was undertaken by Toyo and did not require a direct link between the local company and ICI. The contracts with Toyo also contained clauses binding the National Energy Corporation to secrecy with respect to the technology incorporated in the process, for a period of ten years from the date the project's planning formally got underway. Information on improvements in the ICI process technology, which took place before plant start-up, were to be passed on

---

[107] The qualifications to a traditional turnkey arrangement that might be made are that (1) the local project management team functioned alongside Toyo; its tasks included providing the necessary client approvals; (2)certain areas such as land and site preparation were excluded from the contracts.

to the Trinidad and Tobago facility and such improvements could be incorporated in it with the prior written consent of Toyo and ICI.

The contracts entered into attempted to avoid the pitfalls associated with the use of both fixed-price and cost-plus contracts. While fixed-price contracts offer the apparent advantage of putting a ceiling on the client's liability and avoiding cost overruns caused by a contractor's delinquency, they carry concomitant disadvantages. Three disadvantages may be noted:-

(a) Contractors to cover themselves against the risk of things going wrong are likely to inflate the (fixed) price at which they will carry out work.

(b) Contractors may seek to cut corners by using inferior materials or equipment either to increase their margin, or to preserve their margin if things are going wrong and their costs are rising above planned levels

(c) The failure of a contractor to fulfil the contract at the fixed price, i.e., go into bankruptcy as a result of the job, may leave only litigation open as a recourse. This, while morally satisfying, is not the same as achieving the client's real objective which is getting his plant built.

On the other hand, as is well known, cost-plus contracts provide little incentive for contractors to be careful about costs, in fact, there may be every incentive not to be careful. Consequently, many contracts in recent years attempt to avoid the worst features of both type of contracts by combining certain aspects of each. Some items for example are dealt with as owner's costs usually on a reimbursable basis. Certain other items are dealt with on a fixed-price basis. The arrangements with Toyo incorporated these features. Toyo provided the equipment, spare parts and certain services for a fixed lumpsum price of US$72.3 million under one contract and its construction services for a similar fixed price of US$4.6 million. Other items were provided under the heading of 'reimbursable costs'. The reimbursable costs amounted to some 76% of the fixed-lump sum price. A third category of costs were owner's direct costs which were incurred directly by the local company. This was put at TT$71.3 million in 1982 (US$ 29.7 million).

As is often seen in these arrangements in developing countries, Toyo specified that its fees were to be net of all taxes, duties or other local levies. What is unusual however, was the construction of the plant by Toyo under a suppliers' credit type of arrangement. Toyo received no more than 15% of its fees during the construction of the plant. The remaining 85% was to be paid over a period of eight and a half years starting six months after the plant was commissioned (i.e. September 1984). Payment was to take place in seventeen equal, semi-annual instalments. Interest was levied on the outstanding balance at 7.75% per annum, with the interest accruing during the construction period being rolled up and paid at the time of the first principal repayments.

This arrangement demonstrates one of the reasons why the Japanese have become so difficult to compete against in export markets. None of the other contracts in Trinidad and Tobago's Pt. Lisas projects contained these features. By extending supplier's credits to fees for services and furthermore, by providing such a lengthy repayment period (eight and a half years) and a fixed interest rate below the current market rates (7.75%), the Japanese provided a financing arrangement that traditional contractors from the USA or Western Europe would find difficult to match. The arrangement reduced the quantum of (higher cost) bank credit that would normally have been needed to finance payment of the contractor in the traditional type of arrangement, to say nothing of the various fees and charges generally associated with such commercial bank borrowing.

Toyo's innovative approach to financing was allied with highly efficient engineering and project management. As we have seen, the Trinidad plant was completed more or less on time. This is not very common in large industrial projects undertaken in developing countries. Simultaneously however, although Trinidad and Tobago set up a project management team which worked alongside Toyo (indeed out of the same field-site offices), not very many of the technologies that are involved in, or can be accessed through, the project cycle, were in fact acquired.

Nationals were however successfully trained to operate the new plant. (The plant employed 205-210 persons and was staffed up to the level of general manager). As in the case of Tringen and Fertrin plants, a lot is owed here to the country's prior history of operating process plants such as its oil refineries and Grace's Fedchem operations. Of nineteen top supervisory and managerial positions in the new plant, fully thirteen were occupied by Fedchem alumni and only two persons had not had prior experience in other plants prior to joining the methanol plant.

The successful operationalizing of the methanol plant seems to involve two of the factors pointed to in the fertilizer experience: (a) utilizing an efficient engineering contractor with an international reputation who was given broad responsibility for the completion and start-up of the project; and (b) the country's previous experience with the same or similar types of operations. The absence of the third factor pointed to in the fertilizer case -- the impact of the foreign MNC as joint venture partner-- suggests that this may not be a necessary condition for the successful operationalizing of such a large industrial project.

The Problems of Methanol: Forecasts and Failures

The problems that the new methanol plant confronted upon start-up were not the technical problems of running the operations that were immediately evident with steel. It was rather the impact of erroneous forecasting on the plant's financial viability. As indicated earlier, the investment in the new plant had been predicated upon the scenario for methanol outlined by Chem Systems Inc. as follows:

During the early 1980's a supply shortage is anticipated. Demand is forecast to grow faster than supply, and the projected shortage situation could become acute if there are significant delays in the construction of the announced new plants. Several new plants are, however, expected on stream in the 1983-85 period, which should eliminate the shortages By 1990, a number of projects above those currently announced are required in order to meet the forecast demand.[108]

The profitability of a Trinidad and Tobago methanol project hinged on the accuracy of this forecast. Behind it lay several assumptions about oil price rises, natural gas price rises, the growth in demand for methanol to produce MTBE as a supplement or substitute for gasoline, and a cost advantage in natural gas that would be employed by a methanol producer in Trinidad and Tobago over competitors in the OECD area.

The approach to financing was predicated as in the other projects on the desirability of maximising loan financing and minimizing equity. The project was therefore quite highly leveraged (60/40 debt equity initially), and the approach used in determining the degree of leverage was to calculate the maximum debt the project cash flows could bear.[109] This meant that the success of such a financing plan would depend to a significant degree on the successful realization of the cash flow forecast. These in turn would depend heavily upon the forecast prices being realized.

As it turns out, the Chem Systems forecasts have to date (1985) not materialized. Oil prices have fallen since 1982 rather than risen. The expected rise in natural gas prices in the USA has not materialized. Instead, despite deregulation, the prices have softened in the mid-1980's.

Methanol demand worldwide was projected by Chem Systems to reach 16,730,000 metric tons in 1985.[110] Estimated 1984 demand was put at 13,231,000 metric tons and 1985 at 13,842,000 in De Witt & Company's 1985 Methanol Annual.[111] Chem Systems price projections for Trinidad

---

[108] Chem Systems (1979, p.v)
[109] NEC (1983, p.35)
[110] Chem Systems (1979, p.11)
[111] DeWitt & Co (1985, p.11)

and Tobago's NEC envisaged Gulf Coast prices ranging from US$270-$300 per metric ton in 1985, US$270- $315 on the East Coast and US$270-$300 in North-West Europe.[112] Actual prices in 1985 for methanol averaged US$123 - $126 per metric ton in the first quarter and US$146 - $152 in the second quarter.[113] By the end of 1985, US prices were in the range US$123 -130 and by July 1986, the prices had collapsed to US$99 per metric ton in the USA and US$89 per metric ton in Europe. In 1984, Trinidad and Tobago's methanol plant recorded a loss of TT$26.2 million and in 1985, the loss was estimated to be TT$68.3 million. The Trinidad and Tobago planners originally set out to charge the methanol project a 1980 base price of US$1.50 per mmbtu for natural gas supplied to the plant, with this price escalating by 6% per annum. The price indicated is actually very close to the US$1.47 per mmbtu the 1979 Chem Systems study claimed such a Trinidad and Tobago plant could bear, and the 6% escalation factor was exactly equal to the increase the same study suggested could be borne by methanol destined for Western Europe and Japan.[114] The natural gas prices slated to be charged to the methanol plant were, with the exception of the urea plant, considerably higher than the other plants on the Pt. Lisas estate.

It is possible therefore that the prices set were strongly influenced by the figures in the Chem Systems study. If this were so, then the result would have been to jeopardize the economics of the methanol plant once the forecasts did not materialize. Natural gas prices were indeed critical to the economics of the new plant since the cost of gas was 50% of operating costs (Labour was 16.5% and maintenance, materials and supplies, 10.7%).

At a 1980 price of US$1.50 per mmbtu escalated at 6% per annum, by 1985 the gas price would be US$2 per mmbtu. In early 1985, US gas prices were around US$2.60 per mmbtu compared to the US $3.50 projected by Chem Systems. The gas price advantage it was expected the Trinidad and Tobago methanol project would enjoy would turn out to be much less than projected. The implication of this for overall cost advantage is seen when one takes into consideration the fact the plants in developing countries such as Trinidad and Tobago often suffer a penalty with respect to capital costs as compared with the same facility located in the developed countries.

It is therefore little wonder that by 1982, the project's planners had to resort to making representations to the government to reduce the proposed gas prices for the methanol project by 33%. However, while

---

[112] NEC (1983, Table 17). It should be noted that in its 1979 multi-client study Chem Systems forecast a rather lower 1985 price (US$260/mt US Gulf Coast) than it gave to the Trinidad and Tobago government. See Chem Systems (1979, p. 11). This price is however still double what eventually materialized.
[113] De Witt& Co (1985)
[114] Chem Systems (1979, II, pp. XV-XVI)

this would help nominally the economics of the methanol project, it does little more than shift the problem elsewhere in the system. The country, viewed as an entity, is still confronted by a reduction in the expected profitability of the venture.

It may be noted in closing that despite the hiring of sophisticated metropolitan financiers to prepare a financing plan complete with a custom-built computer model, and despite the contracting of a 'big-name' firm with specialist expertise such Chem Systems, the fate of the project has turned largely on one assumption about oil prices. Nowhere in the Chem Systems 1979 study is there any assessment whatsoever of the dynamics of the international oil market and the future of oil prices, or of the natural gas market and the future of gas prices. The assumption upon which an enormous complex of interrelated projections rests, and upon which, in just the Trinidad and Tobago case alone, a US$179 million plant was built, is taken as given. It is indeed an ironical comment on the 'scientific' methodologies deployed by the late 20th century economics, as well as on the near absolute faith developing countries often seen to have in the pronouncements and analyses of 'big-name' metropolitan firms.

10
TECHNOLOGY POLICY IN THE ENERGY PROJECTS: AN ASSESSMENT

The large industrial projects analysed in the preceding chapters represented the concrete manifestation of Trinidad and Tobago's industrialization strategy, in the heyday of the oil boom. These projects and their outcome can provide the world and particularly the Third World, with a wide variety of lessons. One important area that the Trinidad and Tobago experience illuminates is technology policy in small developing countries. It is to this that we now turn our attention.

First, Trinidad and Tobago's experience abundantly confirms the value of studying actual projects as the concrete expression of a country's real technology policy. Whatever a country's development plans may say, whatever its government articulates about its technology policy in manifestos or white papers or parliamentary declarations, it is in the actual projects formulated and implemented, and its approach to these, that its true technology policy can be found. The proof of the pudding is always in the eating.

It is the decisions made during the project cycle that are the ones which really impact on the development of a country's technological capability. It is those decisions that really determine in what areas such a capability is built, what technologies would be acquired from abroad, at what cost, and how effectively the country would assimilate and diffuse them within its borders. Decisions made during the project cycle also turn out to be of the greatest significance for how an operational facility impacts on the environment, on local factor usage and on local culture and social organisation.

Technology Policy Planning

In the Trinidad and Tobago case, we can identify certain features of the approach taken to the project cycle which had important implications for technology policy. First, while there was some awareness of technology policy issues and the significance of what happened at the project planning stage for the resolution of these issues, there was no comprehensive detailed approach to technology policy planning.

A study of the various plans and reports, as well as interviews with some of the planners, provides considerable evidence that the planners were aware of technology policy problems in such areas as the social and environmental impact of projects being undertaken. They were very sensitive as well to the importance of acquiring the technical skills needed to operate the facilities being built.

However, much less concrete interest was manifested in problems such as how the projects could play a role in building the country's overall technological capability. There was little attempt to carefully define and detail the areas in which such an overall capability needed to be built over the long term, and within this context to identify the specific technologies that the projects being undertaken would contribute. Nor is there much evidence of concern with, and detailed planning for, commercialization of technology problems -- how much should be paid, to whom, and for what technologies.

It is true that there was some interest displayed in identifying and acquiring some of the technologies involved in the project cycle itself, as opposed to the technologies needed to run the actual projects after start-up. For example, efforts were made to offer project management and on-site construction work to local firms in areas in which it was felt they had the capability. The stumbling block was the limited capabilities of local industry at the onset of the boom. In the case of steel, to cite one specific example, a local consulting engineering firm, Trintoplan, was allied with Hatch Associates for the purpose of undertaking various activities, including some project management type work. Similarly, in ammonia and methanol, local project management teams were deployed to work with the foreign project managers. These efforts however, fell short of being a detailed, comprehensive plan to identify and extract all the learning from these activities that was possible, or to systematically develop local capabilities to the fullest extent possible through supplier linkages and spread effects.

Part of the reason for this can be traced to the fact that the major concern of the planners quickly became just getting the projects off the ground successfully. Broader technology policy issues, even where the planners were aware of them, in practice ended up playing second fiddle to this dominant concern. In addition, the main focus with respect to all the projects (in terms of conception) was really to create a set of plants that would generate foreign exchange earnings to replace oil. Technology policy issues, despite occasional rhetoric that suggested differently, were quite secondary, even at the conceptual level.

Another part of the reason for the lack of comprehensive technology policy planning was simply that the handful of people who were entrusted with responsibilities for these projects were not enough in terms of numbers to do the kind of planning that was needed, even if they possessed the necessary consciousness of its importance.   Neither did the planning team encompass the range of skills and experience that would have been necessary.

Finally, the nature of several of the projects and the organisational arrangements made created a dynamic which tended to preclude such comprehensive technology policy planning. This point refers to the kind of technological arrangements current in the modern world for acquiring the capability to design and build methanol, urea and ammonia plants for example.

As we have seen, the process technologies in these areas are the domain of a handful of large, metropolitan firms who have special arrangements with particular engineering contractor firms to design and build plants incorporating their technology While not quite turnkey, the arrangements for building plants using one or other of the highly reputable engineering contractors with the requisite capability, offers little scope for 'unbundling' or using the project cycle to actually acquire capabilities in the various activities.

The plant comes as a package, incorporating the (largely secret) process technologies and with critical areas such as procurement, being choice of technology and the choice of engineers. To break into this arrangement, which has many features of a classic lock-in requires not just the interest in, and determination to do so. It would be necessary to have local suppliers of equipment and services who could be drawn upon, and the willingness to make the trade-off between the short run costs of learning, and the desire for efficiency, in favour of learning. It would also be necessary to overcome the resistance of the firms involved if they should seek to oppose such a strategy.

For all these reasons therefore, technology policy planning in the Trinidad and Tobago situation, was far weaker than it ideally should have been. Such planning as was done lacked comprehensiveness. There was insufficient attention to detail, and the overall conceptualization of the issues that needed to be addressed showed the country's inexperience with respect to planning industrial strategy for today's world. Above all, the technology policy planning that was done, lacked long-sightedness.

Small Size and Technology Policy

A classic example of how technology policy planning in a country such as Trinidad and Tobago has to be rooted in a sophisticated conception both of what is possible and what is desirable, arises in the size issue and its implications. It is by now well understood that the building of a country's technological capabilities is a process which involves learning and which, therefore, involves certain costs of learning. Technology policies which may have the greatest long- run impact on building capabilities will generally involve certain short-run costs. Mistakes will be made, initial inefficiencies will be manifested, higher costs of production and/or lower product quality would be experienced, as a country attempts to develop an indigenous capability in a new industry. These are all inevitable by-products of policies that stress learning and the genuine build-up of local capabilities. Such costs may be minimized but are unlikely to be eliminated altogether.

One area where this can be clearly seen is in the design, procurement and construction phases of large industrial projects involving modern technology. The technologies that these activities involve directly, and those to which they open the door (e.g., through procurement), can be extremely stimulative in the development of country's all-round technological capabilities. The long-run impact would be far greater than the impact of the project itself.

However, procurement based on extensive use of inexperienced, local suppliers of equipment and services (assuming they exist at all) would often run into problems of inferior quality initially, missed delivery dates, and so on. Attempting to use local engineering firms to do detailed engineering and, ultimately, basic engineering is often likely to mean higher costs. Higher costs arise either directly, through the inability to spread overhead costs over several jobs, (which the large, engineering firms can do), or indirectly through the costs of mistakes made because of inexperience. Often these costs can be avoided by going the route of turnkey projects or leaving the setting up of such industries to foreign companies.

In a large country, where the size of the domestic market may mean that several plants would be needed to satisfy demand, a strategy of progressive learning over a series of projects can pay rich dividends. Learning can be invested in, since its costs can be amortized over several ventures, and the technological capabilities built up can be directly applied in successive projects (e.g., design engineering skills).

A small country is often in a different situation. Only one or two plants may be planned in any given industry. The small size of the domestic market, and the imperatives of earning foreign exchange may mean that new industrial ventures have to be export-oriented from the start. They must, therefore, be internationally competitive from the outset, both in terms of cost and in terms of product quality. All of this means that the pressures for immediate efficiency are enormous.

The fact that only a couple of plants in a given industry can be realistically envisaged means that planners cannot look forward to amortizing the costs of learning over several ventures. Also, unless it is planned to export the skills acquired, they cannot depend on finding sufficient opportunities later on, for the exercise of capabilities painfully and expensively acquired in such areas as the design of specialised process plants, or the fabrication of special purpose equipment.

There are therefore, compelling reasons that push project planners in small, developing countries into going the route of turnkey, or semi-turnkey plants built by large engineering contractors specializing in the particular processes, and incorporating the latest technology. It often the best way to produce a product for export that would be competitive in terms of cost and quality. On the other hand, if a country keeps going down this route, it may well find itself remaining technologically dependent forever. The apple of the efficient turnkey plant is often laced with the strychnine of continued dependence.

The Trinidad and Tobago experience with steel, in contrast with its experience in ammonia, urea and methanol, provides a vivid example of this dilemma and the results of alternative choices. In the case of steel, the effort was made to 'unbundle' or 'disaggregate' the technology package. Efforts were made to have locals share in, and even control the project management function. A strategy was utilized of sourcing skills needed to run the new plant based on individual recruitment. The result was an expensive failure.

In the case of the Tringen and Fertrin ammonia plants, the urea plant and the methanol plant, semi-turnkey methods were used, with large, highly reputable engineering contractors being given the overall responsibility for design, project management, construction, and so on. These plants came onstream and operated successfully. While it is possible that if Trinidad and Tobago were to build four more steel mills, it would eventually derive far more benefit from pursuing the route chosen in this project, nevertheless, the trauma of that experience highlights the dilemma that a planner faces and the possible consequences of resolving it as it was resolved in the case of steel. The dilemma is especially acute when, as in a small country, the planners know that four or five steel mills are simply 'not on'.

At the same time as intimated earlier, if a country simply builds its industry on a 'turnkey' basis and eschews the costs of learning, it would forever be dependent, and is likely to incur certain on-going costs. These include: (1) having to pay more for certain services which are imported as compared to if these were developed at home; (2) losing the advantages of fungibility of skills and the resultant ripple effect on the development of country's overall technological capability;(3)losing the advantage of being able to more easily effect adaptations and major modifications of plants, in cases where locals played a greater role in such project cycle activities as basic design, detailed engineering and fabrication, procurement and plant erection; (4) as a result of (1); (3)possibly being rather more flat-footed' when it comes to being able to respond quickly and effectively to either the opening up or the loss of industrial opportunity.

For example, we can see the consequences of choosing the alternative approach by studying the experience of the very same country, Trinidad and Tobago, with its oil industry. Despite being one of the world's oldest oil producers, and being involved in petroleum refining for some seventy years, the dramatic changes that took place in the world refining industry over the last few years (late 1970s and early 1980s), left Trinidad and Tobago completely stranded. The multinationals who had built up and controlled the local refining industry, and who had oriented it towards residual fuel oil production, simply abandoned the local refineries, selling them to the government, as they made the necessary strategic shifts in their global operations. Such shifts were dictated for many refiners by the decline of the fuel oil market.

Not only did the local authorities not discover what was happening in the relevant markets until it was too late, but when they did realise it, they were unable to respond effectively. Fearing rising unemployment because of plant closures, they felt compelled to buy and keep operating two refineries oriented towards fuel oil production. Not only were they unable to respond effectively at a strategic level in terms of say, product diversification, but they were unable to follow the lead of refineries in many other countries and revamp their operations in significant ways based on indigenous capabilities.

The fact that the local industry had for decades been foreign controlled, and there were significant areas of weakness in local capabilities, contributed significantly to this situation, and to the general economic crisis it helped engender in Trinidad and Tobago after 1982.[115]

Technology Policy and the Strategy of Unbundling

Trinidad and Tobago's Pt. Lisas projects do not only point up the classic dilemma between policies that may be wise in the short-run but short-

---

[115] See Farrell (1979)

sighted in the long, they raise challenges as well to some of the now generally accepted strategies for technological learning. Three such issues may be identified.

The first is the strategy of learning or developing a capability over the course of building several plants.[116] This has been dealt with above, and we have seen that the strategy many not be easily applicable to small developing countries.

The second issue relates to the strategy unpackaging' or unbundling. This involves breaking up the technology package that a turnkey operation for example, represents, and identifying the specific technologies, equipment, etc. that need to be acquired. 'Unpackaging' also promises to reduce the costs of projects by eliminating some of the hidden rents that the supplier of the overall technology package may be incorporating into his quotations, including the costs associated with 'sweetheart' links with particular suppliers and contractors. The idea is to source the best and cheapest equipment and services from wherever possible However, the Trinidad and Tobago experience with steel threw up certain novel problems with the use of 'unpackaging' or 'unbundling' as a strategy. For example, it turned out that equipment and systems sourced from different suppliers may just not 'mesh' very well, giving rise to costly problems during operations. There may also be other subtle problems, such as increased maintenance and inventory holding costs for a country, that can result from the widespread use of unstandardized equipment.

The experience with steel in Trinidad and Tobago demonstrates this kind of problem not only with respect to plant and equipment, but even more dramatically with respect to people. The strategy of recruiting expatriates on an individual basis and putting them to work under local control threw up two kinds of problems, one of which is akin to the problem of 'unbundling' where plant equipment and process technologies are concerned.

Expatriates from different steelmaking backgrounds and cultures did not work well together. The Trinidad and Tobago steel experience pointed up starkly the importance of an organisational culture in which certain ways of responding and operating are developed over time with the result that the organisation functions as a well-rehearsed team.

The third issue relates to the other problem that individual recruitment throws up. Local managers proved unable to really utilize the skills that expatriates had. They were also unable to discriminate effectively in their recruitment of these expatriates, or to properly control and manage them. The experience points up the importance of top management itself having certain skills and capabilities. To put it another way, knowledge is required to properly harness, control, and utilize knowledge.

---

[116] Sercovitch (1980)

It may appear superficially attractive to eschew such vehicles for technology acquisition as wholly owned subsidiaries of foreign multinationals, or joint ventures with such firms, by arguing that the same skills can be purchased on an individualized basis, and then put together. The Trinidad and Tobago experience with steel as compared to its other projects demonstrates that it is not as simple as it may appear.

What the foreign company has is not just a set of people with skills and experience. It is an organisation, with an organisational culture, and people at the top who have the capability, the knowledge, and the experience to manage the human assets under their control. It makes little sense to just pluck individuals out of such systems and expect to utilize them effectively, unless you possess, or are able to set up, a similarly effective organisational system with the appropriate management and organisational culture.

Building Technological Capability: Which Way Forward?

Given all this, what would seem to make sense as suitable goal for building technological capability in a small developing country? The weakness of the local industrial base in Trinidad and Tobago precluded any effort at doing the detailed engineering of the large industrial projects domestically. The small size of the domestic market, and the (necessarily) export-oriented nature of the projects precluded a strategy of learning over several projects or absorbing the costs of learning at home in a large domestic market.

These same factors reduce the value of a strategy of unbundling", quite apart from the problems identified with this approach earlier. A strategy of buying skills on an individualized basis seems to require highly skilled and experienced local top management if the desire is to retain local control.

Does all of this mean that only a conservative (some would say, reactionary) approach of building turnkey plants with MNC partners is feasible for small, underdeveloped countries? Is their industrialization best left in the hands of wholly-owned subsidiaries of the multinational corporations? The answer is 'No'.

In the case of the methanol plant (100% state-owned), local management has so far proved capable of running the operations. MNC involvement is hardly a necessary condition. The problems associated with MNC involvement, either in the form of wholly-owned subsidiaries, or in joint ventures, in other local industries (including oil) makes it clear that what one gains on the swings by such a strategy, is likely to be lost on the roundabouts.

The lessons that are derivable relate as much to what does not work as to the *sufficient* conditions for successful localization. It is clearly important for instance, to have an unswerving commitment to choosing and recruiting good, experienced, top people who have the technical knowledge, the managerial skills and the dedication necessary to build and run new organisations. It is equally clear that where these people do not exist locally, they must be developed and trained. This requires many years of carefully planned, self-conscious effort on the part of the country's leaders. In the interim, there may be little choice but to rely on imported management and technical skills. The particular organisational form this takes may well vary. What is important however, is a good local understanding of what has to be achieved in terms of developing nationals, a well worked out strategy for achieving it, and one that is patiently and systematically implemented.

What is involved here is neither difficult nor mysterious. It means recognising that it takes about fifteen years to produce a top-flight senior manager from the end of academic training in disciplines such as engineering, economics, law and business. They need to be moved through a career path that deliberately exposes them to every facet of the business that they may one day run, beginning with production at shop-floor level, and moving through areas such marketing, finance and personnel management. They must be exposed to the world in which they will have to operate, gain familiarity with different cultures and environments, learn to value information and analysis and be steeped in certain values. Further, because of inevitable attrition, for every one that is required, a good rule of thumb is that in a small country, three must be trained.

The career path of these people must involve a progressive increase in the challenges with which they are confronted, and the responsibilities they are given. The set of areas which they must master should be well worked out in advance. Where there is such a clear, detailed planning of human resource development it is then possible to design organisational forms that would achieve this, e.g., how a specific joint venture with a foreign firm is to be structured and how it is to be run. It will also be equally clear whether the desired goals are being met.

While much of this sounds both obvious and 'old hat', it is clear that in the Trinidad and Tobago projects it has been consistently ignored. The top local management selected to run the iron and steel project, both at board and at executive level, can be readily demonstrated to be far from conforming to the profile presented here. In the fertilizer projects, there is nothing in the way of a centrally-articulated strategy for training local top management for these operations, or to be spun off to other operations from them. No system exists designed to learn what can be learnt from the joint-venture partners, from their local operatives and from accessing certain parts of their international operations.

We can also see the impact of failing to have an intimate understanding of industry and industrialization, and how technology policy has to be linked to this in order to build overall technological capability. For example, it is through a detailed analysis of the project cycle for projects in several industries that it is possible to identify those technologies that are fungible and can be developed across a wide variety of apparently different activities. These are the areas that are logical candidates for a small country entering into a number of diverse activities to concentrate on building. There is no reason for example why a small country like Trinidad and Tobago could not set itself the goal of becoming a world leader in catalysis. In so many of its apparently diverse industrial activities, catalysis is critical to oil refining, ammonia and methanol production, and so on. Similarly, setting up and running a system for generating information on foreign firms, is itself a skill.

It can be applied to many firms across many industries and even one day be a valuable export service to other Third World countries. While it may make little sense to master the capability for doing the basic engineering of direct reduction plants or rod mills, it is necessary to have a capacity for dealing effectively with those hired to do so, just as it is necessary to have people skilled in project financing or in doing strategic analyses of the future of various industries.

Most importantly however, is the need to put large 'one-off' projects in their proper perspective in terms of industrialization strategy, and to do this from the outset. This is where the business of having an intimate understanding of industry comes in once again. Projects such as steel milling, ammonia manufacture, petroleum refining, or basic petrochemical production are almost always large, capital-intensive projects which generate little employment and involve certain technologies in their construction (and even back of their operations) that are not easily captured by small, underdeveloped countries.

As foreign exchange earners, they often contain within them, the long-term 'trap' of product inflexibility and the vulnerabilities associated with an undifferentiated product. That is, ammonia manufactured to certain specifications is exactly like ammonia manufactured to the same specifications. Much more than the manufacturer of a high-fashion customized garment, an ammonia manufacturer is vulnerable to his more efficient, cheaper competitor. Furthermore, an ammonia plant produces ammonia, a fuel oil refinery, fuel oil. If the bottom abruptly drops out of the market for such a product, its manufacturers cannot respond flexibly in the short run. An LNG train is a classic example of such product inflexibility.

In a small, export-oriented developing country, large 'one-off' projects in basic industries need to be consciously used as a seed-bed on which to build downstream operations. This reduces the vulnerability of such industries to fluctuations in the export market, and to the long-run degradation of market demand for their production, by diverting more of it to the domestic market. In fact, what this strategy really does is convert the products of the basic industry into higher-valued, more highly differentiated products for the export market.

This has all the advantages of a multiple independently-targeted (MIRV) nuclear weapon over a single missile. Just as a MIRV weapon offers the capability of hitting several different targets simultaneously from one single launcher, so too going downstream of the basic industry permits the manufacture of a variety of different, often differentiated, higher valued products that may be targeted on different markets.

It is from such a perception of industrial strategy and industrialization that the role of the basic industry in building overall local technological capabilities is best defined. Steel production for example, can serve as the seed-bed for the development of metallurgical skills. These would be deployed in a variety of metal manufacturing projects. Similarly, ammonia or methanol can, like oil production, provide the basis for the production of a number of other commodities the manufacture of each of which may require capabilities that cut across all of them. For example, chemicals production or plastics and synthetic rubber processing, require a mastery of certain critical technologies which are common to the production of a family of apparently diverse commodities. Again, moulding technologies can be developed to produce a wide variety of plastic, rubber, and glass products. There are as well basic similarities in the processes and equipment deployed in the manufacture of a wide range of chemicals.

This approach to building technological capabilities is based on an intimate tie-in of the planning of basic industries with an overall industrialization strategy. It requires furthermore a carefully detailed analysis of what technologies are involved in the production of specific product families and an identification of the common 'core' or 'critical' technologies in the various production processes. It is a mastery of these common core technologies that permits the construction of a production platform which is essentially the kind of generalised technological capability a country needs to manufacture a wide range of apparently diverse commodities.

Product design is one example of such fungible core technology. Materials fabrication, which applies to the working of metal, wood, plastics, rubber, etc., provides further examples of fungible core technologies. The engineering industries are the loci of these capabilities. The setting up of certain basic industries such as iron and steel, ammonia, urea, methanol and oil refining has to be tied in to the setting up of certain other linked downstream industries in three ways. First, such industries are to secondary manufacturing what a foundation is to a skyscraper. Second, what basic industries are set up, how it is done, and when it is done have important ramifications for the linked industries. Third, some of the technologies involved in the production of the basic commodities and in the project cycle that sets up those industries are fungible and are a needed part of the complex of core technologies for any industrialised country.

It is important to recognise that the basic industries by themselves do not constitute a 'production platform'. Consequently, they do little by themselves to provide a basis for diversification. Diversification implies productive flexibility, the ability not just to manufacture a wide range of commodities, but to move into or out of various products in line with anticipated changes in market conditions. Failure to recognise this, to plan for it and to implement it, has been a cardinal error in Trinidad and Tobago's industrialization strategy to date.

An example of a country that has understood and utilized this kind of resource-based industrialization strategy is Sweden. Based upon its resources of forests and therefore wood products, good quality iron ore, and water, Sweden built up certain basic industries such as pulp and paper, steel and electricity generation. Upon these basic industries in turn, it built a host of secondary manufacturing industries including shipbuilding, vehicle production, the engineering industries, and so on. The capture of the critical technologies in these areas of secondary manufacturing permitted the production of an enormous range industrial commodities largely because of the sophisticated engineering capabilities the country had developed.[117]

In the Trinidad and Tobago case, there is little evidence to suggest that there was a firmly held conception of this kind of overall development strategy. The emphasis was upon the production of basic commodities for export. This inevitably constrained the whole approach to defining what role the industrialization program could and should play in building the country's technological capabilities. This in turn circumscribed and 'blinkered' what was sought from the projects in terms of technology.

The Acquisition of Technology

Given the constraints implicitly defined for the projects in terms of building technological capability, how can we evaluate the policies (implicit or explicit) for technology acquisition? What lessons, if any, does the experience here offer to other Third World States? Can we distil

---

[117] See Poon (1983)

any fresh insights into the related issue of the commercialization of technology?[118]

As far as acquisition of technology is concerned, there was no detailed plan that attempted to identify what technologies could be acquired through the projects and the project cycle, what technologies should be acquired, and how such acquisition might best be approached. The emphasis on the projects overall, was basically on acquiring the techniques required to operate the new plants. In the case of steel, Fertrin ammonia, and methanol, varying efforts were made to have nationals participate in and/or be exposed to particular activities in the project planning and project management phases of the project cycle.

The strategies adopted involved: (1) seeking to have nationals spend varying lengths of time in the design offices, or the headquarters, of the engineering firms doing design or project management; (2) in the case of steel, organising a joint venture arrangement between a foreign and a local consulting engineering firm; (3) setting up a locally-staffed project management unit alongside the foreign engineering firm charged with design/build responsibilities in the case of methanol; (4) setting up a Technical Advisory Group composed of both locals and the foreign joint venture partner in the case of Fertrin ammonia ; (5) most ambitiously, in the case of steel, setting up an elaborate organisational structure for project management, which sought to centralize coordination and control in local hands.

With respect to acquiring the skills required to operate the new plants, arrangements were made in each case for training of local operators and managers. In the case of methanol, the contract with Toyo Engineering, the design engineer and project manager, explicitly provided for training. In the case of the direct reduction facility in the iron and steel mill, there were well laid out contractual arrangements for training set out by Midrex. Similar arrangements can be found in the other projects.

In general, the arrangements made included provisions for training to be provided at 'the client's expense'. Training was undertaken both domestically and at facilities abroad In the case of steel, it was also envisaged that technology for operations would be acquired by hiring individual expatriates with steel production experience. The original idea also envisaged expatriates occupying the top management positions initially.

Several lessons emerge from a review of the overall experience with these strategies for acquiring technologies from abroad. First, the contrasting fortunes of the steel mill and the other projects, dramatically underline the significance of prior experience with the particular area of industry. In the case of Fertrin and Tringen fertilizers, the acquisition of

---

[118] See Vaitsos (1975) and Farrell (1979) for a definition of this term.

the skills necessary for operation was made much easier by the fact that the country had had many years of prior experience with fertilizer manufacture. In the case of methanol, and the direct reduction facility in the steel mill, where there was no previous direct experience with that type of process, the country's prior experience with similar process plants helped considerably in becoming familiar with the new plants.

The case of steel compared to the other projects also demonstrates the criticality of a well organised, well-timed and well-structured training program. In the actual steel mill operations, poor and ill-timed training programs, together with other problems such as poor choices with respect to expatriate hires and weak local top management, combined to create a disastrous situation post start-up. It is ironical that in the area of greatest unfamiliarity, the weakest arrangements for technology acquisition should have been made.

The Trinidad and Tobago experience suggests that as far as acquiring the technology to operate a plant goes, the ownership structure of a new project is arguably less important than prior experience with the same or similar production processes, and well-organised training programs. While the technologies required for operation were successfully acquired in the joint-venture ammonia projects, and there was simultaneously clear failure in the case of the 100% state-owned steel mill, both the experiences with methanol (100% state owned), and with the direct reduction facility in the steel mill, suggest that a foreign owner or partner is not a necessary condition for successful technology acquisition. This is reinforced by a detailed analysis of exactly what contributed to success and failure in the various cases. It is this analysis that throws up the value of prior national experience with the same or similar production processes and the significance of well-organised and well-timed training programs.

The analysis of the actual experience also suggests that properly arranged and well-timed training programs are themselves derivative of other factors, for example, a well-organised and efficiently coordinated project cycle. In this regard, an experienced and proven engineering contractor with clear overall responsibility and control seems to be important. The experience of steel with its diffusion of responsibilities, weak control and coordination, and ad hoc responses to the crises precipitated by unexpected events, emphasizes the importance of what, once stated, seems to be an obvious principle.

The successful acquisition of operations technology also seems to be affected by the *coherence* of the technological *systems* in a new plant. This refers to the effectiveness of the 'mesh' between various technologies associated with the different processes that together make up the overall production process. Here 'unbundling' and sourcing of different processes and equipment from different suppliers around the world seemed to have created some unexpected difficulties in the case of steel. It is possibly the case that the combination of local inexperience and such difficulties proved much more evocative of failure here, than either would have by itself.

Many suppliers of process technologies and the related equipment, design their processes on the assumption that the interface would be with certain other process technologies and equipment. The marrying of computer hardware and software is a classic example of this. Putting together disparate processes into a coherent system of production can therefore be quite demanding in terms of engineering know-how. Modification and adaptation may be required at considerable expense of time and money. The savings promised by 'unbundling' have to be set off against such costs, and these costs would obviously be higher, the lower the level of technical expertise available to the new plant.

It should be noted as well that while the presence or absence of a foreign partner or owner may not be the *sine qua non* of successful technology acquisition by underdeveloped countries as some writers seem to suggest, nevertheless, foreign companies may often prove to be of value here. Local respondents at Fertrin Ammonia were insistent in interviews, that the systems, procedures and organisational efficiency of Amoco played an important role in the successful acquisition of the technology to run the plant. This however, was just one of several factors. Amoco's presence was contributory, but not decisive, as the contrasting case of the 100% state owned methanol demonstrates. This issue has of course, great significance for the ongoing debate over the role of multinational corporations and foreign direct investment as channels for technology acquisition by underdeveloped countries.

Lesson on Current Issues of 'Commercialization of Technology'

The term 'commercialization of technology' refers to the terms and conditions under which technologies are acquired. The concept recognises the fact that technology is not a free good which is just transferred from its possessor to another. It is a commodity for which a market can be defined, and which carries a price tag. The market for technology has however, certain peculiarities, and as a commodity, technology itself also demonstrates some peculiarities.

For example, since technology (defined as the methods, processes and techniques used in the production of goods and services) is essentially knowledge, one predominant feature is its intangibility. While information may be codified and reposited in books, articles, blueprints, manuals, maps and so on, the understanding and interpretation of this information (knowledge) typically requires that there be a conceptual apparatus that can make use of the information. It is for this reason that the knowledge component of technology is characterized by the fact that its most important repository is human beings. The blueprints for a new aircraft that would be of great significance to a particular team of engineers, would mean nothing to most of their fellow human beings. This is essentially because the latter are not possessed of the conceptual apparatus that permits the conversion of the symbolic representations on the blueprints into information and knowledge.

In addition to knowledge there are three other elements that make up what we commonly refer to as 'a technology'. These are:(a) certain skill(s) or technique(s);(b) particular materials worked with; (c) particular machinery or equipment worked with. The dimension of skill and technique again intimately involves human beings and underscores the intangible dimension of technology. For example, the facility or dexterity of an experienced worker on the trim line in a vehicle assembly plant is a concrete manifestation of how skill is embodied in people.

However, the fact that any specific technology when actually deployed, usually involves certain materials and certain equipment, plus the fact that the information component of knowledge may be codified and represented symbolically (language, writing, drawing, numbers, etc.), gives technology a tangible dimension as well. Hence, technology has both an intangible and a tangible dimension. The intangible, however, is probably more important, in most cases. It is also this dimension that involves human beings most intimately, and that lends a uniqueness to technology as a commodity.

Unlike the normal commodity that is sold, the seller of a technology retains full possession of it (or at least the essential elements knowledge and skills), even after he has sold it. He can also sell the same technology to several different people. The fact that each possesses it does not preclude the other from simultaneously possessing it. This is quite unlike the usual commodity such as a television or a car, where once acquired by one buyer, the seller loses control over it, cannot sell it to anyone else, and the buyer can possess it exclusively.

In the Trinidad and Tobago projects, we can see all these features and peculiarities of the technology market at work and their effects. First, a study of the ten key contracts for the purchase of technology in the steel, methanol and Fertrin ammonia projects demonstrates the intangibility of what is being bought. The relevant clauses in most of the agreements simply specify that know-how will be sold at a particular price. There is nothing that indicates what exactly this know-how comprises or how would the buyer know when or whether he has adequately received it.

While a lot of the discussions on commercialization have focussed on the business of licensing agreements and the patents that lie behind these, in the Trinidad and Tobago projects, licences for patented know-how were not the major feature of the technologies being purchased. Where patents were involved (as in the process technologies and the catalysts in ammonia and methanol), the key agreements signed were really those entered into with the engineering contractors who designed and built the plants. These contractors undertook to procure the relevant licences to cover the patented know-how. However, the cost of such a licence was lumped in with the overall charges for the contractor's know-how. How much was for patented know-how, how much was for unpatented know-how, how much was for particular services (such as procurement), was nowhere specified.

Because of the virtual uniqueness of each know-how in a particular environment, one cannot precisely compare the prices charged for know-how supplied in the construction of a given plant with similar plants elsewhere. Furthermore, because of the phenomenon of one lumpsum charge for both know-how and services, comparisons of the cost of technology acquired from alternative suppliers is rendered even more difficult.

Most of the agreements for purchasing technology however, related to the provision of what was vaguely called 'know-how' and did not refer to patents at all. Part of the reason is that in several areas (e.g., certain processes in steel making), patents had expired. Another part of the reason may be that some firms are not bothering to rely on patents for the protection of their technological know-how. Feeling that the disclosure of information required for a patent can provide too many clues to competitors, they would rather bank on their ability to protect their know-how by keeping it secret. Most importantly, in the Trinidad and Tobago experience, however, a lot of the valuable know-how being purchased comes from skill, experience and practice in doing certain things, from having certain contacts, and from having developed particular systems and procedures for getting things done.

This kind of know-how is characterized by its diffuseness. It ranges over a breadth of areas from technical knowledge of production processes to skill in expediting supplies or handling industrial relations problems, to simply knowing whom to call and whom to hire. Because it is to so large an extent embodied in experienced personnel, it is characterized as well by its intangibility. Much of it is not codified in manuals or books. Some of it may be subsumed in rules or guidelines as to standard operating procedure. But a great deal of it is simply in people's heads.

It is therefore difficult to define it precisely, and even more difficult to assess exactly how much it is worth. In the end, from the point of view of the cost of the know-how being bought, probably the only meaningful yardstick for comparison and control is the competitive bids put in by rival suppliers for the particular job(s), that is, how much was Firm A prepared to accept for providing the package of know-how and services required to do the job, compared to Firm B.

It must be recognised however, that tendering procedures go only part of the way in the struggle to get the best deal, and that in any event, tenders are sometimes not involved in some decisions that subsequently prove most crucial for technology acquisition. One example is the hiring of consulting engineers. Tenders whether open or selective, are not guaranteed to expose the client to the universe of firms who can provide the desired know-how. Entering bids involve costs. Smaller, newer firms, or firms far away, may consider it just too expensive to bid on many jobs, assuming that they know about them at all. Yet those firms are sometimes better channels for technology acquisition by a developing country than the large, transnational engineering firms.[119]

Furthermore, the evaluation of bids often requires considerable experience and information. Especially when hiring consulting engineers or project managers who would then be available to help with other evaluations down the line, a developing country may not have the required experience, expertise and information. Poor choices for these services then have echo effects on subsequent evaluations of tenders for providing services and know-how. Thus the most important decisions may be made when the country is in the weakest position knowledge wise.

This is especially so when entering an unfamiliar industry. Trinidad and Tobago's experience with steel, and its hiring of a consulting engineer who subsequently proved to not have the levels of experience and expertise needed, is a good example of this problem.

However, choosing among suppliers of know-how is just one part of the problem. There is as well the problem of knowing when and whether the know-how being provided is what is needed. Here again, lack of experience, expertise and information on the client's part, a condition easily recognizable by any sophisticated consultant or supplier, can prove detrimental to success in obtaining the know-how sought, or it can permit the provision of a lower quality of services than is required and is being paid for. The contrasting experiences of steel and the construction of the ammonia plant in Trinidad and Tobago are good examples of this. In the case of the ammonia joint ventures, the experience and expertise of the foreign transnationals involved as partners played a role in ensuring that the services and know-how bought were in fact received. In steel, as we

---

[119] The description of Sercovitch of the Brazilian approach to acquiring the technology required for olefins production, and the choice of a firm that was not one of the-industry leaders is a case in point See Sercovitch (1980).

have seen, the local company was well and truly exploited by various foreign suppliers of services and know-how.

Several noteworthy features of the contemporary commercialization of technology problem, which emerge from a study of the Trinidad and Tobago experience, may now be briefly summarized:

(1) In many cases, what Third World countries are now having to deal with is not the purchase of precisely specifiable proprietary technology that is the subject of patent protection. There seems to be a clear trend towards corporations recognising that certain intangible non-balance sheet assets that they possess, such as their organisational and managerial skills, their methods, procedures and contacts, are just as valuable and just as saleable, as the tangible assets shown on their balance sheets, for example, physical property, plant and equipment. These intangible assets which include know-how can be packaged and sold. The 'know-how' being sold may itself consist of two components patentable, proprietary technical knowledge, and non-patentable, much more generalized, knowledge of organisational methods, management procedures, and so on.

(2) We also see, as in the case of the large engineering contractors, the setting up of a package consisting of somebody else's proprietary technology and their own generalized know-how and engineering skills. In the case of both ammonia and methanol we saw in this study examples of this where the engineering contractor was the one who procured and passed on a licence for the use of proprietary, patented know-how that was the property of other firms specialising in the particular process technology.

(3) These packages of know-how comprising proprietary and non-proprietary components, can be and are sold over and over to many different buyers. They are partially expressed in certain services provided (e.g., engineering services management services, marketing services, training, project management services, etc.) Some of these service for example certain engineering services are customized i.e., they are tailored to a particular operating environment.

(4) These features have at least two implications for the pricing of technology and know-how packages:-

(a) Companies can exercise the option of pricing various components of services and the related know-how either separately, or lumped together in various fashions, as is most conducive to profit maximization;

(b) Those services that are customized, plus those areas of know-how that are rather broad and vague make it especially difficult to determine whether the price demanded is fair or unfair in terms of what is being bought. Both features can be seen in the Trinidad and Tobago projects, and particularly in the case of steel;

(5) The use of tendering procedures may seem, at first glance, to be one method that permits effective price comparisons and as such, some shopping around for the best deal. While this is true to some extent, the use of tenders is not fool proof, nor does the process guarantee that the best deal is being obtained.

(6) Finally, the vagueness of the know-how packages being bought exacerbates a serious problem that Trinidad and Tobago experienced with steel exemplified by the lack of what may be called 'consumer protection'. Not only was what was being paid for vaguely specified (e.g., in the case of Korf) but there was little or nothing set up that would provide a litmus test of whether the client had obtained what he was supposed to get, how he would know when he had gotten it, or whether the quality of the services provided was what was desired. Neither was there an effective system for providing redress if the seller of the know-how failed to deliver adequately.

Technology and Information Systems

One of the features of the Trinidad and Tobago experience that stands out, was the weakness of local information systems. In the light of our discussion of the 'commercialisation' and 'acquisition' issues, the value and importance of proper, well-organised information systems is clear, especially where the country was entering new unfamiliar industries. Experience and expertise are important in knowing what technologies to buy and how much they are worth. But these things, if not already possessed, take time to build. Without them there are certain inevitable costs of learning.

These however, can be reduced by a willingness to invest in information and its co-requisites, study and analysis. In the case of Trinidad and Tobago, the country was not only entering new industries such as steel and methanol, it was also undertaking a large number of projects simultaneously. It was dealing in consequence, with a large number of different foreign firms.

Despite this, there was no system for generating detailed and comprehensive information on all these various firms. No mechanism existed for throwing up information on their track records, what they had done elsewhere, with what results, what else they were currently engaged in, and so on. Such information as was obtained was often ad hoc, limited and, in a couple crucial cases, received late. This is a problem that is shared by many Third World states. It is also exacerbated by the penchant for keeping details of contracts secret, and from the lack of systematic mechanisms for the exchange of information between states.

Foreign companies that have operated in one or more states with negative results, generally need not fear that other potential clients elsewhere in the Third World would automatically be informed about their performance on previous jobs. Direct information exchange among Third World states about such matters can only be described as haphazard.

Ironically, such information, plus information about contract provisions is often available in the metropolitan countries to certain privileged groups. It is not unusual for a handful of consulting engineering firms, or financial institutions, domiciled in a few metropolitan countries, to be involved with a wide variety of deals being made in a large number of Third World countries.

Third World governments who believe or are persuaded by the foreign firms with which they negotiate, that details of contracts should be kept secret, are often unwittingly helping to keep themselves in a position of systemic disadvantage vis a vis such firms. The same firms who argue for this are often themselves dealing with several countries, and through this, plus various other channels, have good information about each specific government, its political and economic situation, and all its deals. They can therefore play one country off against another, tailor the details of each agreement according to their assessment of the knowledge, acumen, financial circumstances and probity of the governments they are dealing with, and indulge in what is effectively price discrimination.

While therefore, competition among foreign firms to supply technology helps the buyer, and the fiercer the competition internationally, the better for him, it should not be thought that the existence of competition (as formalized through the tendering process) guarantees the best deal, or even a good deal. In some cases (e.g., fertilizer plant construction) one is dealing with international oligopolies. Furthermore, experience, expertise and information are critical to getting a good deal both in terms of choosing among competing suppliers, so that those contracted really have the capability of doing what they say they can, and what is really needed, and after the contract has been awarded, ensuring that the buyer gets what he is paying for.

11
INDUSTRIALISATION STRATEGY, PROJECT ANALYSIS AND THE MNC: FURTHER LESSONS OF EXPERIENCE

Forecasting, Project Analysis and the Impact of Changing Technologies

The Trinidad and Tobago experience also offers some illuminating insights into an issue which cuts across several different areas, viz. the techniques generally used for project analysis, the impact of modern metropolitan technologies and overall transformation strategy. This is the issue of forecasting failure and its impact.

As we have seen, in none of the projects examined have the forecasts of prices and market conditions made at the time of the investment decision, been realized. The result has been extremely serious. By 1983, Trinidad and Tobago's economic boom was not only over, but had turned into a slump. Real GDP fell by 3.8% in 1983, a further 10.8% in 1984 and a further 6.3% in 1985. Unemployment moved into double-digit figures in 1983 and the numbers unemployed leapt by some 20% in 1984 over 1983 levels to reach just under 13% of the labour force. Foreign exchange reserves which had reached TT$7.2 billion at the end of 1982, plummeted to TT$2.9 billion at the end of 1984 and TT$2.1 billion by the second quarter of 1985. In 1982, the government's fiscal surplus turned into deficit and remained so through 1984. The public debt which had been under TT$2 billion in 1981 ($1.7 billion or 9.6% of GDP) began to rise. It topped TT$2 billion in 1982, and by the end of 1984 it had reached TT$3.1 billion. The debt thus rose by 48% in 2 years and by the end of 1984 it amounted to 17% of GDP. By June 1984, it had climbed further to $3.6 billion.[120] In December 1985, it was thought necessary to devalue the Trinidad and Tobago dollar by 50% measured in local currency units, from TT$2.40 to the US$ to TT$3 60.

The economic slump was precipitated mainly by falling oil prices, assisted by falling oil production and a crisis in the refining sector of the industry. This was precisely the kind of situation in which the Pt. Lisas energy-based projects were supposed to have marched to the rescue. They failed to do so. In fact, as seen most dramatically in the case of steel, the projects were up to 1985/86 a drain on the national treasury rather than a net contributor.

What went wrong? While one might expect to find that if a country or a company undertook five or six large projects, one or two might fail, it is significant that of the five Trinidad and Tobago projects not one can presently be considered a financial success. In the case of steel, the largest and costliest of them all, we have seen what can only be described as spectacular failure.

While one might point to several factors, two may be seen as critical. The first relates to the overall conception of the industrialization path i.e., the strategy chosen. The second relates to certain problems associated with project analysis techniques and their use in investment decisions.

Failures of Conception

The notion that a country should produce those commodities in which it has an advantage based on some abundant resource seems at first blush eminently sensible. In the case of Trinidad and Tobago, an energy-rich, technology-deficient country with expensive labour and weak domestic organization, the argument for energy-intensive industry would even seem conclusive. The country would seem to possess no natural advantages in the production of low labour cost skill-intensive products, or in the production of technology-intensive commodities, or in the production of services. Not even in low-technology commodities dependent upon cheap, unskilled labour would Trinidad and Tobago enjoy any natural advantage (given its high wage rates).

This intuitively appealing conception is, however, seriously misleading. There are two reasons why this is so. First, it leads to a 'supply-side' approach to the identification of what commodities to produce. Second, static comparative advantage is easily subverted by the passage of time and changing circumstances, and the requirements for true, *dynamic* comparative advantage may not at all be the same as those for static comparative advantage. This is briefly examined.

---

[120] Central Bank Annual Reports 1984 and 1985 and Quarterly Bulletin, June 1985; See also Ministry of Finance, Review of the Economy, 1984, Table 48.

Product identification using a resource-based strategy is straightforward. It simply involves generating a list of commodities, the production of which requires relatively large quantities of the abundant resource, and then making investment decisions on projects drawn from such a list. This is literally what was done in the Trinidad and Tobago case. However, simply because something can be produced does not mean that there is a demand for it, or that existing levels of demand will be maintained into the future.

Here is where simple static comparative advantage misleads. It fails to lead organically to a consideration of demand. The essence of the approach a la Ricardo and Heckscher-Ohlin is to identify whether a country can *at a given point in time* produce a particular commodity *cheaper* than its competitors. The demand for that commodity is implicitly assumed. In the real world, it is often a different story. Demand may be non-existent or declining over time. For example, better, cheaper substitutes based on different raw materials may be capturing market share from the particular commodity. Oil-based plastics displace steel and aluminum. Optical fibres displace copper. High Fructose Corn Syrup displaces sugar in the commercial sweetener market. In other cases, demand may decline over time, either relative to other commodities or even absolutely, as incomes rise. Certain agricultural commodities are cases in point.

Comparative advantage may thus be meaningless if demand for the commodity is non-existent or evaporates over time, as any manufacturer who stuck to making buggies, marble baths, spears or cross-bows would have long discovered. Even where comparative advantage is not subverted over time by changes in demand, it can be subverted by the supply side. Changes in production technology and comparative production economics are relevant here. These changes may lead to the loss of comparative advantage to cheaper, more efficient, suppliers. Such competitors may or may not also possess abundant reserves of the natural resource in question. In some cases, their burgeoning advantage may lie in their discovery of new, larger, lower cost reserves. This happened in the case of Sweden for example, where Swedish advantages in iron and timber were eroded in the 1960's by the developments of new iron mines in Brazil, and new forest resources in the USA and other countries.[121]

In other cases, since almost all production processes require more than one raw material input and require as well other factors of production such as technology and labour, the advantage one producer possesses in a particular resource input, may be vitiated by gains his competitors make in other resource inputs, or in technology, or in labour costs. A particular resource or raw material may at a particular point in time be critical to a

---

[121] Boston Consulting Group (1978)

production process, accounting for example for a large proportion of production costs. However, the advantage of being able to supply it more cheaply than others, may be eroded if competitors are able to sufficiently lower their costs of acquiring other, less important inputs, or introduce new production technology.

New technology may lead to a reduction in the demand for all raw material inputs, for the key input, or for some subset of inputs. A classic example here is the impact of conservation technologies on energy-intensive production processes in the 1970s and 1980s. By the introduction of conservation and new energy-efficient production processes, manufacturers in many industries were able to erode the advantage that access to cheap energy gave to competitors, in what had been energy-intensive processes in the early 1970s. Economists and policy makers often behave as if factor intensities and the advantages or disadvantages that flow from them are immutable. They are not.

For these reasons industrialization strategies based on static theories of comparative advantage can easily flounder. It is also for these reasons that product cycle theory, suitably adapted, is a much more fruitful approach to the planning of industrial development, especially where this is export-led. It may, however, be argued that these considerations do not really explain why wrong production choices are made and the investment projects fail. After all, changes in demand, and changes in raw materials supply or production technology, are all likely to be reflected in price changes. Feasibility studies are done precisely to tell planners and decision-makers what to expect with respect to demand and markets, and consequently, what to expect with respect to relative prices and project profitability. It is here however that we find that contemporary project analysis techniques are arguably, fatally flawed.

The Weaknesses of Project Analysis Techniques

In Chapter Two of this study, we saw that when once feasibility studies or project analysis were put into the context of the overall project cycle, it was immediately apparent that there were three very serious problems which bedevilled contemporary methodology.

The first was that investment decisions were usually taken at a point in the project cycle when the estimates of capital costs were likely to be rather weak. Really good estimates of the cost of a project were often not available until the basic design engineering was done, firm quotations were received from suppliers based on precise specifications, etc. However, to reach this stage, a 'Go' decision had often already been taken. Such a decision would be based on preliminary study estimates, the use of rules of thumb for costing equipment and supplies, etc. These estimates as we saw, generally turned out rather wide of the mark, so that for this reason alone, mistakes would arise in making investment decisions.

Our concern here however, is less with this first problem than the other two. The second problem relates to the implication of the often-long gestation period that elapses between project conception, preliminary analysis, investment decision, and plant start-up, and then between plant start-up and full capacity production. With large industrial projects this entire cycle could take anywhere from 3-10 years.

The significance of this is that when the feasibility studies are done, on the basis of which the investment decision is made, start-up and full capacity production may be several years away. Prices have to be forecast several years ahead (to the point of plant start-up) and then several years beyond that (theoretically over the normal working life of the plant). All told, it is not unusual for feasibility studies to be purporting to forecast both output and input prices fifteen years into the future.

This brings us to the third problem. Over such a long period the kind of changes in demand, raw materials supply and production technology we have been discussing above are very likely to impact on the structure of relative prices. Yet current forecasting methods are quite unable to generate the set of relative prices that these changes will produce. In fact,often the attempt is not even made.Instead, the customary device is to extrapolate future prices based on past price trends, or to attempt to forecast supply/demand balances for the commodity and the consequent direction of prices. However, even in the latter case, demand forecasts for the commodity are usually quite primitive, and the supply side work little better.In none of the industry forecasts this author has examined, has there been any reasonably acceptable method of incorporating the impact of technological change on either the demand or the supply side.

It is therefore ironical that economists would have spent so much time devising measures for shadow exchange rates, shadow wage rates, numeraires, and other exotica, in an attempt to do proper social cost-benefit analysis, while the most important numbers, the set of future prices, receive little, if any, serious attention.

The impact of this is quite clear and may be bluntly stated. Current project analysis methodologies are an unreliable guide to investment decisions. Therefore, they cannot be depended upon to pick up and signal the kind of demand changes, technology changes and general supply conditions, that we have seen subvert investment decisions based on static comparative advantage.

The Special Problem of Small Countries

These weaknesses in methodology are not specific to project analysis undertaken in developing countries. The same happens in the metropolitan countries. Many projects there fail as well, because the assumptions and forecasts upon which they have been based turn out to be inaccurate.[122] The problem is with the methodologies employed, not where they are employed. It may be noted, en passant, that the hiring of large metropolitan consulting firms, with big names, therefore, does not help. As long as the traditional methodologies are used and depended upon, the same mistakes are liable to be made. However, the situation in the metropolitan countries is attenuated by five factors:

1) If a large number of projects are undertaken, a certain number are likely to succeed. This argument for example is advanced by Peters and Waterman as an important explanation of the success of their so-called excellent companies. They simply try more things.[123] The business of large numbers of projects operates in another subtle way as well. In a large economy, or a large company, three or four projects failing, five or six bad investment decisions, do not have the same effect as in a small company or a small company. The failure of Concorde did not bankrupt Britain or France. Exxon's failure in the office systems markets did not bankrupt Exxon. In a small economy or a small company, one or two mistakes can be devastating. The closure of a single refinery can lead to the collapse of an island economy. The bankruptcy of a steel mill can be a national crisis in another. Failure in any single project can be much more expensive to a small organisation than to a large, simply because a larger proportion of its eggs are inevitably in that one basket.

2) In a large economy, there is another f actor that operates to its advantage, particularly in a large, advanced economy. The substitutes that eat away market share, the firms that introduce new production technologies that undercut the old, the new commodities characterized by income-elastic demand that capture a larger proportion of growing incomes, may all be located within the borders of that single, large dynamic economy. Therefore, the losses imposed on one industry as a result of its mistaken investment decisions may sometimes (though not always) be compensated for by gains in other industries, which deliver the blow that destroys or debilitates the former.

3) Also, in the metropolitan economies, investment decisions are to put it bluntly, often more sophisticated. In large companies, they are often the product not just of the feasibility study contained in consultant's prospectus, but of careful, detailed strategic analysis. This takes primacy over the numbers, and in fact the identification of the projects for analysis is often derived from such strategic analysis which are characterized by their broad-based nature, the variety of factors considered, the amount of information collected, and judgements based more on qualitative than on purely quantitative considerations.

---

[122] See Harrison (1981); Morgan and Robinson (1978) and Petroleum Economist October 1985, pp. 358-359
[123] Peters and Waterman (1982)

4) In the metropolitan countries as well, because the relevant organizations are often better managed, mistakes are often recognized earlier, and dealt with sooner. (One tangential factor that may be mentioned here is the greater speed of reaction that seems to characterize private sector corporations as compared to state-owned corporations. The latter of course often predominate in large industrial projects in developing countries).

5) Sometimes too, large metropolitan firms, as indeed large economies, can use *power* to alter certain variables so as to make certain projects succeed, or at least not fail.

In the case of Trinidad and Tobago, we see dramatically the impact of these various, subtle problems on its industrial planning during the oil boom years. Investment decisions were made on the basis of a presumed advantage in energy-intensive industries. Feasibility studies, mechanistically applied, by well-known metropolitan firms, forecast incorrectly that there were good prospects for steel, ammonia, urea and methanol. None of these studies took into account the impact of new metropolitan technologies, the growth of substitutes, metropolitan reactions to the energy crisis, or even metropolitan reaction to the threatened loss of comparative advantage in the proposed industries.

The impact of new materials for example, on steel was never addressed in the engineering or economic analyses on the basis of which Trinidad and Tobago went into steel. Neither was the implication of the changing economic structure of the developed countries away from the smoke-stack industries and towards services and technology-intensive production. Both these factors have subtle, long-run effects on the demand for steel.

The forecasts of the demand for methanol were predicated on the assumption of continued high oil prices. No analysis was offered to support this presumption, and the projection of increased demand for methanol that was based upon it. Nowhere in the planning of the projects or in the actual feasibility studies, was any serious consideration given to the impact that metropolitan investments in conservation and energy-saving technologies would have on the overall energy picture and energy prices. And yet these investments promised to have the effect of vitiating over time, comparative advantage predicated on large differential in energy costs. Neither was there a recognition that high energy prices would call forth increased supplies of energy, which would in turn undermine the high energy prices Without any detailed analysis, Trinidad and Tobago's planners accepted the conventional wisdom of the time that 'the world was running out of oil' and that energy supplies were implicitly characterized by near zero elasticity.[124]

---

[124] See Farrell (1985)

In the case of fertilizer, the forecasts similarly ignored fundamental issues, including the strong possibility of protectionism in important metropolitan markets such as the USA and Western Europe. The fact is that without protection, metropolitan fertilizer manufacturers stood to be bankrupted by foreign competition based on cheap natural gas in Russia and the oil producing countries. The destruction of metropolitan fertilizer producers would then lead inexorably to the increasing dependence of US agriculture for example on imported fertilizer, (including imported Russian fertilizer). It requires no real political acuity to see that this situation is unlikely to be tolerated by the metropolitan countries that would be affected.

It also possible to see in the forecasts made the 'fallacy of composition' at play. The forecast of a shortage often leads to individual decisions on an atomistic basis to expand supply. These individual decisions ignore the fact that if everyone does the same, the shortage is likely to be replaced by a glut.

Neither can one find in the forecasts done for fertilizer any serious assessment of the impact of technologies (a) on agricultural productivity, and consequently on land, in production and fertilizer demand; (b) on the creation of substitutes through the genetic engineering of nitrogen-fixing bacteria. Neither was the impact of Russian entry into the world fertilizer trade and its implications seriously addressed.

In short, the failures of Trinidad and Tobago's large industrial projects on the oil boom years can be placed squarely at the door of poor forecasting and on erroneous conception of what industrialization strategy should be. The failure owes as much to flawed techniques as it does to misperceptions of how the world functions. Ironically, the philosophical bases of both technique and perception are to be found in metropolitan theory of comparative advantage and how projects should be analyzed. We see here a classic case of the effect of modes of thought imported from abroad and applied uncritically in circumstances for which they are ill-suited.

These are modes of thought which are arguably, just as flawed when deployed in their countries of origin, but a variety of factors operate, as we have seen, to attenuate their worse effects there. In a small, developing country, the impact has not been ameliorated and has been devastating.

What Trinidad and Tobago clearly needed, and needs to do, is to build the foundations of true, dynamic comparative advantage. This involves recognizing that demand changes, technology changes, and consequently comparative advantage is temporary, even ephemeral. To be able to produce competitively, over time, and to follow demand as it evolves and changes, it is necessary even for a small country, to build what we might call a production platform.

This comprises the set of skills and activities, including product design capability, materials fabrication, the production of certain basic commodities and the capacity to utilize a core of identifiable techniques to produce a wide range of commodities. It involves as well, building a cephalous structure the information systems, the planning and deciding mechanisms, that permit the constant scanning of the international environment and its trends, and the generation of the appropriate responses in the area of production.

Foreign Capital and the MNC: Some Contemporary Lessons

Trinidad and Tobago's experience with its industrialization strategy of the oil boom years sheds light not just on technology policy issues but on several other areas. Another area worth examination is the insights we can derive about the contemporary operations of foreign capital and the multinational corporation (MNC). Several features of MNC operations noted elsewhere were manifested in recent Trinidad and Tobago experience. This experience provides us with useful documentation that adds to our knowledge of the contemporary practices of foreign capital.

(1) First, Trinidad and Tobago dealt during the boom years, with a large number of different companies, from several metropolitan home countries. The country dealt with firms from Japan, Austria, France, the United Kingdom, Germany, Holland, Canada, Italy, Brazil and of course, the United States. The variety of backgrounds demonstrates at microcosmic level, the rapid growth of non-US multinational firms in recent years, a phenomenon noted and recorded at global level by the UN Centre on Transnational Corporations.[125] The significant role played by Japanese firms in the steel and methanol projects (and also infrastructural works such as port construction) mirrors at micro-level the growth in the international competitiveness of the Japanese vis a vis the Europeans and the Americans.

It is however interesting to note that in the joint-venture ammonia projects, Tringen and Fertrin, where the joint venture partners were American firms (Grace and Amoco), the Japanese did not play a significant role at all. Neither did the Europeans. US engineering firms were used in both these cases (Fluor and Kellogg). While these firms are among the handful of firms internationally that have major reputations in ammonia plant technology, this list does include Japanese firms such as Toyo, as well as European firms.[126]

---

[125] UNCTC (1983, p. 2-3)
[126] UNCTC (1982) and UNCTAD (1985)

Whether this experience suggests a predilection of the part of at least some U S firms to favour other US firms in today's world, is not clear. Certainly, it has been often suggested that Japanese firms do precisely that when operating internationally (i.e., seek to boost other Japanese firms over those of rival nationalities). In the case of Trinidad's ISCOTT, we in fact saw one such example where Japanese firms when asked to state precisely what they wanted to get out of the project, made it clear that they wanted to see other Japanese firms given business, even if they, the proponents, were not being given it themselves.[127] This raises interesting questions as to exactly how much today's MNCs in fact put the national interests of their home countries behind them, and operate as the purely self-interested, profit-maximizing capitalist firm classical economic theory, or the supra-national global corporations suggested by some business theorists.[128] The Trinidad and Tobago experience raises the question of whether business, in the form of the MNC does not still play a role, not just of 'following the flag' but of 'carrying the flag'.

The notion that multinational corporations are increasingly supra-national in their orientation and outlook is probably rather exaggerated. In fact, it can be argued, with at least as much truth, that what we are increasingly seeing in today's world is not large corporations doing battle with each other to promote and safeguard their individual corporate interests while remaining aloof from or even antagonistic to the national interests of their home states.

Rather we have nation states operating as economic collectives, doing battle with other nation states - Japan Inc., Korea Inc., France Inc. From this perspective, the distinction between government and business is increasingly blurred, and firms are, at least in part, agents of arms of their home states' economic machines.

Even if this is not the whole truth, it is surely part of the truth. Even in the metropolitan countries themselves, it is not uncommon to hear views articulated which are close to this in the course of debates on the need for national industrial policy, or for the protection of domestic industry against 'unfair' foreign competition. Of course, it is usually in the context of suggesting that other firms and their home countries are operating in this fashion. In the USA for example, it is not uncommon to hear charges that US firms are forced to do battle with enterprises that are part of a national economic machine (e.g., Japan Inc.). This machine is usually depicted as centrally directed, heavily subsidized and operating in the pursuit of national interests as opposed to individual, corporate interests.[129]

---

[127] See Chapter 4 above.
[128] See Levitt (1983) and Vernon (1977)
[129] See Wolff (1983)

What may be closer to the truth however, is neither of the 'extremist' views of corporate behaviour, but rather a synthesis of both, that is, corporations may operate out of multiple motivations. Individual, corporate interests, and the national interests of their home countries may operate side by side as influences on their decision-making. Which would take precedence over which, and in what circumstances, is an interesting issue for further research. The Trinidad and Tobago experience cannot by itself, provide answer to these questions, but does raise them.

(2) Another feature of contemporary international transactions that is manifested in the Trinidad and Tobago projects is the shift to the provision of cross-border services -opposed -to the more 'traditional' manufacture of physical products in other countries by MNC subsidiaries. Firms have increasingly learnt to disaggregate and sell their 'intangible' assets, such as generalized know-how, management skills and marketing contacts. Many firms have also sought to use these assets, and the services derived from them, as their contribution to joint ventures, instead of equity capital.

Foreign firms provided a wide range of lucrative services in the Trinidad and Tobago projects. These covered, inter alia, financial advice and financial planning, the sale of multi-client studies on the prospects for certain industries, customized feasibility studies and market reports, engineering services, training and personnel recruitment services, the procurement of supplies, technical assistance, and project management.

In both of the joint ventures studied, the foreign partners provided management and marketing services as well as technical assistance, all for contractually specified fees. The old notion of foreign direct investment bringing a package which included capital, technology, management, marketing, etc., and for which profits (dividends) were the accepted recompense is in many areas outmoded as a description of what takes place. Instead, firms consciously minimize their equity contribution, make maximum use of debt, break up the package of services/skills they provide, and price each component separately (e.g., management, marketing, technical assistance).

Not only can this offer greater total rewards as compared to just a share of profits, but it has the important advantage of reducing the risks that foreign firms perceive themselves as facing in developing countries. There are at least two types of risks that are significant here. The risk of nationalization and the loss of physical assets on the one hand, and ordinary business risk on the other. Given the 'intangibility' of services (much of it is embodied in people), there is little chance of the assets that produce them (the people involved) being physically confiscated. Also, payment for services becomes a cost of doing business, like paying for labour or raw materials first lien on revenues and pre-tax profits. Should untoward events reduce or eliminate profits, the provider services, like the providers of labour, raw materials, or loan capital enjoy precedence over its shareholders in terms of claims on the firm's resources. Thus, in a joint venture with a foreign MNC as we have seen in the case of fertilizer, the firm may suffer a loss, but this does not necessarily mean that the foreign joint-venture partner suffers a loss, or that the loss is equitably distributed among the shareholders in proportion to their nominal shareholding.

(3) At the same time, the foreign partner may be able to control the joint venture and direct its dynamic as though it were a wholly owned subsidiary. This was seen in the case of both joint-venture fertilizer firms. The notion, therefore, that joint ventures represent a mechanism whereby a developing country could, using majority equity ownership, obtain technical assistance, marketing skills, etc. while securing control over the overall direction an enterprise, is increasingly being threatened with irrelevance.

As we saw in both the cases of Tringen and Fertrin, the foreign joint-venture partner obtained effective day to day control over the plants. The foreign firms, therefore, stood to lose little in terms of control by structuring their investments in a developing country as part of a joint venture, and indeed may have a great deal to gain. For a developing country such as Trinidad and Tobago, the joint venture may have more symbolic or cosmetic value to the government, in terms of its dealings with its public, rather than representing a mechanism for simultaneously obtaining benefits such as technology or market access and retaining local control. It permits the pretense of local control, through advertising majority ownership. This is often sufficient to deceive a relatively unsophisticated public into confusing the form and trappings of majority shareholding with the substance of control.

(4) The Trinidad and Tobago experience also demonstrates graphically the impact the informational and organizational disadvantages that characterize small, developing states in their dealings with foreign multinationals. In the Trinidad and Tobago case, several things combined here:- (a) the large number of firms being dealt with in the same time period; (b) the variety of backgrounds of these firms, in terms of countries of origin; this has implications for the cultural nuances involved in dealing with say Japanese as opposed to American firms; it also has implications for the ease of generating information about the activities and strategies of the firms involved; (c) the inexperience of the Trinidad and Tobago planners in terms of dealing with sophisticated metropolitan firms and setting up large, complex industrial projects which incorporated sophisticated technology; (d) the lack of familiarity of the planners with the new industries such as steel and methanol which the country was entering for the first time; (e) the remnants of what is often termed the colonial mentality and the psychological readiness to give greater weight to metropolitan analyses and forecasts, and to the pronouncements of

'big-name' metropolitan firms than these deserved; (f) the lack of a local culture which stressed information gathering and intense cerebration in approaching problems; this permitted the planners and their political masters to be content with information and analysis of a quantity and quality which would be rejected in a more developed society; (g) the cultural orientation to information and the value placed on it, reflected itself as well in the kind of organizational structures set up, the procedures followed, and most importantly, the personnel entrusted with making key decisions in terms of contracts, negotiations and arrangements with foreign firms personnel often lacked the knowledge base, the training and experience necessary for successfully carrying out the tasks with which they were entrusted.

The result of all these factors combined was to lead to the kind of deals we have examined in the fertilizer joint-ventures, the weakness of the arrangements made for technology acquisition, and the series of mishaps and misadventures which we saw characterized the iron and steel project.

Transformation and the People Factor

In conclusion, it might be said that the Trinidad and Tobago experience with its industrialisation strategy in the oil boom years demonstrates above all the importance of the 'software' factor in transformation in today's world. By this is meant the role of people, the culture that shapes them, their thinking, their perceptions of the world and their attitudes. In addition, there is the role of information and organization, the procedures devised for getting things done, a people's experience with running things and dealing with the modern world, and the resultant wisdom and understanding of subtleties that comes with this.

More than anything else, the Trinidad and Tobago experience provides a classic demonstration of the truth that capital is not the critical bottleneck to successful transformation. Here was a country that found itself with a large windfall of the capital needed for transformation. It failed quite comprehensively to use this windfall effectively. The contrast between Trinidad and Tobago (and other Third World oil producing countries) and a country such as Norway, which enjoyed the same windfall, is instructive. While it is not possible to do a detailed comparative assessment here, it is enough to say that Norway did not make the kinds of mistakes that Trinidad and Tobago and other Third World oil producers made.

The difference can arguably be traced to the 'people' factor. Industrialization requires a cadre of people with well-developed technical skills. Experience is important, but experience has to be acquired through learning and doing. The pains and costs which inevitably accompany the acquisition of the necessary experience can be greatly eased by a value system which stresses information gathering, cerebration, feedback, and the choice of the best people for positions. The kind of organisational apparatus set up plays a critical role, as does the set of procedures adopted for getting things done. It is on these foundations that building technological capabilities or successfully acquiring and assimilating foreign technologies rest.

In Trinidad and Tobago, we have seen the results of the violation of these basics. An apparatus was set up in which a handful of people were entrusted with billions of dollars' worth of projects involving new industries, sophisticated modern technologies and a web of complex transactions. We see a Cabinet formally overseeing these programs but without its membership possessing either the collective experience of setting up and running large industrial projects, or the expertise on the particular industries being entered. In any event, one had the phenomenon of a political arrangement in which Cabinet, Parliament and the traditional Civil Service bureaucracy played second fiddle to the judgements and decisions of just a handful of men (including the then Prime Minister). Even had the necessary expertise existed in these institutions (and it largely did not), it would have been given no chance to be brought into play.

Most devastating however, was the impact of the industrialization strategy chosen. Here we see once again how things that seem intuitively obvious may turn out to be wrong or misguided. The truth, one learns, is sometimes counter-intuitive. It is counter-intuitive to suggest that an industrialization strategy based an abundant material resource such as gas, which seems to be all that a small, underdeveloped country has, may not after all be the easiest strategy. And yet, strangely enough, so it is, and so it has turned out to be at least in the form so far attempted.

Lastly, the problems and failures experienced in the Trinidad and Tobago case, offer tremendous insights into issues that transcend the specific case of Trinidad and Tobago So do the successes. For example, Trinidad and Tobago's industrialization strategy represented a practical and very literal application of metropolitan comparative advantage theory, a la Heckscher-Ohlin. Whether the planners knew this or not is beside the point. The results point up some fundamental weaknesses in that theory, at least in its superficial textbook form.

The experience illuminates as well the weaknesses that inhere in contemporary approaches to project analysis and forecasting, and the enormous impact of the mistakes that result, especially for small countries. There are as well many fruitful lessons for those concerned with formulating and implementing technology policy and industrialization strategies in small countries, and even more for students of organization and management.

The story is recorded in the Book of Exodus of the Israelites, who despite the gift of manna from heaven and other manifestations of the benevolence of a Divine Providence, turned away during their search for the Promised Land, and worshipped a golden calf. There are interesting similarities between this story and the experience of Trinidad and Tobago (and other Third World oil producers in the 1970s). The enormous windfall of capital from the oil boom was dissipated in a few short years in an orgy of excessive consumerism, waste, and the pursuit of expensive, prestige projects many of which were born out of erroneous conceptions of what industrialization and transformation were all about.

Two thoughts however are apropos as we come to the end of this review. First, mistakes are inevitable. They are part of the human condition. The important thing is that we learn from them. (In the Book of Exodus, God was finally persuaded to forgive the Israelites their mistakes, on condition that they renounced them, and did not make them (i.e., the same ones) again.

Secondly, it is said that experience is the best teacher. She must however, have willing students. It is also said that a wise man learns from the experience of others. If Trinidad and Tobago can be persuaded to study the experience recorded here and learn from it, and if other Third World states also derive some benefit from the study of this experience, then the mistakes, the expensive failures and the other evils associated with this experiment in industrialization, would not have been altogether in vain.

POSTSCRIPT: DEVELOPMENTS IN IRON AND STEEL, AMMONIA, UREA AND METHANOL AFTER 1985

Terrence W. Farrell

Trevor Farrell's conclusions in *The Worship of the Golden Calf* (WGC) were somewhat pessimistic. The iron and steel project was deemed a failure, both operationally and financially, and based on the initial financial results for the ammonia and methanol projects, he expressed concern that these would not be as successful as planned unless prices were to recover. Today, the Point Lisas strategy of resource-based industrialization is viewed overall as successful both operationally and financially.[130] However, while this positive evaluation certainly applies to the petrochemicals industries and to LNG which began in the 1990s, it does not apply to iron and steel, and does not apply to the issues of technology transfer and technological capability addressed in *WGC*.

Iron and Steel

As documented in the Cabinet-appointed Esau Committee report, by 1984, it was clear that ISCOTT, the wholly-state-owned iron and steel company was in serious trouble. Indeed the report stated baldly "ISCOTT is insolvent and continues to operate on a day to day basis by heavy Government financial support."[131] The Committee had invited several companies to inspect and evaluate the facilities and make proposals. Many companies having made enquiries or visited declined to submit proposals. However, proposals were received from Bechtel-Nucor and Bechtel-Laclede, Neue Hamburger Stahlwerke (HSW) and Voest Alpine (VA). The proposals were evaluated based on the following criteria: (1) Equity Participation (2) Cost of Services over a two year period (3) Scope and adequacy of services (4) Know-how and qualifications (5) Profitability of the partner (6) Availability of key personnel (7) Foreign experience and language (8) Marketing capability in the USA (9) Corporate Reputation (10) Financing (11) Viability of joint venture company (12) Loss sharing during turnaround (13) Suitability as a

---

[130] See Wendell Mottley, *Trinidad and Tobago Industrial Policy 1959 – 2008*, Ian Randle, Kingston, 2008; Trevor Boopsingh and Gregory McGuire (eds.) *From Oil to Gas and Beyond*, University Press of America, 2014. Earlier assessments of the Point Lisas strategy, reflecting the performance in the first decade, were not as positive. See Dennis Pantin, Whither Point Lisas? in Selwyn Ryan (ed.) *The Independence Experience, 1962-1987, ISER, 1988.*

[131] There were three reports. The first submitted in March and the second in April 1984 were to propose measures to deal with the countervailing and anti-dumping duties and reduce government financial support to ISCOTT. The second report of November 1984 was to make recommendations to secure a partner to remove entirely the need for government support. I am grateful to Joe Esau for making the report available to me.

partner. Based on these criteria, the committee proposed Bechtel as the partner in the proposed new joint venture company.

The Government decided to proceed with HSW and VA and entered into a two year agreement with these companies in 1986. However, losses continued to mount over the period.[132] In 1989, the Government entered into a lease/purchase agreement with Mittal Steel. This was a small steel producer then operating in Indonesia and run by Lakshmi Mittal. Mittal's Indonesian operation which was based on scrap iron had in fact started to imported DRI from ISCOTT since 1983, sparking Mittal's interest in DRI technology.[133] The lease rental payment was US$11.0 million per year and the operating company was Caribbean Ispat Limited (Ispat). Ispat was able to turn the operations around and in December 1994, Mittal exercised his option to buy and the Government sold the plant to Ispat for US$70 million.

Ispat made additional investments to the plants to increase capacity and to address emissions and effluent. The IFC in 1995 approved a loan of US$27.3 million to assist in financing the overall project cost of US$147.4 million.[134] Ispat's success in Trinidad and Tobago launched its international expansion. Ispat International acquired iron and steel plants in Mexico (1992), Canada (1994) and Germany (1995), as well as the USA (1998) and France (1999) following an IPO on the New York Stock Exchange in 1997.[135]

Chart 1 below shows the evolution of iron and steel production over the period 1985 to 2015.

In 2006, Mittal's Ispat acquired Arcelor and formed ArcelorMittal. In 2015, in the face of competition from China and Turkey, the operations at Caribbean Ispat were halted after several years of mounting losses. The operations were closed in March 2016, bringing an end to Trinidad and Tobago's attempt to be a player in the iron and steel industry.

---

[132] See Ashley Bobb et. al, Impact of the Closure of a Large Foreign Direct Investment: The Case of ArcelorMittal in Trinidad and Tobago, Central Bank of Trinidad and Tobago, Working Paper 01/2020
[133] Carnegie Would be Jealous, Forbes, August 23,1999 (https://www.forbes.com/forbes/1999/0823/6404054a.html?sh=27c58805f0a0)
[134] See IFC https://disclosures.ifc.org/project-detail/SPI/4653/caribbean-ispat-ltd
[135] Ispat International Annual Report, 2002

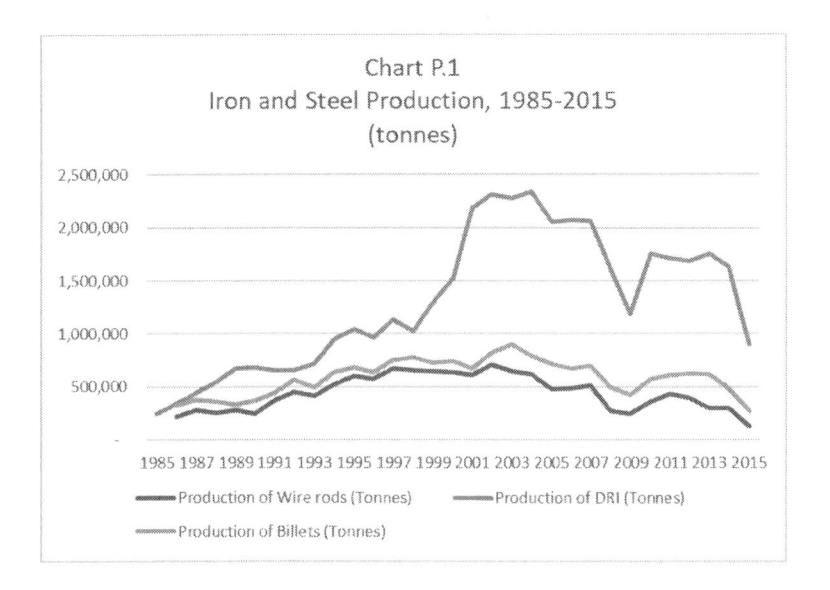

**Chart P.1
Iron and Steel Production, 1985-2015
(tonnes)**

- Production of Wire rods (Tonnes)
- Production of DRI (Tonnes)
- Production of Billets (Tonnes)

Fertilizers (Ammonia and Urea)

Tringen which began operations in 1977 was established as a joint venture between the Government and WR Grace. Grace was an experienced operator which had set up and run Federation Chemicals (Fedchem) since 1960.
Fertrin (Fertilizers of Trinidad and Tobago) was established from the outset as a joint venture between the Government and Amoco. The O1 ammonia plant began operations in 1981 and the O2 plant in 1982.

The urea plant was wholly-owned by the Government, Trinidad and Tobago Urea Company (TTUC), but was built and operated adjacent to the ammonia plants since urea uses carbon dioxide derived from ammonia production as one of its inputs. The urea plant commenced operations in 1983.

These plants, according to WGC, were built on a turnkey or "semi-turnkey" basis and had few of the operational difficulties which severely impacted the iron and steel project. However, they commenced operations in a difficult market environment marked by low product prices and recessionary conditions in the major markets. It appears that both Fertrin and TTUC incurred losses during that period. However, by the end of the decade of the 1980s, production had increased significantly and with the additional capacity installed during the 1990s, Trinidad and Tobago was on its way to become the second largest exporter of ammonia in the world.

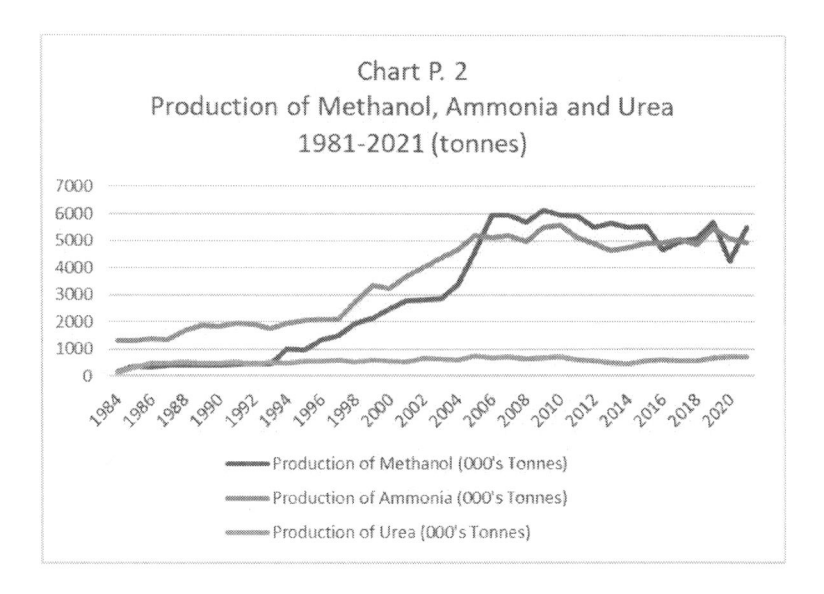

Chart P. 2
Production of Methanol, Ammonia and Urea
1981-2021 (tonnes)

Chart showing production trends from 1984 to 2020, y-axis 0–7000, with three lines:
- Production of Methanol (000's Tonnes)
- Production of Ammonia (000's Tonnes)
- Production of Urea (000's Tonnes)

However, because of the Government's fiscal difficulties brought on by the collapse of oil prices and hence government revenues, together with higher government spending and debt, the government entered into adjustment programmes with the IMF and a restructuring programme with the World Bank.[136] This then led to the divestment of its equity interests in the fertilizer plants. Arcadian acquired both Fertrin and the urea company and subsequently, Arcadian's interests were acquired by PCS Nitrogen.

Additional supplies of cheap natural gas were discovered and brought on stream and prompted a significant expansion of capacity in the ammonia. PCS Nitrogen added the O3 plant in 1996 and the O4 plant in 1999. Farmland Misschem added ammonia production capacity in 1998. In 2002, Caribbean Nitrogen came on stream and in 2004, Nitrogen 2000 came on stream. Ammonia production peaked in 2010 at 5.5 million tonnes after Consolidated Energy had brought its AUM Ammonia plant on stream in 2009. This level of production was ten times the output produced in 1981.

Moreover, with the recovery in economic activity in the 1990s and higher oil prices, the prices of ammonia and urea improved compared to the 1980s and continued to improve into the first decade of the 21st century (Chart 3).

---

[136] See Terrence W. Farrell, *The Underachieving Society: Development Strategy and Policy in Trinidad and Tobago, 1958-2008*, UWI Press, 2012

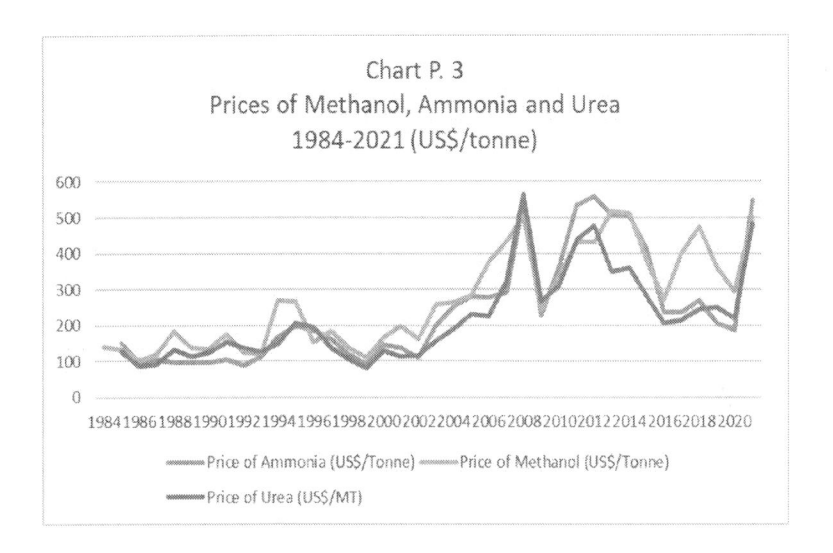

Chart P. 3
Prices of Methanol, Ammonia and Urea
1984-2021 (US$/tonne)

— Price of Ammonia (US$/Tonne) — Price of Methanol (US$/Tonne)
— Price of Urea (US$/MT)

Methanol

The production of methanol commenced in 1984 through a wholly-government owned company, Trinidad and Tobago Methanol Company (TTMC), supported by a management contract. The plant (M1) was constructed on a turnkey basis and though there were cost overruns, there were few of the problems experienced in the iron and steel project.

Production of methanol has increased significantly since inception (Chart 4). Additional capacity was added in 1994 (M2), 1996 (M3) and 1998 (M4). Methanex brought on the Titan plant in 2000 followed by the Atlas plant in 2004, while Consolidated Energy added even more capacity in 2004 with its M5 plant. The last investment to be made at Point Lisas was also in methanol with the CGC plant commissioned in 2019.

Capacity expansion in methanol was induced by favourable prices which have increased since the levels obtained in the 1980s.

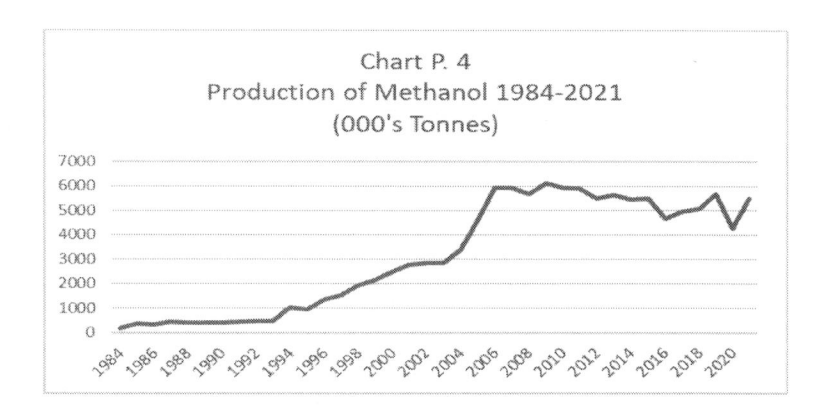

Chart P. 4
Production of Methanol 1984-2021
(000's Tonnes)

[Line chart showing methanol production rising from near 0 in 1984, gradually increasing through the 1990s, sharply rising around 2004-2006 to about 6000, then plateauing around 5000-6000 through 2021]

Development Impact

The petrochemicals industry, that is ammonia, urea and methanol, has had a significant positive impact on Trinidad and Tobago's growth, tax revenues, and foreign exchange earnings.

Inspection of the production charts indicates that output had more or less plateaued since around 2010. There has been only one new major investment in gas-based industries since 2011 when the CGC plant obtained final investment decision from Mitsubishi. The petrochemicals industry has been adversely impacted since around 2010 by gas curtailments which led to periodic plant shutdowns. More important, the price of natural gas at the fence has increased, impacting cash flows and profitability.[137]

With the demise of CLICO Energy following the collapse of CL Financial, the industry is foreign-owned. Local professionals have successfully operated these plants over the past 45 years and in some instances led those local companies as their CEOs. However, the issues raised in Trevor Farrell's *Worship of the Golden Calf* in respect of technology transfer and the building of local technological capability have not been addressed.[138] There have been no meaningful attempts to leverage the skills and knowledge acquired in plant construction and operations to go further downstream as had originally been mooted in the 1970s, or to engage in commodity marketing and trading. Governments has been content to harvest the rents from the sector through taxation and dividends from the National Gas Company, but have not sought to invest some significant proportion of those rents in diversification within or outside the energy sector.

---

[137] See Terrence W. Farrell, At A Point of Inflexion: The Downstream Petrochemicals Industry in Trinidad and Tobago, https://papers.ssrn.com/abstract=4046233

[138] See also Government of Trinidad and Tobago, Vision 2020 Energy Sub-committee Report, and Kerston Coombs, Energy and Development in Boopsingh and McGuire, op. cit., Chap. 9.

REFERENCES

American Iron and Steel Institute, Steel Processing Flow Lines, Washington DC, USA (AIST), no date.

Baloff, Nicholas, Start-ups in Machine Intensive Production Systems, *Journal of Industrial Engineering*, vol. 17, June 1966

Beckerman, Paul, Some Arguments for (moderately) capital-intensive development even in Labour-Abundant Nations, *World Development*, Vol. 6, 1978.

Bell, R. M., and Hoffman, K., Industrial Development with Imported Technology: A Strategic Perspective on Policy" mimeo, Science Policy Research Unit, University of Sussex, September 1981

Best, Lloyd, Size and Survival, in *New World Quarterly*, Guyana Independence Issue, 1966

Bhalla, A.S., *Technology and Employment in Industry*, 2nd edition, Geneva, ILO, 1981

Boston Consulting Group, *A Framework for Swedish Industrial Policy*, mimeo, Boston, October 1978.

Braverman, Harry, *Labour and Monopoly Capital*, New York, Monthly Review Press, 1974

Brill, Winston, Agricultural Micro-biology, *Scientific American*, 1982

Central Bank of Trinidad &Tobago, *Annual Report*, 1974 to 1985, Port of Spain, Trinidad.

Chem Systems Inc, *Methanol: A Global Analysis, 1977-1990*, unpublished May 1979.

Cooper, Charles and Maxwell, Phillip, Machinery Suppliers and the Transfer of Technology to Latin America, mimeo, Science Policy Research Unit, University of Sussex, 1975.

Coordinating Task Force, Progress Report #1 to the Minister of Industry and Commerce and Petroleum and Mines, 15th October 1975 -15th November 1975, mimeo, unpublished, 1975.

Coordinating Task Force, Progress Reports No. 4, 5, 6, 7 to Minister of Finance, mimeo, unpublished, 1976-1980.

Demas, William G., *The Economics of Development in Small Countries*, Montreal, McGill University Press, 1965.

Desai, M. B. Preliminary Cost Estimating of Process Plants, *Chemical Engineering*, July 27th, 1981.

DeWitt & Co. Methanol Annual, 1985, Texas, July 1985

Esau, J., (Chairman), Second Report: Committee appointed by Cabinet to Review 1984 Expenditure Proposals and to secure a suitable international partner for Government in the Iron and Steel Company of Trinidad-Tobago Ltd., mimeo, 1984.

Farrell, Trevor, Small Size, Technology Policy and Development Strategy, CTPS-II Research Paper, UWI St. Augustine, Trinidad, Dept. of Economics, August 1982.

Farrell, Trevor, The Unemployment Crisis in Trinidad and Tobago: Its Current Dimensions and Some Projections to 1985, *Social and Economic Studies* vol. 27 no. 2, June 1978.

Farrell, Trevor, Foreign Direct Investment, the Transnational Corporation and the Prospects for LDC Transformation in Today's World - Lessons from the Trinidad-Tobago Experience, mimeo, UWI St Augustine, Trinidad, Department of Economics, 1984.

Farrell, Trevor, A Tale of Two Issues: Nationalization, the Transfer of Technology and the Petroleum Multinationals in Trinidad and Tobago, *Social and Economic Studies*, Vol 28, No. 1, March 1979

Farrell, Trevor, Technology Policy and Economic Transformation the Fundamental Issues, mimeo, Department of Economics UWI St. Augustine, Trinidad, 1984.

Farrell, Trevor, The World Oil Market 1973-1983 and the Future of Oil Prices, *OPEC Review* vol. IX No. 4, Winter 1985.

Food and Agriculture Organization (FAO) Commission on Fertilizers, *Current Fertilizer Situation and Outlook*, Fert/81/3, June 1981

Freeman, Christopher, *The Economics of Industrial Innovation*, Middlesex, England Penguin, 1974.

Government of Trinidad & Tobago, Minister of Finance, *Budget Speech*, 1974 to 1985.

Government of Trinidad & Tobago, Report to the Minister of Industry and Commerce on Development of a Steel Complex in Trinidad & Tobago, mimeo, July 8, 1976.

Government of Trinidad and Tobago Report on the Status of the Iron and Steel Project, mimeo, May 1977.

Government of Trinidad & Tobago, White Paper on Natural Gas, Port of Spain, Trinidad, Government Printing Office, January 1981

Harrison, F.L., *Advanced Project Management*, London, Gower Publishing Co 1981.

Hatch Associates Ltd., Steelmaking at Point Lis as Trinidad- Study and Recommendation to the Industrial Development Corporation of Trinidad & Tobago, Project No. 6928, mimeo, unpublished May 1974.

Hatch Associates Ltd, Trintoplan Consultants Ltd., Scope of Services and Estimated Cost for Engineering Project Management Services and Supervision of Construction and Inspection for Direct Reduction Facility at Point Lisas, Trinidad, mimeo, 1976

Heden, Carl-Goran, Report to UNIDO on the Potential Impact of Microbiology on Developing Countries, mimeo, April 1981.

Hollander, S., *The Sources of Increased Efficiency: A Study of Dupont Rayon Plants*, Mass., USA, MIT Press, 1965.

Industrial Development Corporation (IDC), Status Report on Iron and Steel Complex to Minister of Industry and Commerce, mimeo, October 21st, 1974

ISCOTT, Report to the Minister of Finance, mimeo, unpublished, May 1977.

ISCOTT, Contract dated 2nd March 1978 between ISCOTT and Korf Industries Inc.

ISCOTT, Contract between ISCOTT and Midrex Corporation.

Junta del Acuerdo de Cartagena, *Technology Policy and Economic Development*, Ottawa, International Development Research Center, 1976.

Koch, James, *Industrial Organization and Prices* 2nd ed. New Jersey, Prentice-Hall, 1980

Laird, Roy De and Betty A. *Soviet Communism and Agrarian Revolution*, Middlesex, England, Penguin 1970 .

Levitt, Theodore, The Globalization of Markets, *Harvard Business Review*, No. 3, May-June 1983.

Lewis, Arthur, The Industrialization of the British West Indies, *Caribbean Economic Review*, vol. 2, No. 1951.

Little, I. M.D. and Mirrlees, J. A. *Project Appraisal and Planning for Developing Countries*, London. Heinemann, 1974

Mahabir, Errol, Speech at the Formal Commissioning of Fertrin, September 19th, 1981 (mimeo)

Mahabir, Errol   Speech to Parliament on Industrial Development Policy, 16th March,1979 (mimeo)

Maxwell, Philip, Technology and the Gestation Period in Latin American Steel Plants _mimeo, Seminario del Centro de Investigaciones Economicas, Instituto Torcuanto di Tella, November 1980.

Morgan, J. and Robinson, C. *North Sea Oil in the Future*, London, Macmillan, 1978.

National Energy Corporation (NEC), Methanol Project Comprehensive Report to the Ministry of State Enterprises, March 1983.

National Energy Corporation (NEC), Trinidad &Tobago Methanol Project, Agreement for Supply of Equipment and Materials and related services between the National Energy Corporation of Trinidad-Tobago Ltd. and Toyo Engineering Corporation, Port of Spain, Trinidad, unpublished, May 1981.

National Energy Corporation (NEC), Agreement for Construction, Commissioning and Start-up Services between the National Energy Corporation of Trinidad-Tobago Ltd. and Toyo Engineering Corporation Port of Spain, Trinidad, unpublished, May 1981.

National Energy Corporation (NEC), Economic Analysis of Project Consolidation, mimeo unpublished July 3rd, 1981.

National Energy Corporation (NEC), Ten Year Plan 1981-1989, mimeo, Port of Spain, Trinidad, 1981.

Parsan, Elizabeth, An Evaluation of the Organisation and Development of the Fertilizer Industry in Trinidad and Tobago, unpublished MSc Thesis, UWI , St. Augustine, Trinidad, 1981.

Peters, Thomas and Robert Waterman, *In Search of Excellence*, New York, Harper & Row, 1982.

Petroleum Economist, January 1985.

Petroleum Economist, October 1985

Plipdeco, Annual Report 1983,1984.

Poon, Auliana, Towards a Strategy of Export -Led Industrialization for the Caribbean with Special Reference to Trinidad and Tobago, unpublished MSc. Thesis, UWI, St. Augustine, September 1983.

Ramlogan Ronald, Trinidad and Tobago Iron and Steel in Perspective: Analysis and Prospects, unpublished Thesis, Department of Economics UWI, St. Augustine, November 1984.

Sercovitch, Francisco, State Owned Enterprises and Dynamic Comparative Advantage in the World Petrochemical Industry, mimeo, Harvard Institute for International Development Discussion Paper no. 96, May 1980.

Shelby Stewman, David Lincoln et al., Recombinant DNA Breakthroughs in Agriculture, Industry and Medicine- A Delphi Study, *Futures*, April 1981.

Solomon, Cyril, Analyzing Engineering Consulting Firms, mimeo, CTPS Il, August 1983.

Squire, Lyn and Van der Tak, Herman, *Economic Analysis of Projects*, Washington DC. World Bank, John Hopkins University Press, 1975.

Stewart, Frances, and James J. (eds.) *The Economics of New Technology in Developing Countries*, London, Frances Pinter, 1982.

Technical Insights Ltd, *Direct Nitrogen Fixation*, New Jersey, USA, 1978.

Thomas, C Y., *Dependence and Transformation*, New York, Monthly Review Press, 1974

Trintoplan CH2M (Cornell, Howland, Hayes and Merryfield, U.S.A.), Report for year 1978. Caroni-Arena Water Project, submitted to Water and Sewerage Authority of Trinidad and Tobago, March 1979.

Trintoplan CH2M, Report for November 1980, Northern Range Valleys and North Oropouche Interim Water Supply Projects, submitted to Ministry of Finance, Trinidad & Tobago, December 1980

UNCTAD, *Fertilizer Supplies for Developing Countries: Issues in the Transfer and Development of Technology*, New York, United Nations 1985.

UN Center on Transnational Corporations (UNCTC), *Transnational Corporations in the Fertilizer Industry*, New York, United Nations, 1982.

UN Center on Transnational Corporations, *Transnational Corporations in World Development*, Third Survey, New York, United Nations, 1983 .

UN1DO, *Technological Profiles on the Iron and Steel Industry*, New York, United Nations, 1978

US Congress, Office of Technology Assessment, *Technology and Steel Industry Competitiveness* Washington DC, US Government Printing Office, June 1980.

US Department of Agriculture Economics Research Service, *Fertilizer Outlook and Situation*, Washington DC., December 1981.

US Department of Commerce, International Trade Administration Import Administration (c-274-002), Carbon Steel Wire Rods from Trinidad and Tobago: Final Affirmative Countervailing Duty Determination and Countervailing Duty Order, Washington DC December 17th, 1983

Vaitsos, Constantine, The Process of Commercialization of Technology in the Andean Pact, in Hugo Radice, ed. *International Firms and Modern Imperialism*, Middlesex, England, Penguin 1975

Vernon, Raymond, *Storm over the Multinationals-The Real Issues*, Cambridge, Mass. Harvard University Press 1977.

Williams, Eric, The Problems of Industrialization, Political Leader's Address to the 20th Annual Convention of the PNM, September 29th, 30th and October 1st, 1978, Chaguaramas Convention Center, Trinidad, mimeo, 1978.

Wolff Marvin, *The Japanese Conspiracy* Empire Books, 1983.

Postscript References

Coombs, Kerston, Energy and Development in Boopsingh and McGuire, 2014, Chap. 9.

Boopsingh, Trevor and Gregory McGuire (eds.) *From Oil to Gas and Beyond*, University Press of America, 2014.

Dennis Pantin, Whither Point Lisas? in Selwyn Ryan (ed.) *The Independence Experience, 1962-1987, ISER, 1988.*

Farrell, Terrence W., *The Underachieving Society: Development Strategy and Policy in Trinidad and Tobago, 1958-2008*, UWI Press, 2012

Farrell, Terrence W. At A Point of Inflexion: The Downstream Petrochemicals Industry in Trinidad and Tobago, https://papers.ssrn.com/abstract=4046233

Government of Trinidad and Tobago, Vision 2020 Draft National Strategic Plan, Energy Sub-committee Report, 2005

Mottley, Wendell, *Trinidad and Tobago Industrial Policy 1959 – 2008*, Ian Randle, Kingston, 2008;

INDEX

A

Amoco 37, 38, 43, 47, 48, 52, 66, 121, 122, 123, 126, 132, 141, 142, 143, 169, 184, 192
Arthur Lewis 37, 60

B

Black Power 36
Blackman effect 31
Booz, Allen and Hamilton 81, 104, 106

C

Carlos Hee Houng xiv, 48
Chem-Systems 151
Commercialization 32, 110, 158, 167, 169, 170, 172
Commissioning 9, 12, 15, 17, 35, 75, 88, 94, 124, 127, 134, 152
Construction 3, 4, 9, 12, 13, 15, 17, 23, 26, 30, 32, 33, 34, 35, 41, 42, 54, 57, 64, 72, 86, 88, 89, 90, 91, 97, 102, 107, 108, 119, 123, 124, 125, 126, 127, 129, 130, 131, 132, 133, 134, 144, 152, 153, 154, 158, 160, 161, 165, 166, 171, 172, 174, 183, 194
Coordinating Task Force x, 47, 48, 49, 70, 108, 123, 124, 126, 131, 150, 195
cost overruns 26, 27, 34, 54, 83, 108, 147, 152, 193
Cost-plus contract 30

D

Design engineers 11, 13

E

Eric Williams 37, 39, 60, 105, 122
Esau committee 98
Ex-Im Bank 29, 142

F

Feasibility Studies 11, 24
Fedchem 120, 121, 122, 123, 124, 132, 140, 153, 192
Fertrinx, xiv, 42, 43, 49, 52, 122, 123, 124, 125, 126, 132, 133, 135, 136, 141, 142, 143, 150, 153, 161, 167, 168, 169, 170, 183, 186, 192, 193, 197
Financing x, 18, 28, 83, 139, 140, 142, 190
First Boston Corporation 70, 83, 151
Fixed price contract 30

H

Hatch x, 61, 64, 65, 66, 67, 68, 78, 81, 85, 89, 90, 92, 93, 94, 98, 99, 104, 106, 107, 109, 158, 196

I

ICI 128, 148, 152
Industrial Development Corporation 17, 48, 49, 59, 64, 70, 96, 196, 197
Industrialization strategy 7
ISCOTT x, xiii, 49, 52, 53, 54, 55, 56, 57, 58, 61, 66, 67, 69, 70, 71, 73, 75, 76, 78, 79, 80, 81, 82, 83, 84, 85, 86, 87, 88, 89, 90, 91, 92, 93, 94, 95, 96, 97, 98, 99, 100, 101, 102, 103, 104, 105, 106, 107, 108, 109, 110, 111, 113, 114, 115, 116, 117, 118, 119, 143, 184, 190, 191, 197

K

Ken Julien 48
Korf 66, 67, 68, 69, 72, 76, 78, 79, 80, 85, 86, 89, 91, 92, 93, 98, 102, 107, 109, 173, 197

M

Midrex 68, 69, 72, 78, 79, 80, 81, 85, 89, 90, 91, 92, 97, 106, 107, 168, 197

N

National Energy Corporation xiii, 46, 47, 49, 51, 57, 96, 135, 147, 150, 152, 197, 198
Neue Hamburger Stahlwerke 103, 190

O

OPEC xii, 2, 17, 39, 196

P

Project Conception 11, 16
Project management 13, 90
Project Planning 2, 11, 12, 16, 18, 20

R

Resource-based industrialization 39, 41, 149, 166, 190
Rust International 86, 95, 107

S

Small size 6

T

Tringen x, 43, 49, 52, 122, 123, 124, 135, 138, 139, 140, 141, 142, 143, 153, 161, 168, 183, 186, 192
turnkey contract 30, 116, 125, 130

V

Voest Alpine 88, 103, 190

W

World Bank xiii, 29, 103, 136, 192, 198

Made in the USA
Columbia, SC
14 October 2022